THE NEW HOLLYWOOD

Jim Hillier

STUDIO
VISTA

First published in the UK
1993 by Studio Vista
Villiers House
41/47 Strand
London WC2N 5JE

Produced by Cameron Books, PO Box 1, Moffat,
Dumfriesshire DG10 9SU, Scotland

Copyright © Movie 1992

Distributed in Australia
by Capricorn Link (Australia) Pty Ltd
PO Box 665, Lane Cove, NSW 2066

British Library Cataloguing-in-Publication Data
A catalogue record for this book is available
from the British Library

ISBN 0 289 80049 8

Edited and designed by Ian Cameron

Filmset by Cameron Books, Moffat
Halftone reproduction by
Thomas Campone, Southampton
Printed and bound in Britain
by Hartnolls, Bodmin

Stills by courtesy of ABC Pictures International
(*The Jericho Mile*), Alligator Associates and
Group 1 (*Alligator*), American International
(*The Trip*), Charles Burnett Productions (*Killer
of Sheep, My Brother's Wedding*), Carolco
(*Terminator 2*), CBS Television (*The Equalizer*),
CBS Theatrical Films (*The Keep*), Columbia
(*The Big Easy, Boyz N The Hood, Sleepwalkers*),
Columbia-TriStar (*Look Who's Talking*), Dino
De Laurentiis Entertainment Group
(*Manhunter*), Disney (*Tex*), 40 Acres and a
Mule Filmworks (*Do The Right Thing, Jungle
Fever*), The Goldwyn Co. and Matty Rich
(*Straight out of Brooklyn*), Hemdale (*River's
Edge*), Imagine Entertainment (*The 'burbs*),
Lorimar (*Cookie, Smithereens*), James McBride
Productions (*David Holzman's Diary*), MCA
Television (*Miami Vice*), MGM (*Shaft, The
Slams, Liebestraum*), The Moving Picture
Company (*Stormy Monday*), MTM Enterprises
(*Hill Street Blues*), New World (*The Hot Box,
Angels Hard as They Come, The Lady in Red,
Android, Dead Heat, The Punisher, Piranha*),
New World Television (*Crime Story*), Orion
(*Miami Blues, Something Wild, Over the Edge,
Great Balls of Fire, Navy Seals, Desperately
Seeking Susan, Making Mr Right, She-Devil,
Heartbreakers*), Orion Television (*Cagney and
Lacey*), Palace Pictures (*A Rage in Harlem*),
Paramount (*Children of a Lesser God, Internal
Affairs, Explorers, Citizens Band*), Pioneer Films
(*The Loveless*), Public Forum Productions (*The
Killing Floor*), Renegade Women/Artists
Entertainment Complex (*Caged Heat*), Santa Fe
Productions (*Slumber Party Massacre*), The Taft
Entertainment Co and Sunn Classic Pictures
(*Cujo*), SVS Films (*To Sleep with Anger*),
Touchstone (*The Doctor*), Twentieth Century-
Fox (*Jewel of the Nile, Point Break*), Universal
(*Fast Times at Ridgemont High*), Vestron (*Blue
Steel, Fear*), Warner (*Ratboy, Gremlins, Gremlins
2, Innerspace, New Jack City, Swing Shift*),
Working Title/Polygram (*Drop Dead Fred*).

A book of this kind depends on a lot of help from a lot of different people and sources. For a book so heavily dependent on interviews, I am particularly grateful to those film-makers who gave up time during the summers of 1990 and 1991 to talk to me about their careers in the movie business, often at some length and despite pressures of work: George Armitage, Charles Burnett, Rob Cohen, Joe Dante, Ate de Jong, Bill Duke, Mike Figgis, Mark Frost, Mark Goldblatt, Randa Haines, Amy Heckerling, Tim Hunter, Amy Jones, Jim McBride, Michael Mann, Aaron Lipstadt, Sondra Locke, Rockne S. O'Bannon, Joseph Ruben, Susan Seidelman and Lewis Teague. Where I was not able to interview people I wanted to feature in the book, I used the British Film Institute Library as my main guide to material and, as ever, it proved invaluable as a source of information; my thanks to the staff there. The University of Reading Research Committee contributed to my expenses in research. I am grateful to Julia Gibson and Karen Brumer for their warm hospitality, without which my research would not have been possible.

As well as being interviewed, Mark Goldblatt, an old friend, was generous with ideas and contacts. Extra special thanks are due to two people. Aaron Lipstadt and I have been friends and occasional collaborators for many years; without his encouragement and generosity with time and ideas, I doubt whether the book would have been begun. Any value the book may have owes much to him, though its shortcomings are due entirely to me. Without Fiona Morey, I doubt whether the book would ever have been finished; her encouragement and generosity with time, particularly after the birth of our daughter Martha, in the middle of getting the book together, made its completion possible.   J.H.

Contents

Preface

This book is about contemporary Hollywood, taking 'Hollywood' in its broadest sense to mean the American film industry as a whole. In this sense, Hollywood is by no means restricted to Los Angeles; it comprises independent production as well as production by the major studios (though the distinction is often intentionally blurred by the industry itself); its output is aimed as much at television as at theatrical distribution. In the industry today, film-makers typically move, albeit sometimes uneasily, between studio pictures, independent pictures, episodic television, television movies, cable movies, commercials and music videos. While I have tried to make some of the crucial distinctions between such different kinds of work, I have taken all of these to be Hollywood.

My intention has been to explore the way that film-makers themselves experience working in the Hollywood system, rather than to take a critic's approach to their output. At one point, I wanted the book to be called 'Working Hollywood' to signify that it was both taking a look at Hollywood at work and investigating the way film-makers worked the system. One side of this enterprise has been to synthesise a mass of material about the economics of the industry, focusing on the twenty years or so since the major crises and changes of the late 1960s and early 1970s, and more specifically on the present situation and on prospects for the rest of the 1990s. On the other hand, by talking to film-makers at length, I wanted to explore the ways in which the changing economic structures have affected the day-to-day experience of the people who make the products on which the industry depends. By their very nature, film-makers' accounts are anecdotal and individual, but I have tried to place them within contexts which give them a more general explanatory or exemplary force. I do not make any assumptions about the absolute accuracy or objectivity of what they say – film-makers have their own agendas to define and interests to defend. The very fact that have wished to make them seems to me to endow their statements with significance.

In this book, I have concentrated on the careers of directors. It has become common-place for writing on the cinema to accept, at least implicitly, that the principal or even sole authors of films, whatever the mode of production, are their directors. The industry itself has bought the idea in many ways, and directors are commonly given, in effect, an authorial credit: a work will be, for example, either 'A Susan Seidelman film' or 'A film by Susan Seidelman'. The origins of this practice go back to the changes in Hollywood which stemmed from Orson Welles's 'egocentric conception of the director' (as Jacques Rivette put it in *Cahiers du Cinéma* in the 1950s) and to the critical debates in France, Britain and the United States from the 1950s that revolved around the director as author, and particularly around the status of Hollywood directors as the authors of their films on a par with their European counterparts. Part of the reason why Hollywood itself appeared to go for the idea may be that the disappearance or decline of any distinguishing studio identities for films (and to some extent of genre identities too) left a kind of vacuum which director identity helped to fill.

The idea of the director as author is treated with great scepticism by many directors who know the extent to which films depend upon the input of writers and producers as well as of directors of photography and editors. The vast majority of Hollywood projects will have had producers attached to them since they were no more than the germ of an idea; by the time that directors become involved, the scripts may have existed for some time and have already gone through many changes and writers; some of the intended casting may even have been agreed. Directors do (though to wildly varying degrees) have vital roles in determining the final forms that films take, but to accept them as authors for Hollywood product as a whole is seriously to misunderstand the processes involved. Even so, since the 1970s, the status and power of the director have become firmly established, a development encapsulated in the titles of interview books edited by Joseph Gelmis and by Eric Sherman and Martin Rubin, *The Film Director as Superstar* (1970) and *The Director's Event* (1972) respectively. This is a situation that most directors are obviously happy to go along with.

Over the last twenty years, increasing numbers of writers, actors and others, cognisant of the greater power and control that has become attached to the role, have wanted to become directors. To a remarkable degree, both inside and outside the industry, being a director has become the main aim of people wanting to make movies. As Lili Fini Zanuck, producer-turned-director, put it, 'Directing has become such a cliché. They have T shirts in Hollywood that say "What I Really Want To Do Is Direct", so coming out and saying that is a joke.' Almost all the directors whose stories are told at some length here have first been producers, actors, writers, editors or something else. In that their other work is discussed here only as what they did previously, or do when they are unable to direct, this book could be said to be going along with the current Hollywood enthronement of the director, but I hope that enough is revealed about the processes of commercial film-making to point to the crucial roles of other contributors and other factors arising from the nature of the industry.

Given the way that I have conceptualised Hollywood, the film-makers covered needed to represent a wide range of experience and status, from well-established studio directors to those just beginning their Hollywood careers, from those who have worked almost entirely in theatrical features to those who have worked extensively in television. I have therefore not concentrated on a select group of exceptional figures in the way that Michael Pye and Lynda Myles did a decade or so ago in *The Movie Brats*. The criteria for selection for interview (subject inevitably to people's availability) had to do with range of experience as well as reflecting my own assessment of the interest of the directors' work. I hope that they recognise themselves in the contexts in which I have placed them and that readers will gain some sense of what it is like to work as a director in contemporary Hollywood.

FORTY YEARS OF CHANGE
Hollywood from the 1940s to the 1980s

The American film industry has never remained in a particularly stable state for any length of time. It has always had to struggle and manoeuvre to establish and retain control, to keep out competition, to survive economic problems of its own and others' making, and to counter or negotiate with the government over policies that would upset its preferred modes of operation. Even in the period from the late 1920s to the early 1940s, which is thought of as the heyday of the studio system, the industry had plenty of difficulties to cope with: the change to sound production and exhibition had to be financed, the Depression brought a temporary decline in audiences, there were changes in the ownership and control of studios, and New Deal government policies seemed to demand fairer, more competitive codes of practice (in the movies as in other industries). On the other hand, the familiar industry pattern of the studio system was well established with the Big Five studios (Twentieth Century-Fox, MGM, Paramount, Warner Brothers, RKO) all vertically integrated, exercising control not just over production but also over distribution and, through their ownership of, on the whole, the largest and best-sited movie theatres, over crucial segments of exhibition. The complement of major studios was made up by the Little Three (Columbia, Universal, United Artists), which had no theatres of their own. Releases of feature films from the majors (which also produced much other material, such as animated cartoons – Bugs Bunny at Warner Brothers, Tom and Jerry at MGM, Woody Woodpecker at Universal) stabilised at between 320 and 400 per year, dropping significantly in the years of World War II. The number of cinema theatre seats rose steadily to a peak in 1945, although the number of separate venues never surpassed that at the end of the silent period, and after a dip caused by the Depression, box-office receipts grew steadily to reach a maximum in 1946, while total revenues and profits generally grew or remained stable.

In contrast, the four decades or so after 1945 present a picture of almost constant and frequently radical change. The period since World War II is most often talked about as one of decline, and in some senses – number of releases, average weekly attendances – the description is appropriate. Even so, in the 1990s, the movie industry as a whole remains dynamic and profitable, and the names of the majors (with the exception of RKO, which ceased operating in the mid-1950s) remain as familiar to us as they ever were. The industry may have changed, but it is still very much there, and in a highly recognisable form.

The movie industry is, above all, an *industry*. It changes to preserve or increase profitability, not to produce better entertainment or art. But perceptions of it (among film-makers as well as consumers) are complicated precisely by its producing art and entertainment as well as being a business; the relationship between these two aspects is always involved There were always critical voices in Hollywood that were critical of it, and these grew in number and in volume during the crucial postwar period, arguing against the studio system and the factory-like way in which movies were assembled, very often looking towards Europe as an alternative model, perhaps recognising the artistic status attached to many of the European film-makers who had been assimilated into the American industry at various points. In the two decades after 1945, European cinema – in the form of Italian neo-realism and later the French *nouvelle vague,* as well as individual film-makers like Federico Fellini, Ingmar Bergman and Luchino Visconti – seemed to many to offer a particularly strong artistic contrast to Hollywood. The studio system, it was argued, was hamstrung by its production-line methods under the iron control of studio bosses and money men, by its reliance on make-believe artifice, and by its bland, conservative subjects usually equipped with happy endings and chosen and marketed with the emphasis on stars and genres. Without the studio system, the argument continued, creative people could be given control, and ideas and energies would be released, leading to more imaginative and realistic films; it is only more recently that critics have talked about 'the genius of the system'. Some accounts of the changes in Hollywood in the 1970s take the view that some of what was wrong with the movie industry under the studio system did change, that power did shift from studio bosses to film-makers like Steven Spielberg, George Lucas, Francis Ford Coppola, Martin Scorsese and Brian De Palma – the so-called 'movie brats' – and that films were being made with more artistic freedom and individuality. The authors of *The Movie Brats* quoted the writer/director John Milius: 'Now, power lies with the film-makers, and we are the group that is getting the power.' Certainly, in the 1990s, some of these names continue to wield considerable industrial muscle, and it is often hard to remember the names of the often rapidly changing studio heads.

So, did the studio system collapse? The question is sufficiently complex to admit of different answers. Take for instance, independent production (that is, by production companies independent of major distributors): there were very few independent productions in the 1930s and only about forty independent producers in 1945, but, by 1958, some 58 per cent of productions were 'independent', a percentage that continued to rise, and there were some 165 independent producers. On the other hand, between 1969 and 1975, with independent production at around two-thirds of the total feature output, the six majors (Fox, Universal, Paramount, Warner, Columbia, United Artists – MGM being temporarily more or less out of production) averaged over 70 per cent of North American rental revenues. By the early 1980s, some 90 per cent of those revenues was accounted for by six majors (MGM now having returned in partnership with United Artists) plus Disney. If the majors so completely dominate the market in terms of revenue and profitability, how can one talk about the majority of productions being independent? To make some sense of this, we need to understand something of what happened to the majors and the studio system in the postwar period.

Divorcement and the Independents

Despite the code of practice for the movie business agreed with the government in the 1930s, the Justice Department, which had a history of anti-trust suits against the industry, brought a suit against all eight major studios in 1938, charging them with conspiracy to restrain and monopolise trade through a variety of restrictive practices in the distribution and exhibition of films. In the 1940 US v. Paramount case, the Big Five agreed to change their trade practices, but by 1944 the government was still dissatisfied and the suit was reinstated. Thus began, in 1947-48, the series of consent decrees or divorcements in which the Big Five agreed to sell off their theatre chains (though the last divestitures were not completed until 1957), as well as to end various restrictive practices, thus breaking down the vertical integration that had seemed so essential to the success of the business. Although the Little Three had prospered with no theatres, they had, of course, benefited from the restrictive practices in force throughout the industry. One immediate problem for the Big Five was that the theatres had contributed more to profits than either production or distribution – production, of course, can only become a profitable activity as a result of distribution and exhibition. The divorcements therefore set in train a shift in the power structure of the industry in which distribution (that is, the marketing of films and the physical distribution of prints) was to become critical.

Even without the consent decrees, the dramatic decline in attendances, which happened precisely when the divorcements were going through, would have forced the majors to adopt different strategies. An obvious move was to reduce the output of films, but this made it increasingly uneconomic to maintain studios with stars, creative personnel and technicians on long-term contracts and with extensive physical studio space and facilities in constant use or on permanent standby, which all added up to big, continuing overheads. Rapidly in some cases, more slowly in others (such as MGM and Universal), the studios abandoned both contracted staff and permanent studio facilities. Many employees were forced into independent production or unemployment. For well-known stars and other creative personnel, there were considerable tax advantages (mainly in the form of investment credits) in setting up, or becoming associated with, independent production companies, and many took this option quite early on. Thus Burt Lancaster and his agent Harold Hecht formed the Hecht-Lancaster Company in 1948, while Randolph Scott and producer Harry Joe Brown formed Ranown Productions in 1955, a year that also saw the founding of John Wayne's Batjac and Kirk Douglas's Bryna Productions. In some respects, the divorcements did result in the freer market conditions they were intended to create. By the late 1950s, two-thirds of features were being made by independents, although fewer A picture releases were being made – less than 200 a year by the end of the 1950s, around 150 by the mid-1960s, settling at around 100 from the mid 1970s on.

These figures need to be increased somewhat if films made by American companies abroad are taken into account. These 'runaway' productions tended to be cheaper than American-made movies; labour costs were lower, and ways were found to exploit foreign government subsidies. The runaway trend was especially marked in the 1960s and 1970s: it has been estimated that between 1967 and 1972, some 45 per cent of the 1,200 features made by US companies – not all A pictures – were made abroad. Major studio pictures made abroad in the 1950s and 1960s included Columbia's *The Bridge on the River Kwai* (1955), *The Guns of Navarone* (1961), *Lawrence of Arabia* (1962) and *Oliver* (1968), Paramount's *War and Peace* (1956) and *Romeo and Juliet* (1968), MGM's *Dr Zhivago* (1965), *2001* (1968) and *Ryan's Daughter* (1970), Fox's *The Longest Day* (1962) and *The Bible* (1966), and Warner's *My Fair Lady* (1964) and *The Great Race* (1965). Interestingly, this was the period when investment credits were being challenged by the tax authorities; they were declared legal in the early 1970s, but only for product made in the United States, and film-making abroad declined rapidly. The closing down of overseas production also reflected the more general retrenchment of the early 1970s.

The main advantage that independent producers had was the ability to make films more cheaply than the major studios: by many reckonings, independent pictures came in on average at somewhere around half the cost of major studio pictures. With audiences declining (even though rising admission prices covered some of the loss), cheaper movies could appear to make sense. Independent productions did not have to carry fixed overheads: they hired personnel from the pool of casual labour produced by the break-up of the studios and rented what space and equipment they needed. The independent producers had two main problems: getting finance and getting their finished films into theatres. The two were intimately connected (as they still are): a guarantee of distribution, and thus of access to theatres, made it infinitely easier to get finance. With the film industry very evidently in crisis, banks were not particularly eager to lend to production companies that did not have rolling production schedules or significant assets. As independent companies were often set up for just one or two movies, this was where the new-style major 'studios' came in. Finance and distribution had not been problems for the majors in the heyday of the studio system; their continuing programmes of production and release provided rolling funds for new production, and their vertical integration guaranteed access to theatres. Although Columbia, Universal and United Artists did not have theatre chains, they did have well-established distribution organisations. After the consent decrees and divorcements, all the majors were still powerful as distributors and, while continuing as producers (even if on a diminished scale), all remained crucial as sources of finance, albeit usually of co-finance.

The usual pattern for independent production was that a project would be brought as a package to the studios for financing and eventual distribution. Typically, a producer or agent would line up a property (a novel, play or original screenplay), stars and often a director, then pitch the package to a studio. One variation on this – much like the deal enjoyed by a few prestigious producers, like David O. Selznick, in the days of the studio system – involves studios doing deals whereby film-makers (usually producers and/or directors) with successful track records are provided with office space and administrative support in the studio complex in return for 'first look' at new projects. Steven Spielberg's Amblin Entertainment organisation has enjoyed this arrangement at Universal, as have, for example, Joe Dante and Richard Donner at Warner. The rolling production programme of the studio system was replaced by one-off independent productions backed by a studio for all or part of their financing. An independent production company might or might not then rent facilities from the financing studio. In such situations, the majors were no longer producers in the old sense. But while they may have lost their dominance as production units, they certainly continued to dominate film finance and distribution (and still do); the overall changes which came in the wake of the consent decrees and other factors amounted essentially to a restructuring rather than a revolution and allowed the majors to retain command of the market.

The growth of independent production had several important consequences. Given the simultaneous sharp decline in the number of films being made, creative personnel got a very different, much more intermittent, experience of production than they had had under the studio system, where people could expect to work almost constantly and could, for example, move up from B movie production to major pictures. Since the late 1960s, it has been common for directors to average only one feature every year and a half or two years, whereas, at the height of the studio system, a John Ford or George Cukor might regularly have made two or even three major features a year. There were serious implications here for the way in which directors (and, of course, others) learned their craft. Certainly, directors tended now to take on a wider range of production responsibilities. There were advantages, too: one of the attractions of independence was greater creative freedom. However, given the crucial role still played by the majors, whose finance came with the expectation that they would have their input on the nature of projects, we should not overestimate how much freedom became available.

The growth of independent production also increased the importance of agents. As freelance work (as opposed to work under studio contract) became the norm, it was increasingly the agents who brought together the elements of film projects. It has been estimated that by the 1960s some two-thirds of the films being made were pre-packaged by agents. In the forefront was MCA (Music Corporation of America) which had started out as a firm of musical agents. MCA entered television production in the early 1950s, for which it bought Universal's production facilities in 1959; it later took control of Universal itself (as well as Decca Records). Anti-trust problems then forced MCA to divorce itself from its original agency business, and it was left as the owner of a major studio. Agents continued to grow in importance in the industry to such an extent that, by the 1980s, Michael Ovitz, president of CAA (Creative Artists Agency), was being talked about as the single most influential person in the movie industry. The trend was for many smaller agencies to merge, and now, in the 1990s, CAA, the William Morris Agency and ICM (International Creative Management) dominate the field and, as the prime suppliers of both talent and story material, do much of the work that used to be done by the major studios. Such is their power that agents now feel that it is they who make the movies, with the studios functioning as little more than bankers. Some agents have actually moved across to the studios as producers and executives.

The Majors in the Balance

Although the majors abandoned continuous, routine production, they did not stop producing films, and tended to make bigger, more expensive ones than the independents. In a studio's steady production programme, the profitable films had offset the unprofitable ones, but now, with fewer films to share the ups and downs of profitability, there was a greater need for at least some to make big profits. To revive their fortunes in the 1950s, the majors increasingly made films in colour (half the major releases in 1955 as against only ten per cent of releases in the 1940s). The same effort to make movies as different as possible from what the small, monochrome television screen had to offer led to technical developments beginning with Cinerama (which with its original three-camera, three-projector system was used in the 1950s only for travel documentaries that were shown in a few specially adapted theatres). This was followed, much more significantly for feature production, by anamorphic widescreen processes beginning with CinemaScope, which became widely established after the success of Fox's *The Robe* in 1953, as well as by more short-lived novelties like 3D (which was used for 36 releases by the majors in 1953-54). More generally, there was an increasing vogue for blockbusters, which had the advantage that spectacular movies in colour and widescreen provided the opportunity for increasing ticket prices as a financial antidote to the continuing falls in admissions.

The conviction grew that only big, expensive movies could make big profits. There was some evidence to support this, but there was the unfortunate corollary that only expensive movies could make really big losses, as Fox (among others) discovered in the 1960s: its *Cleopatra* (1963) lost $40 million. Although Darryl and Richard Zanuck, brought in after this disaster, more than recouped the loss with *The Sound of Music* (1965), later attempts to duplicate its success with other massive musicals *(Dr Dolittle,* 1967, *Star!* 1968, and *Hello, Dolly!* 1969) all flopped, as did such other films as *The Only Game in Town* (1969) and *Justine* (1969), causing Fox to lose $27 million in 1969 and $77 million in 1970. Also in 1969, United Artists lost $85 million and MGM $72 million, marking the culmination of a crisis that had been developing throughout the 1960s (and before). It only made matters worse that, in this same period, ABC, CBS and National General, essentially television concerns, started to produce theatrical features (about ten each per year). They were motivated by television's huge appetite for material, and by the increasing value of movie sales to network television: in 1967, a total of $270 million was spent by the networks on leasing rights to show features on television, and there was the prospect that such sales could cover production costs on features. In the resulting glut of movies, ABC, CBS and National General collectively lost over $80 million and in 1972 they dropped out of theatrical production.

Despite their immediate financial problems in the 1960s, the major studios retained significant assets, such as prime real estate, libraries of old films (whose value was just beginning to be understood), interests in thriving television production and well-established distribution networks. Temporarily undervalued, because of cash crises, they represented a good (as well as apparently glamorous) investment, and it is not surprising that there were changes in ownership and structure. One trend was the takeover of studios by conglomerates – corporations with a range of different industrial interests. Thus, in 1966, Paramount was taken over by Gulf + Western, a conglomerate with diverse interests that included leisure areas such as sports, music and television; film production and, to a lesser extent, production for television were boosted, although the studio was forced to sell some of its real estate after the failure of *Darling Lili, Paint Your Wagon* and others in 1969. When Frank Yablans replaced Stanley Jaffe as president of Paramount in 1971, he declared that 'For a picture to be profitable, it should be made for $2.5 million.' In 1967, Transamerica, with a base in insurance, bought United Artists. In 1969, Warner Bros (which had already merged in 1967 with Canada-based Seven Arts) was taken over by Kinney National Services, which was in car rentals, parking lots and funeral parlours, and in 1971 became part of Warner Communications Inc, the new name of Kinney's corporate entity. The film, television and recording divisions of Warner Communications reverted at this time to the name of Warner Bros, rounding off a series of transactions that signalled important future shifts in entertainment industry strategies and recognition of the power and value of studio names associated with the past. Control of MGM passed into the hands of financier Kirk Kerkorian in 1969. Although Fox had suffered such big losses, it was not taken over at this time; both it and MGM retrenched, selling land to realise capital and cutting back on production. The banks refused MGM rolling credit, lending to it only on a picture-by-picture basis and sending a chill through the whole industry. Soon, MGM was mainly a real-estate company more interested in Las Vegas hotels than in movies (though the Las Vegas hotels traded heavily on the MGM name). Fox profited from its television stations and from production for television. Columbia had already gone into leisure areas, such as pinball machines, and had a wide range of interests in television, but suffered its heaviest ever annual loss in 1973 and was put under new management.

These various changes of ownership and diversification helped re-establish the industry, which was by now firmly diversified to include not just theatrical feature production but also the still-growing television business and traditional leisure concerns such as publishing and music. It was also beginning to extend into newer electronic media such as cable and video, laser and computer technology. Given this new situation, it was not surprising that further changes of ownership should take place in the 1980s and 1990s. 1981-82 was particularly busy. MGM, which had almost ceased production and was releasing its few pictures through United Artists, now formed MGM/UA by acquiring United Artists from Transamerica, which was just coming out of the unhappy *Heaven's Gate* affair, in which it was reputed to have lost $40 million. Coca-Cola, faced with a levelling-off in its soft drinks business and looking to diversify, decided to build on its considerable experience in media and marketing by buying Columbia. Oil tycoon Marvin Davis acquired Fox, but was bought out in 1985 by Rupert Murdoch's News Corporation; Murdoch had been anxious to get an entry into the industry for some time and had earlier tried to acquire MGM/UA.

Television and the Majors
By the 1980s, the movie industry was indissoluble from the newer television industry; this had in fact been the case long before the 1980s, to some extent for as long as television had been going. The major studios had wanted to buy into television in its early days, but, in the context of the active anti-trust suits against them in the 1940s, it is not surprising that the government preferred to entrust the new television networks to the existing radio corporations, CBS, NBC and ABC. Although television was seen as competition and the majors were initially reluctant to cede ground by selling it old movies, the film industry recognised from the outset that television was here to stay and that it would have a great appetite for filmed entertainment, which was Hollywood's stock-in-trade. United Artists set up a television department as early as 1948. Screen Gems, set up by Columbia in 1949 as a subsidiary company to produce telefilms and commercials, was, by the mid 1950s, heavily involved in the production of television series like *Father Knows Best* (1954-59); also in television production were Twentieth Century-Fox Television, Warner Bros Television and MGM, usually trading on their major-studio credentials. MCA entered production for television in the early 1950s through a subsidiary company, Revue, which by 1960 was the largest producer of films for television, with shows like *Alfred Hitchcock Presents*. It was mainly for television production that MCA bought Universal's studio facilities in 1959. Disney developed a twin-track strategy involving theatrical film and television production (as well as other interests): it integrated a television show (in conjunction with the ABC television network, which helped to fund Disneyland) with movie production and distribution. The television show, not particularly

profitable in itself, helped bring in the audience for theatrical movies (in this case, the family audience which had all but vanished for most films) and the visitors to Disneyland, and later other theme parks.

Production for television, mostly series until the mid 1960s and the advent of the made-for-television movie, was by its nature more steady, and the studio facilities and personnel set free by the demise of the movie studio system were to a very large extent taken up by it. In the mid 1950s, Hollywood was producing 20 per cent of prime-time network television shows; by 1963, the proportion had risen to almost 70 per cent, and live television, which was less flexible from a scheduling viewpoint (given the different time zones across the United States) and associated mainly with New York, had effectively been displaced from the position of dominance that it had held in network prime time in the early 1950s. The majors thus achieved their objective of entering and dominating telefilm production to balance declining theatrical business, earning as much as a third of their total revenue (some $300 million a year) from this source by the mid 1960s. Indeed, the difficulties in their theatrical businesses in the 1960s turned most of the majors more emphatically towards their television interests. By 1971, only 24 per cent of the income of SAG (Screen Actors Guild) members was being derived from theatrical features, the remainder coming from work for television of one kind or another. For production companies, television was certainly less glamorous and less publicised than movies; it had significantly less potential than theatrical movies for spectacular individual profits, but also significantly less potential for spectacular losses. Even so, new series for television required considerable investment, which often took some years to recoup. As with big budget features, the majors had significant advantages over the independents which enabled them to establish a comparable level of control over the supply of television shows to that which they had over theatrical distribution.

Television had a great need to fill air-time, and existing movies were an obvious candidate. At first, the majors resisted supplying films, and only minor studios like Monogram and Republic – more immediately hit by audience decline and cinema closures – sold their pictures to television. However, by 1955-58, all the majors had made deals for mostly pre-1949 features and shorts to be screened on television. Initially, as with the RKO library, film rights were sold outright, but the majors learned very fast that a better long-term strategy was leasing films for specified numbers of screenings, retaining the rights which could be leased again and again. Movies very soon became a crucial part of television programming in prime as well as other time, and the rental or leasing costs of features for television screening began to rise sharply. The $4 million paid by ABC television in 1966 for screening *The Bridge on the River Kwai* was exceptional, but the average leasing fee in the United States by the mid 1960s was about $400,000, up from about $150,000 only a few years before, corresponding to a very significant percentage of the average production costs per film at the time of $2.5-3 million. Back in the 1930s, when the only way in which movies could realise profit was by being shown in theatres, films were assumed to be able to make only more or less immediate profits, and studios wiped 80 per cent off a film's value after one year, 100 per cent after two years. Old movies were not really a marketable category except in the very occasional cases when films were re-released. Hence, it was not really surprising that the entire RKO library should be sold outright in the mid-1950s for only $15 million (an average of about $10,000 per feature), nor that only ten years later prices had inflated so enormously. From the mid 1960s, the prospect of future sale to television became part of the calculation in almost all film production.

Just how early in the history of sales to television these were taken account of in the budgeting of theatrical features is suggested in the movement from black-and-white to colour film production. By 1955, over half of major theatrical releases were in colour. But at about the same time, movies began to be sold to television (then, of course, broadcasting only in monochrome), and feature production in colour declined, only to rise again, very rapidly (to 94 per cent by 1970) when the networks switched decisively to colour broadcasting in the mid 1960s. In the rush to colour programming, NBC, in association with MCA/Universal, began producing made-for-television movies. It was soon followed by the other networks, which went even further, with their disastrous ventures into theatrical features. In 1974, 130 new television movies were shown in prime time, compared with only 118 theatrical features (by then about a year's worth of theatrical features) receiving their television broadcast premieres. Many of the television movies were made in association with major studios; television (series as well as movies) had now decisively taken the place in the studios' routine production that, until the 1950s, had been occupied by theatrical features.

Audiences and Theatres

Average weekly cinema attendances in the North American market had reached a high of 80 million in 1930, declined sharply during the Depression (to 50 million in 1933-34), but then rose steadily to 84 million in 1943-44, staying very high for the next few years. But between 1946 and 1957 attendances halved, and they halved again between 1957 and 1964-65. The low point was 17 million in the early 1970s, after which the figures stabilised, and some of the lost ground was regained between the late 1970s and the mid 1980s, when the level was around 20-23 million. The effects on box-office receipts were significant, but not quite as dramatic as these figures imply, mainly because of increases in admission prices (from around 25 cents in the mid 1940s to around 50 cents in the mid 1950s, $1.00 in the mid 1960s, $2.00 in the mid 1970s and $3.50 in the mid 1980s). As ticket prices rose, the majors increased their share of box-office takings, a development which they justified as compensating for their loss of revenue from theatre ownership. Thus a 73 per cent drop in attendances between 1946 and 1962 produced a box office gross decline of only 48 per cent.

The dramatic decline in film-going has almost always been put down to television. The figures are indeed striking: the number of television sets being used in the United States soared from only 14,000 in 1947 to 172,000 in 1948, a million in 1949, 4 million in 1950 and 32 million in 1954; by 1955, over half of American homes had television. It would have been extraordinary if expansion on this scale had not brought with it economic and social changes of great significance for the movie industry, in both the short and the long term. But television was not the sole cause of the decline, which was already in progress between 1946 and 1949, before television penetration was really significant, and continued after most households had sets.

The postwar period was marked by a major population shift from the old cities to new suburbs, the consequences of which for inner cities remain with us today. This demographic change and generally increasing affluence were accompanied by more diversified patterns of both leisure (including both movie-going and television-watching) and family expenditure, with rapid growth in home ownership and spending on cars and other consumer goods. Of every dollar spent on recreation the amount devoted to movie-going declined from 20 cents in 1946 to 12 cents in 1950, 4 cents in 1974 and $2\frac{1}{2}$ cents in the mid 1980s.

Over 3,000 conventional movie houses (or hard-tops) closed between 1948 and 1954 (and closures continued after that date). Most of these were urban neighbourhood theatres which had specialised in third-run movies, B features and so on (their closure was one of the factors that made the demise of B movies inevitable). The one growth area was the number of drive-ins, which were cheap to set up by comparison with conventional theatres. The first drive-ins had appeared in the early 1930s, but, by the end of the war, there were only 100 in operation. However, between 1948 and 1954, against the background of a boom in car ownership and the movement from the cities, some 3,000 drive-ins were opened. Because the length of the drive-in season mainly depended on the weather, many were in the south and south west: in general, drive-ins catered for widely spread, mostly rural populations and, increasingly, new suburban areas. They were popular because they were both cheap and convenient for family audiences; later they appealed particularly to working-class and teenage audiences. It was for this reason, perhaps, that the majors tended rather to look down on drive-in locations, or, in *Variety* parlance, 'ozoners', even though by 1958, when drive-ins reached their peak numbers, they provided some 20 per cent of all American box-office revenues. Drive-ins thrived through the 1970s and radically declined in numbers only in the 1980s, when land values rose and drive-in sites often became more valuable for housing and for the shopping malls that followed the postwar shift of population to the suburbs. There were some 1,500 shopping malls by 1965, 2,500 by 1970 and 22,500 by 1980. Whether or not malls took the sites of drive-ins, these developments rapidly affected patterns of exhibition (which then had their own effects on drive-ins). The 1970s and 1980s saw the rise of multi-screen complexes, very often associated with shopping centres, exploiting the integration with other consumer and leisure activity, and making use of the extensive car parking space on which the malls depended. By the early 1970s, it was standard industry practice to talk of *screens* rather than cinemas. Cinema theatres reached their low point of about 12,500 in the mid 1970s, by which time there were around 14,000 screens. But multi-screen developments came rapidly and by 1984 there were over 20,000 screens, many of them owned by big chains like General Cinema and AMC (American Multi-Cinema), with the Canada-based Cineplex Odeon becoming increasingly important from the mid 1980s. The multiplexes, with their auditoria of different capacities, allowed for both greater flexibility in programming – depending on their success, films could be shifted between screens – and economies in running costs.

Research showed that in the postwar period audiences were becoming generally both better educated and younger, but there is little evidence that Hollywood, or any-way the majors, took account of this, or, indeed, took much trouble to investigate the market, an attitude that almost certainly contributed to the decline in attendances. As in the 1960s, when trying to repeat what in retrospect appears to be the freak success of *The Sound of Music*, Hollywood often seemed to be going for the family audience which, as a *regular* audience, had been definitively lost to television. A survey in 1957 showed that 52 per cent of the audience was under 20, and 72 per cent was under 29 – in other words, a group that constituted only 40 per cent of the total population of the United States was making up about three-quarters of the movie-going public.

Of course, Hollywood did make movies aimed largely at a youth audience in the 1950s and 1960s, though not to the extent that it did in the 1970s and 1980s, when it took greater note of audience research. In the 1950s and 1960s, it was the independent 'exploitation' companies like AIP (American International Pictures, which averaged about ten releases a year in the 1960s), that were in many ways more successful at targeting the youth audience with cheaply made movies intended primarily for drive-in double bills. Roger Corman learned the business by producing and directing exploitation movies for AIP in the 1950s and 1960s and carried the experience forward into the 1970s and 1980s with his own independent companies.

The young, better educated audience provided the opening in the 1950s and especially the 1960s for the rise of independent distributors specialising in predominantly European 'art movies'. By the mid 1960s there were some 800 art-house venues, particularly in college towns. At first, the majors were little interested, but eventually they began to take note that what was once a 'mass' audience was now much more segmented and had to be catered to in a variety of ways. The art-house market was another that some of the majors, such as United Artists and Orion, made an effort to exploit in the 1970s and 1980s with their 'classics' divisions.

Overseas markets declined less rapidly in the postwar period than the American market and consequently grew in economic importance, although the industry's prime focus always remained on North American box-office performance. By the early 1960s, American movies often derived half their rental revenues from overseas (with Europe providing 80 per cent of this). The percentage declined somewhat in the early 1980s mainly as a result of increases in domestic revenue. The majors were helped in overseas distribution by being able to combine their efforts in ways forbidden by anti-trust considerations in the United States. Thus, in 1977, Paramount and Universal combined to form CIC (Cinema International Corporation), with about a third of the overseas market, transforming CIC into UIP (United International Pictures) in 1981, when MGM/UA joined them for overseas distribution. American cinema increasingly dominated European markets, cornering about 85 per cent of film rentals in Britain throughout the 1970s and 1980s, with similarly high percentages in European countries without significant indigenous industries. In countries with substantial film industries (with substantial government subsidies), the American share of the market was smaller: 40-45 per cent in France, 50-60 per cent in Italy.

Television film production has also sought to make back its costs in the North American market but has depended very often for profitability on foreign sales (and on syndication in the North American market, after initial network broadcasts). As a 1983 study discovered, domestically produced television shows invariably dominate ratings in European countries and make up over 70 per cent of programme time, leaving television less open to American domination. Nevertheless, the ability of American companies to offer 'quality' television material at comparatively low cost has meant that they provide almost half of the imported material; almost all of it is fiction that occupies prime-time slots. US imports of television programmes are negligible.

From Movies to Communications

By the 1980s, the movie industry (and, inextricably, the television industry) had firmly established itself as profitable, but the only way to share in the profits on a large and continuing scale was to be a major. Companies wanting to break into the industry could not set themselves up in business as new players; they needed to buy an existing studio as a going concern. To get back into the action in the 1980s, MGM acquired United Artists to form MGM/UA. Orion was a new company formed in 1978 by United Artists executives who left after a difficult period in the early 1970s and strained relations with Transamerica; it could function only by making a distribution deal with Warner.

The television networks remained important sources of revenue through buying features for broadcasting – *American Gigolo,* which cost $5 million to make, was reputed to have made $6 million from three broadcasts by ABC – but the status quo was changing rapidly. During the 1980s, the rapid growth of cable television, satellite technology and video meant that, for the first time, revenues from these sources began regularly to overtake those from theatrical release. Already, in the early 1980s, cable or pay television was emerging as a very important market force, accounting in 1982 for over 17 per cent of total movie revenues, and in 1983 buying exclusive cable rights to 37 of the year's 106 releases. Video cassette recorder sales had increased from 30,000 a year in 1976 and 1·4 million in 1981 to over 12·5 million in 1986, reaching over half the households in America. (The 1980 screen actors' strike and the 1988 writers' strike were directly related to such developments, centring on rights in 'residuals', as the films they had contributed to achieved more varied, longer and more lucrative lives.) The increasing value of merchandising – the marketing of commodities such as toys and T-shirts associated with particular movies – and tie-ins with publishing and music also fitted in with the multi-media interests of the majors.

These developments seemed to present the opportunity for expanding production, and out of this was born Tri-Star in 1982. In essence, Columbia Pictures, HBO (Home Box Office, the dominant cable movie channel, which was owned by Time Inc.) and the biggest television network, CBS, joined forces to form the new 'studio'. Joint financing of production tied up with joint exploitation of product: theatrical distribution was guaranteed through Columbia and cable delivery by HBO, while CBS would distribute the films on video (rental, then retail) and show them on the CBS network. Rupert Murdoch's acquisition of Twentieth Century-Fox was also characteristic of the times. Fox lost $189 million between 1982 and 1985, when owned by Marvin Davis, and this gave an opening for Murdoch's Australian News Corporation to buy a half share in the company for $250 million in 1985. Almost immediately, Davis and Murdoch spent $2 billion buying Metromedia Television, the largest group of independent television stations in the United States, reaching almost 20 per cent of households. To be allowed to own American television stations, Murdoch had to take American citizenship. Soon afterwards he bought out Davis for $325 million and was in a position to create a new television network, Fox Television. Now Fox was able to produce both films and television to feed not only Fox's theatrical distribution, but also Fox Broadcasting in the United States and Murdoch's new European satellite station, Sky Broadcasting (now BSkyB).

In the late 1960s, some small-scale movies (such as *The Graduate* in 1967 and *Midnight Cowboy* and *Easy Rider* both in 1969) had been comparatively big successes, while some big-budget movies like *Hello, Dolly!* had been financial failures. But there was a general lesson being learned by the majors: only a very few pictures, maybe one in ten, will make big profits, while most will lose money (theatrically at least). Many of the big hits of the late 1960s and early 1970s – like *Airport* and, especially, *The Godfather* – had been big-budget movies. Despite a general climate of crisis and retrenchment, the belief grew, partly supported by some spectacular successes, that studio pictures should have big budgets to have any chance of taking off. Cheaper films tended to be made by the independents. In 1977, it was calculated that out of 199 major films released, the top six accounted for one-third of the year's rentals to distributors, the top thirteen for half, and the top twenty-eight for three-quarters. Not surprisingly, twelve of the top thirteen were distributed by the majors, for only they have the organisation to release films optimally on both the domestic and the international markets, not to mention the cash and product flow to allow losses to be set against profits on a large scale.

Theatrical distribution remained vitally important and continues to form the focus of industry attention. This is in part because a movie that is successful theatrically can generate stupendous profits, even though big hits are few and far between. Connected, and in many ways more important, is the fact that the theatrical life of a movie does most to establish its value as it goes through its distribution cycle, from theatrical exhibition through home video rental, pay television and cable showing, video retail sale, network television transmission, to re-release on cable and syndication for television.

Releases from the majors settled down at a little over 100 a year in the 1980s as against 350 or more fifty years earlier. No longer was there the regular flow of product to the regular audience that was characteristic of the 1930s and 1940s, when cinema-going was very much a habit; now, it had become much more of an event – each film needed in some way to be special and to be marketed as such. This strengthened the role of the distributor, who could have a powerful role in determining success or failure by deciding in advance which films merited large publicity campaigns, and when and where films should be released, with Christmas and summer (and Easter to a lesser extent) being favoured for event (and especially family) movies. Certainly, from the 1970s, so much more was riding on individual films that immensely larger sums were thought necessary for promotion and publicity. It was reckoned that *Alien* (1979) cost $10 million to produce but $15 million to promote.

Only the majors have the resources to spend at this level and have gained worldwide dominance through economies of scale and consolidation of overseas distribution with other majors. The current industry calculation is that the average movie needs a worldwide box-office take of $2^{1}/_{2}$ times its negative – production – costs to break even (that is, to cover the costs of production, prints, distribution and promotion).

Production costs also rose fast, with the average for Hollywood features inflating from $2 million in 1972 to $10 million in 1980 and $23 million in 1989; on average a further $9-10 million were needed for advertising and prints. A big contribution to the rise in costs came from the financial demands of the big stars who, in the post-studio era, offered one of the few guarantees, or apparent guarantees, of success. As in the 1950s, many stars (Robert Redford and Jane Fonda among them) used their new power to form their own companies and become their own producers and/or directors. The need to maximise audiences had already led in the 1950s to a sharp decline in the proportion of original scripts, and the tendency to pre-selling by basing films on known properties of some kind (most obviously plays and novels) grew stronger in the 1970s and 1980s, with big films such as *Airport* (1970), *The Godfather* (1972), *The Exorcist* (1973), *Jaws* (1975), *Saturday Night Fever* (1977) and *Superman – The Movie* (1979). The pre- and post-selling power of existing novels or music could often be extended by publishing tie-ins, 'novelisations', soundtrack albums and so on. With so much riding on each film, another sure route to profitability appeared to lie in sequels or in television series based on hit movies. Indeed, sequels became almost emblematic of the industry from the 1970s into the 1990s, with often multiple sequels to such pictures as *Star Wars* (1977), *The Godfather, Jaws, Rocky* (1976), *Smokey and the Bandit* (1977) and, more recently, *Nightmare on Elm Street* (1984), *Predator* (1987), and *Die Hard* (1988). It has been estimated that in recent years some 10 per cent of the majors' production was made up of sequels – in some ways, sequels could be said to have taken over the role that genres played in earlier production. With very rare exceptions, sequels cost more than the originals and do not make as much profit, but they can nevertheless be relied upon to be profitable in their various markets, with the added advantage that experience gained from the success of the original makes it much easier to plan for profitable ancillary activities.

On the whole, the majors stuck to very cautious, very conservative, very expensive film-making, and any vitality that the industry retained came from the many smaller, cheaper films that continued to be made, usually by independent producers. The industry's reliance on a few big hits suggests that proportionately less revenue accrues to smaller films. In the context of reduced output, the purpose of smaller movies sometimes seemed to be keeping theatres supplied with product, but, fortunately, small movies refused to die and continued to show the majors that they could make significant profits.

By the mid 1980s, the majors had demonstrated that movie production and distribution was still profitable, and the business was still essentially in their control. As parts of conglomerates and communications companies, they were well positioned to take advantage of rapidly developing new technologies for the delivery of their products. They might well have been targets for new anti-trust suits, since they constituted an oligopoly as restrictive as the vertically integrated studios of fifty years earlier, but the nature of the market and the means of dominating it had shifted significantly. In any case, this was the era of Reaganite *laisser faire* economics, with government much less keen to restrain the natural tendencies of capitalist industry. In a striking historical reversal, some majors began to take advantage of the well-established upturn in cinema audiences and the change in the political climate by reacquiring theatres without challenge.

TOWARDS 2000

In spite of all the changes that have taken place, Hollywood in the late 1980s and early 1990s does not look that different from the Hollywood of the previous forty years. Fears of recession are endemic in the industry, and weekly box office returns are scrutinised for the worst. The central worry is that there might be a recurrence of the crisis of the late 1960s and early 1970s, when overproduction and escalating costs were accompanied by a downturn in admissions. In general, however, the industry has remained relatively buoyant and profitable.

The studio names remain familiar, and their market shares (though eagerly watched and compared) imply, as in the past, a group of studios, rather than any one or two, dominating the market. In 1991, Warner Bros led with a 13·9 per cent market share (against 13·1 per cent in 1990 and 17·4 per cent in 1989) from 28 releases, but in large part due to *Robin Hood: Prince of Thieves*, which grossed $165 million in North America in 1991, bringing profits of some $18-23 million to the studio) and *New Jack City* (gross $50 million, profits $8-10 million). Disney/Buena Vista was in second place with a 13·7 per cent share (15·5 per cent in 1990 and 13·9 per cent in 1989) from 23 pictures, with *Beauty and the Beast* its most profitable film ($25 million to make plus $10-15 million to release, but grossing $120 million to give $30 million profits, a figure liable to rise to more like $100 million when foreign and video markets are added). Third was Paramount, with a 12 per cent share (14·9 per cent in 1990, 13·8 per cent in 1989) from 21 pictures, the most profitable being *The Addams Family* (which grossed over $110 million to return about $22 million in profit), followed by *Naked Gun 2¹/₂* ($86 million gross, $12 million profit).

Fourth equal on 11 per cent were Universal (23 pictures, 13·1 per cent in 1990, 16·6 per cent in 1989) and Fox (20 pictures, 13·1 per cent in 1990, 6·5 per cent in 1989), with *Sleeping with the Enemy* grossing over $100 million and returning $20 million profit for Fox, and *Backdraft* ($70 million gross, $20 million profit) and *Cape Fear* (over $70 million gross, $20 million profit) the most successful films for Universal, though Universal also achieved good grosses on low-budget movies like *Problem Child 2* ($24 million), *The People under the Stairs* ($22 million) and *Child's Play 3* ($13 million), all of which were likely to do exceptionally well on video. Columbia's and TriStar's shares are listed separately, at 9·1 per cent and 10·9 per cent on 14 and 13 pictures respectively (Columbia from 4·9 per cent in 1990, 8·1 per cent in 1989, TriStar from 9 per cent in 1990, 7·9 per cent in 1989). However, both are part of Sony Entertainment, whose market share was thus 20 per cent if the totals were added – enough in itself to start rumours circulating about Sony integrating the two entities even more closely than they already are. *Terminator 2* ($204 million gross) and *City Slickers* ($130 million) were the biggest grossing films but, being made independently, are likely to return on domestic theatrical revenues only $15-20 million and $19 million respectively in profits to their major distributors, while the low-budget, studio-made *Boyz N the Hood* (production costs $6 million, release costs $12 million, box-office gross $57 million) is likely to return over $25 million profit on domestic theatrical release alone.

Whether Orion, formed only in 1978 (and destined for bankruptcy in 1992) should be grouped with the majors is open to debate, but the success of *The Silence of the*

Lambs (about $25 million profit), helped by continuing receipts from *Dances with Wolves*, gave it 8·5 per cent of the market (5·6 per cent in 1990, 4·2 per cent in 1989) with only nine pictures. MGM/UA, barely in business, achieved only 2·3 per cent from sixteen pictures, its only major release being *Thelma and Louise*. The leading independent studio/distributor was the expanding New Line, which achieved 4 per cent market share, from 18 releases (4·4 per cent in 1990, 1·3 per cent in 1989).

As 1992 ends, it looks as if only five of the original eight majors – Warner, Paramount, Twentieth Century-Fox, Universal and Columbia – will survive, plus Disney, which definitely took its place among them in the 1980s, and TriStar to the extent that it can be considered an entity separate from Columbia. Orion could still survive, and New Line must be a contender for at least 'mini-major' status (it has indeed, been taking over bits of Orion's business). The power of the majors, their control of the market for motion pictures in North America and the rest of the world, has become, if anything, more concentrated over the 1980s. This is largely because they have further changed their nature. In fact, though theatrical box-office revenues, and especially those from the domestic North American market, remain an important pointer, they have not for some years been the prime source of the majors' profits.

Independents

The further concentrated power of the major studios has obvious consequences for independent producers and distributors in the market. However, three of the five films that grossed over $100 million in 1991 were in fact only distributed by the majors: *Terminator 2* was made by Carolco, *Robin Hood: Prince of Thieves* by Morgan Creek and *City Slickers* by Castle Rock, all independent production companies. Two other high-grossing films of the summer of 1991 were also made by independent companies – *Backdraft* by Imagine and *Point Break* by Largo. Together, these five films generated about a third of the 1991 summer season's $1·8 billion box-office gross – independently made films were certainly no less important to the industry than they had been at any time since the 1950s, and were perhaps more important. However, a big hit made by an independent brings less profit to the major that distributes it (and gets only a distribution fee) than it would had the film been produced in-house.

Carolco, Morgan Creek, Castle Rock, Imagine Entertainment and Largo are all recently formed companies, established in the mid and late 1980s. They are a distinctively new breed of independent, all sufficiently well capitalised to be able to produce pictures on their own, without recourse to studio finance, but generally with an established relationship with a studio for domestic theatrical release. The new independents often also cover, and therefore control, the costs of making prints and of advertising: importantly, they retain the rights to foreign distribution, home video, television and cable sales, all rights that are often pre-sold and play a part in the financing package. The majors take their distribution fees but the independents' retention of rights enables them to build up the important asset of a library of titles.

Morgan Creek (responsible for titles such as *Pacific Heights, Young Guns II, Freejack,* and *Enemies, A Love Story*) was formed in 1987 and is secured by mostly Japanese finance: it has an output deal with Fox, as has Largo, which started in 1989 and is funded by JVC. Castle Rock *(When Harry Met Sally, Misery, Sibling Rivalry)*, was formed in 1987: it is 51 per cent owned by its five partners (who include the director Rob Reiner), 34 per cent by Columbia (now Sony) and 15 per cent by Westinghouse Broadcasting, and has an output deal with Columbia/Sony. Imagine Entertainment *(Parenthood, The Dream Team, The 'burbs, Problem Child)* was founded in 1985 by Ron Howard and Brian Grazer; it is part-owned by, and has a (non-exclusive) output deal with Universal which, with the cable channel Showtime, finances an important part of Imagine's productions. Carolco's first huge success was *Rambo: First Blood Part II*, which has led to the company being dubbed 'the house that Rambo built'; its other productions have included *Total Recall*, *Air America*, *Mountains of the Moon*, *The Music Box*, *Basic Instinct*, *The Doors*, *LA Story* and *Rambling Rose*. Carolco has as partners Japan's Pioneer Electronics, France's pay cable Canal Plus, the UK's Carlton Communications, Italy's Rizzoli/Corriere della Sera, and has an output deal with TriStar.

The roster of products and backers makes it clear that the independence of these companies does not lead to significant risk-taking: their pictures are more or less indistinguishable from those of the majors. Their production processes are less subject to studio interference – a major advantage of working independently – and freedom from some of the pressures of distribution allows them to focus more clearly on making the product. Their attraction for the majors is that they make quality pictures usually more economically than the studios could themselves, partly because they are very lean companies with low overheads. Castle Rock, for example, has only 55 full-time staff, and Joe Roth, a co-founder of Morgan Creek and until late 1992 head of Fox, reckons he was hired by Fox 'because at Morgan Creek we had only a handful of people and we made eleven movies in eighteen months. When I came to Fox, with all their enormous staff, they hadn't produced as many.' Rob Reiner describes Castle Rock as 'a kind of mini-studio, a kind of satellite of Columbia with real autonomy . . . our initial funding came from Coca-Cola. From that we raised a lot more money and struck deals with cable television and video companies. We put up all the money to make the films and we pay for all the prints and advertising, distribute through Columbia Pictures in America and make separate deals for international distribution. Because we pay for the prints and ads, the studio takes only a 15 per cent fee instead of the usual 35 per cent. I must say this is very unusual in Hollywood. All the money we earn goes towards the next picture.'

Firms like Castle Rock and Morgan Creek are happy to point out that their independence is strictly limited, just like that of the majority of independents in the 1950s. Alan Horn, one of the founding partners of Castle Rock, summarises the situation very clearly: 'I would define an independent as a company that has the capability to finance its own motion picture product, whether it does so via presales or using its own capital from the beginning or some combination of traditional borrowing, subordinated bank debt or equity. But from one source or the other, they have the wherewithal to make their own movies and therefore to greenlight their own movies . . . I think of Castle Rock as a dependent independent because we are dependent upon a major motion picture company to get our product distributed in the domestic theatrical marketplace. For us, it's a positive. We are making so-called A pictures: medium-to-high budget, $15 million to $30 million movies with A elements, a combination of director/star, director/cast, writer/director/cast, with some marquee value, box-office appeal, or even just production value that makes it very special. This would put us in direct competition with the majors if we were to distribute on our own because we would be distributing the same product they're making, only we'd be hitting them head-to-head in distribution. We're not making enough pictures to be an effective force in distribution.'

'A true independent operates outside the established studio system and competes directly with it for a share of the market. But the word has been corrupted. Independent no longer means "independent". It now means "appendage".' This is from Lloyd Kaufman, president of Troma, low-budget producers of *The Toxic Avenger* series – true independence seems to have become the preserve of very low-budget film-makers. Roger Corman, who formed and led low-budget New World Pictures in the 1970s and now runs Concorde (whose recent productions/releases include *Brain Dead*, *Slumber Party Massacre III* and *Rock 'n' Roll High School Forever*) concurs: 'A true independent is a company that can finance, produce and distribute its own films. Most are partial independents, connected in some way to a major studio. They are independent producers but not truly independent companies. There are very few independents in the classical sense left in Hollywood, and it may well be that it's a dying breed.' Concorde, with average budgets of $2-3 million per picture, normally organises its own distribution, but even it works with the majors for home video where, in fact, its main business lies.

More in the traditional image of the adventurous, risk-taking independent producer is Ed Pressman's Edward R. Pressman Film Corporation, which in 1991 made a financing deal with the Japanese Ascii Pictures Corporation, a subsidiary of computer chip manufacturer Ascii that has also invested in other companies. Pressman, a producer as far back as *Badlands* and *Sisters* in 1973, has been more recently involved in productions like *Wall Street, Talk Radio, Walker, Good Morning Babylon, Paris By Night, To Sleep with Anger, Reversal of Fortune, Blue Steel*, and lately with David Mamet's *Homicide*. John Frankenheimer's *Hour of the Gun* and Mark Frost's *Storyville*. Interviewed in 1987, Pressman argued that, over the last few years, the industry had changed and that 'it's not such a clear monopoly by the major studios, and that has allowed me and a number of other people to gain some prominence that would not otherwise have been allowed.' Pressman favours a close working relationship with directors, whose work is respected: 'In the old days, the studio bosses had directors under contract; they could come up with a great idea and choose Howard Hawks or whoever to direct. That gave the producer a kind of dominance that doesn't exist today . . . You can't just hire Martin Scorsese or Stanley Kubrick. They are independent in a way that requires a common point of view . . . It's an unspoken kind of thing; it's a common purpose that sets you on the same side as them; the objectives are mutual; there is no division between producer and director.' Pressman favours more independence right up to the delivery of prints: 'After that, practically any of the majors can give you what you want . . . if you want that type of handling.' Pressman's deals with distributors change with the nature of the project: as the titles of his films imply, he often does not want the kind of distribution the majors have to offer. More recently, however, Pressman, responding to a further change in the industry, has been reported as negotiating with Warner Bros for an exclusive, five-year financing and distribution arrangement covering up to twenty major motion pictures, which would put his corporation in the same kind of position as Morgan Creek and the others.

The advent of independents like Morgan Creek and Castle Rock has spawned the term 'neo-indie' to distinguish them from the earlier independents who did operate – or tried to operate – outside the orbit of the majors, in some cases setting themselves up as 'mini-majors'. As these companies failed in the late 1980s, they were in a sense replaced by the 'neo-indies' with their close ties to the majors. Orion, formed in 1978 by disaffected United Artists management, was one such mini-major. It was set up in 1978 with Wall Street backing and was its own North American distributor, but had pre-sale arrangements with Home Box Office (HBO) for pay cable, RCA/Columbia for overseas home video and for overseas theatrical. Through much of the 1980s, Orion was remarkably successful, gaining the reputation of being a sanctuary for creative film-makers like Woody Allen and, remarkably, capturing the largest market share of domestic theatrical distribution in 1987. Orion also diversified into television production (making, for example, the long-running *Cagney and Lacey)* and formed the highly suc-cessful Orion Classics division, for the distribution of 'niche' pictures. Only in the late 1980s did Orion begin to suffer significantly from its burden of debt, and its future, following its bankruptcy, remains uncertain despite the spectacular success in 1990-91 of *Dances with Wolves* and *The Silence of the Lambs*.

The fate of other mini-majors was more decisive. Menaham Golan and Yoram Globus's Cannon, a minor independent in 1979, had a rapid rise and fall. It started off by making low-budget 'Cannon-fodder' to exploit foreign markets hungry for American product, and financing on the basis of territory-by-territory pre-sales. In the early and mid 1980s, Cannon upgraded its product and energetically acquired theatres in both Europe and the United States to sustain the distribution of its films. Although it was apparently very successful financially, Cannon's stock fell disastrously after a Securities and Exchange Commission investigation. Cannon was just about saved by backing from Giancarlo Parretti and became part of Pathé Communications, the base from which Parretti launched his extended but ultimately unsuccessful bid to take over MGM/UA in the early 1990s.

A similar challenge to the system was mounted by the Dino de Laurentiis Entertainment Group (DEG), formed in 1985, and New World, after Roger Corman sold it in 1983. De Laurentiis, abandoning film production in Italy, built sound stages in North Carolina and embarked on an ambitious production schedule; it bought Embassy Pictures as a film library and distribution arm, but was soon forced to sell it off. DEG continues, but in a much scaled-down form. New World expanded rapidly in the mid 1980s, producing its own films (rather than simply acquiring titles), forming New World Television and New World Video, establishing New World Pictures Australia to produce features and television movies cheaply, and generally aspiring to make itself an international player. With movies like *Hellraiser* (1987), it increased its revenues from $41 million in 1984 to $106 million in 1986. By the late 1980s, New World, too, was in bankruptcy. A similar fate befell companies like Kings Road Entertainment, Lorimar, the Weintraub Entertainment Group, Vestron, Atlantic Releasing and others, despite such big hits as Vestron's *Dirty Dancing* (1987) and Atlantic's *Teen Wolf* (1985).

The expansion of the neo-indies was based on the buoyant box-office of the 1980s (when production by the majors was cut back temporarily but the number of screens in the United States expanded) and on the availability of low-cost credit to finance expanded activity. More important still was the explosion of growth in the home video and pay cable markets. Although the majors were always crucial to the rapidly expanding home-video market, a diversity of product was required, and the independents were able to provide it. There was enormous demand, too, from the four recently established national pay cable channels for new material – much more than the majors could provide. With the possibility of pre-selling projects to both cable and home video and with often very low-budget pictures, risk was frequently minimal. Theatrical distribution was useful but not always a necessary precondition for a sale. As the 1980s wore on, several factors began to work against the independents. Flushed with early success, several of them, like New World, expanded too ambitiously, while Vestron was essentially a video company that expanded into the more difficult world of theatrical features and distribution (with John Huston's *The Dead* as well as more obviously commercial vehicles like *Dirty Dancing)*.

Observing such changes, Corman commented that 'as they move up in budgets, what used to succeed for independents won't succeed anymore. They're leaving what had been a safe, profitable niche to try to compete on the fringes of the majors – that's their undoing. They tried to find an area between the traditional independent and the majors and they couldn't.' There was a glut of product, with the annual output of the mini-majors and independents growing by nearly 180 between 1984 and 1987 – approximately 300 of the 500 features produced in 1986 were independently made. At the same time, the home video market was levelling off and the majors were moving increasingly to dominate it. Crédit Lyonnais Bank Nederland had been a significant supporter of the independents, but the Parretti-MGM/UA debacle, in which the bank loaned $1 billion to Parretti, led it to pull back, and this made other financial bodies more cautious. As usual, the independents were an inherently more risky investment than the majors or, as the late 1980s showed, than the neo-indies which surrendered distribution to the majors.

The Majors
The majors had been forced to adapt to divorcement and to television in the 1940s and 1950s, and had adapted again in the era of mergers and conglomerates in 1960s and 1970s. In the 1980s and early 1990s, as the core activities of media empires, they were changing yet again in response to new pressures and new opportunities. Entertainment

has become the second largest American export category (after military hardware), and the studios are organised to promote and expand their activity both at home and abroad.

Although theatrical distribution and exhibition are now less significant for the revenues derived from them, they remain in some ways the key activity in establishing the value and therefore the profitability of films as commodities. The legal decision that had forced the studios to sell off their theatre chains after 1948 was reversed in 1985 – reflecting the Reagan era's attitudes to business – and the majors immediately bought into theatre chains once again. Coca-Cola, then the owner of Columbia, bought the Walter Reade chain, MCA/Universal bought a 49 per cent share in Cineplex Odeon (with 1880 screens in 1989); Columbia/Sony now owns Loew's Theaters (839 screens) and Paramount, with Time Warner, has several chains (adding up to 466 screens). The acquisitions helped the majors to increase their control over which films would be shown, where, and for how long, at the expense (once again) of independent producers and distributors.

Getting back into theatre ownership – a re-assertion of vertical integration – inevitably smacked of past practices. But other – even more fundamental – changes in the structure of the industry had their origins elsewhere, in media industry trends and particularly in new technologies. Under the studio system, the majors made movies, then controlled their distribution to and exhibition in theatres, and that was most of what they did. Today, these activities are only one element, even if arguably a pre-eminent one, in integrated media empires that also include television production and syndication companies, cable distribution networks, home video distribution, record companies, book and magazine publishing, theme parks, and much else. We need to think increasingly of the movies themselves either as software to feed the appetites of distribution structures (which in a restricted way they always were) and hardware systems, or as pretexts for other operations such as merchandising or theme parks. As screenwriter Lewis Cole summed it up (in *The Nation*): 'Old Hollywood – independent companies owned and run by entrepreneurs who relied on stables of "creative elements" (actors, writers and directors) to produce films reflecting the boss commercial and artistic convictions – was being replaced by New Hollywood: film divisions of multinational corporations that specialized in leisure-time products – books, records, magazines, theme parks and children's toys.'

Warner, which, in the 1970s, had extended into a range of fields, mostly connected with leisure, had a disastrous experience with Atari video games in 1982-83, losing $300 million. It then sold off various subsidiaries, including cosmetics and sports, to concentrate on film and television production and distribution plus music and publishing, buying out American Express's half interest in Warner Amex cable to position itself for future developments in cable such as pay-per-view. In 1989, Steve Ross, who had been head of Kinney Services when it took over Warner and became chairman of Warner Communications, masterminded the corporation's purchase by Time Inc. on terms that were very advantageous for Warner – and himself. This aligned Time's magazines and cable television channels with Warner's records, film and television studios and world-wide distribution network. Time Warner constitutes the largest communications and media enterprise in the world, with 1990 sales of $11.5 billion. Ross remained chairman until his death in December 1992; it is thought that power is now likely to shift towards the Time side of the empire.

When Gulf + Western acquired Paramount in 1966, entertainment was only a minor element in the conglomerate's overall portfolio, but twenty years later entertainment accounted for over a third of its total revenues: Paramount in the late 1980s was very successful with such pictures as *Top Gun*, *Beverly Hills Cop II* and *Fatal Attraction*, capturing the largest market share among the studios in both 1986 and 1987, and Paramount Home Video did likewise in its sector, while Paramount Television was also in a strong position. When Gulf + Western changed its name to Paramount Communications in 1989, this signalled both its aim of concentrating its energies on communications and entertainment – having shed many other interests in the process – and its recognition of the continuing power in the media field of the old studio names. Paramount Communications then divided its energies between entertainment – mainly Paramount movies and television and theatres – and publishing – notably Simon & Schuster.

Disney was not considered a real major before the 1980s, even though it had early on diversified into television, theme parks, music and merchandising (which had helped it to survive the 1969 recession). Disney's market share was smaller than that of the majors and it was strongly identified, unlike the others, with what was now a single niche market, the family audience. By the 1980s, Disney's profits from family movies were declining, and profits from Disneyland and Disneyworld were levelling off. Forced to change direction, Disney launched the Touchstone name for adult-oriented movies with *Splash* in 1984. A management shake-up installed a new team headed by Michael Eisner, and Disney quickly expanded production, achieving the top market share of 20 per cent in 1988 with a series of hits such as *Down and Out in Beverly Hills* (the company's first R-rated film), *Ruthless People*, *Three Men and a Baby*, and *Who Framed Roger Rabbit?* Disney also extended its theme park operation to Europe, went extensively into merchandising on the basis of its brand and character names, syndicated its library of cartoons, films and television programmes, produced hit television shows such as *The Golden Girls*, and progressively re-issued its classic animated cartoons on home video. In 1989, in a move to expand its production and share of the box-office at a time when the market seemed to be growing, Disney launched a new 'studio' name, Hollywood Pictures, though its marketing and distribution operations remained integrated. Thus far, Hollywood Pictures has failed to establish much of a separate identity, and only *Arachnophobia* has been a significant success (while, for example, *One Good Cop* and *V.I. Warshawski* failed at the domestic box-office). Overall, however, under Eisner, Disney's profits grew spectacularly, from $98 million in 1984 to around $650 million in 1990, a year that included receipts from *Pretty Woman*, *Dick Tracy* and some home video successes. Disney, too, has sought to become vertically integrated in the old sense of the word, steadily building up theatre holdings and concentrating heavily on in-studio production, rather than acting as distributor for films made by independents.

The recent history of the other majors – Columbia-TriStar, MCA/Universal and Twentieth Century-Fox – demonstrates the increasingly global context in which Hollywood needs to be seen. Although all the majors are global players, what Time Warner's Steven Ross calls 'the $35 billion fire sale' of American media interests since 1985 has left these under foreign ownership. In part, this simply reflects a much broader shift in economic and financial power away from the United States as the world's economic powerhouse towards Japan (and the Far East in general), and towards Europe. Thus, Japan, since the mid 1980s the world's largest creditor nation, is a major force in American banking and stock dealing, as well as producing 20 per cent of the semiconductors sold in the United States, over 30 per cent of its cars, and over 50 per cent of its machine tools and consumer electronics. European interests have also increasingly invested in the American economy. It would, indeed, be surprising if the entertainment industry, with its global reach, had not attracted foreign investors.

American entertainment (and American-style entertainment) is dominant in large parts of the world. Japan and Europe are the most lucrative markets for American movies. From the 1980s, European broadcasting, previously heavily regulated, if not run, by the state, underwent a radical transformation, with satellites and cable opening up many more channels of entertainment. As in North America, this created an enormous hunger, and thus much competition, for material – in itself enough to make Japanese and European interests want a stake in filmed product which would bring with it guaranteed access. Such, in large measure, was the motivation of Rupert Murdoch's News Corporation in buying Fox in 1985, simultaneously buying important television stations, and then launching a fourth television network, Fox Broadcasting, to challenge CBS, NBC and ABC. Fox's film and television production goes not only to its film distribution and television organisations in the United States but also, for example, to its Sky (now BSkyB) satellite-broadcasting operation in Europe and, like other media corporations, it aligns these interests with its others in magazine and newspaper publishing. Slowly, though still saddled with large debts, News Corporation and Fox have established a more profitable base: Fox Broadcasting lost $100 million in 1988, broke even in 1989, and began to be profitable in 1990, coming in as the second most profitable of the four networks, after ABC, but ahead of NBC and CBS. In television production, the great success of the animated series *The Simpsons* promises much when eventually syndicated, with profits from it and other shows potentially contributing revenues of $300-400 million. 1990 was also a good year for Fox's theatrical film division, with *Home Alone*, which cost $18 million grossing $280 million domestically and $200 million abroad: it is expected to ship over 10 million units on home video, possibly bringing in a total $250 million in profit. Although many observers remain sceptical about the viability of Murdoch's global aspirations, there is certainly now a stronger feeling that Murdoch/Fox operations could be brought finally to stable profitability.

A rather different impulse is represented by the Sony Corporation's $3.4 billion acquisition of Columbia Pictures in 1989 (Sony had previously bought CBS Records for $2 billion in 1987), and by Matsushita's 1990 take-over of MCA/Universal, the largest single take-over of an American company by a foreign concern – and said to have been orchestrated by Mike Ovitz of CAA. Both Sony and its larger competitor Matsushita (whose brand names include JVC, Pioneer and Technics) are – or were – essentially electronic hardware manufacturers, and there have been persistent rumours that Toshiba, another Japanese electronics giant, is interested in Paramount. Traditionally, Sony has been seen as the innovator and Matsushita as the company that follows up and exploits new ideas cheaply – one reason often given for Matsushita's purchase has been a feeling that it could not afford not to follow suit after Sony made its move.

Sony's motives can be traced back to the VCR battle of the 1970s, when Sony's Betamax system lost out in the fight to establish a universal standard format for video cassettes to Matsushita's VHS, which many saw as technically inferior to Betamax. Sony felt that guaranteed access to software – essentially movies – for its system would have put it in a stronger position. In the late 1980s, new technical rivalry loomed. Sony's Digital Audio Tape (DAT), effectively killed off by the record companies, and its Minidisc, were launched in the face of Philips's Digital Compact Cassette (DCC), which was licensed to Matsushita (hence Sony's interest in CBS Records, now Sony Music Entertainment). Sony was initially held back in the contest by legal challenges on copyright laws (as with the VCR battle) as well as by its attempt to establish Video8 as a new VCR standard. More important will be the coming, furious competition over high-definition television (HDTV), in which Sony and Matsushita are both clear that Hollywood software is likely to play a decisive role.

Undoubtedly, there were other reasons for the arrival of the Japanese: Sony's action can also be read as a classic example of a company diversifying when its primary market – in this case video recorders both in Japan and elsewhere – has reached saturation. Both Sony's acquisition and the price it paid are still much debated and will need to be assessed in the long term – this probably suits Japanese management style, which could hardly be more different from Hollywood's notorious fixation with immediate bottom-line performance. Sony's Akia Morita has pointed out that the price tag of $6 billion ($3.4 billion for Columbia, $1.3 billion in assumed debt, $1 billion to get the company up and running, $200 million to acquire The Guber Peters Entertainment Company) was 'very, very small' compared to the expenses involved in developing hardware. In the short term, the profits of Sony and Matsushita have fallen after their studio acquisitions, but Sony certainly acquired some very solid assets – a library of 2,720 movie titles,

Columbia Pictures Television, with a stock of 23,000 episodes, two studio facilities (Columbia Studios and Culver Studios), the Loew's theatre chain, half of RCA/Columbia Home Video (now wholly owned and renamed Columbia-TriStar Home Video), and Columbia-TriStar International Releasing, as well as the TriStar operation. Under Coca-Cola, Columbia had tried to expand production and maximise revenue by integrating theatrical film, cable and network television and home video by joining with HBO and CBS in 1982 to form Tri-Star (renamed TriStar by Sony). Despite some hits like Carolco's *Rambo: First Blood Part II* and Tri-Star-Delphi II's *The Natural*, the arrangement did not work out quite as planned, and CBS sold its shares back to Columbia in 1985 and HBO half its shares in 1986.

MCA/Universal had been very successful at the box office in the early 1980s, particularly with *E.T.* (which went on, in 1988, to sell 15 million home video units), and had produced some very successful television shows like *Magnum* and *Miami Vice*, but had been less successful in the late 1980s. MCA had diversified rapidly in the mid 1980s, acquiring toy companies (for movie-linked merchandising), music companies, WOR-TV (a major television station in the New York area, to ensure access for its television shows) and a half interest in the Cineplex Odeon theatre chain, as well as developing the Florida Universal Studios tour, to try to repeat the highly profitable Universal tour in Hollywood. Matsushita took over a company whose box office share had declined but which had managed to survive a lack of big hits with fairly cheap but profitable pictures like *Field of Dreams*, *Back to the Future 2* and *3*, *Twins*, *Uncle Buck*, *Parenthood*, *Kindergarten Cop*, *Problem Child* (these last three produced by Imagine), and only a few expensive flops like *Havana*. Current Universal policy favours the occasional high-profile film, like Scorsese's *Cape Fear* or Ron Howard's *Far and Away*, alongside inexpensive guaranteed hits like *The People under the Stairs*, *Problem Child 2* and *Child's Play 3*.

Sony and Matsushita clearly want their acquisitions to go on producing Hollywood movies, which have a global profit potential. They have not, therefore, sought to impose a Japanese style of management, though elements of it may yet appear, and reports in mid 1992 spoke of growing tension between MCA executives and the parent company. On the whole, the Japanese have retained existing management and/or looked to producers of past successes to make future successes. Like other studios, Sony Pictures Entertainment (as it is now) and MCA/Universal have gone along with a trend to longer-term first-look deals with producers (such as Sony's with Francis Ford Coppola and the Zucker brothers, or Universal's with Imagine and Steven Spielberg's Amblin) and even exclusive deals (such as Sony's with James Brooks and Universal's with Martin Scorsese).

Japan is now the biggest single national market for American movies, and it is not surprising that Japanese interest in Hollywood goes beyond Sony's and Matsushita's acquisitions, whether it involves hardware manufacturers looking for ties to software producers, investors looking for tax breaks, or distributors looking for early access to film and television rights. In 1991, after long negotiations, Time Warner finally concluded a deal with Toshiba and C. Itoh (a trading company with cable interests), in which the two Japanese companies invested a total of $1 billion in return for 6.25 per cent equity stakes each in Time Warner, and 25 per cent each in Time Warner Entertainment Japan (which integrates the handling of theatrical film distribution, television distribution, home video and merchandising). Time Warner argues that it is gaining the expertise of two established Japanese companies in their own market and reckons that its revenues in Japan, at present $200 million a year or 20 per cent of its worldwide revenues, will quadruple, while Toshiba gains a software link-up and C. Itoh gets access to the American cable market, all without any company takeovers. In other developments, even though some earlier Japanese investments had not paid off with hit movies, Japanese money has been raised for Disney and for a number of the independent companies which have deals with the majors to guarantee theatrical release, including Pioneer's 10 per cent stake in Carolco, JVC's partnership with Larry Gordon in Largo, Nomura Securities' funding of Morgan Creek, Ascii's partnership with Pressman and others, and media giant NHK's $600 million deal with Thom Mount's Mount Enterprises. On the other hand, in a reaction against high spending and company acquisition, the media conglomerate Fujisankei has set up its own operation, Fujisankei California Entertainment, modestly at first (though Fujisankei had also helped finance other films, such as four by Enigma, the first of which was *Memphis Belle*). Overall, Japanese investment in Hollywood is now calculated to exceed $20 billion in total; in 1992, and over a third of the 138 films made by the majors were backed by Japanese money.

The Giancarlo Parretti/Pathé Communications attempt to gain control of MGM/UA with the backing of Crédit Lyonnais Bank Nederland exemplifies the interest shown by European media and entertainment interests in Hollywood and its products. The record label Polygram (80 per cent owned by Philips), Bertelsmann (the German media enterprise that is second largest in the world after Time Warner), Canal Plus (the French pay television channel, with pay television services also in Germany, Spain and Belgium) and Francis Bouygues (construction boss and controller of France's most successful television channel) have all been rumoured contenders for the rump of Orion's business. Like the Japanese media concerns, the Europeans are mainly aiming to secure access to Hollywood product for their television, cable and video services, but they want to participate in production rather than simply entrust their fates to the majors – one reason why much of their co-production activity is with independent producers. Many European companies are already involved as partners in Hollywood companies. Canal Plus, which shows about 400 films a year (of which over a third are American-made), has a five per cent stake in Carolco, co-produced films including *JFK* and has plans to co-produce with Warner and with Arnon Michan's Regency. Polygram has committed $200 million to become a major Hollywood producer, with output deals with Columbia, Showtime and Viacom. Penta, an Italian venture involving Silvio Berlusconi (whose Fininvest media empire ranks fourth largest in the world), has a deal for European rights to Castle Rock pictures; it also has deals with Fox which include Penta co-producing Irwin Winkler's *Night and the City* and taking the foreign rights, and Fox distributing three films a year made by PentAmerica, including Bob Rafelson's *Man Trouble*. Bertelsmann is looking for movie co-production deals with majors, also to feed television and cable interests in Europe: it is a partner with Time Warner in a new European all-information television channel.

Many people expect European production to increase – Berlusconi is said to expect European film production to equal that of the United States by 2000 – and this is likely to be production of Hollywood-style entertainment; Hollywood sets the agenda and creates the model for movies. Thus, UGC's Franco-British co-production, *The Arrowtooth Waltz*, is a $16 million western with American stars. The Japanese also want Hollywood movies: the head of Fujisankei California Entertainment hopes 'that we can bring something Japanese to these pictures, but we will not be making Japanese films.' Bouygues's Ciby 2000, which is backing Bernardo Bertolucci and Pedro Almodovar as well as David Lynch, is exceptional in being interested in more European product and in American projects that stand a little outside the mainstream.

With the transformation of the majors into media and communications empires and their takeover by hardware companies, the buzzword of the early 1990s is 'synergy', which implies that different elements can come together to do better than they could do apart. In a development of the thinking that went into the formation of Tri-Star a decade before, synergy for Time Warner means aligning Time's magazines and cable television channels with Warner's records, films and television studios and worldwide distribution network, making it possible to re-market talent and programming through a range of media and countries. Thus, for example, Madonna (with whom Time Warner negotiated a new contract in 1992) not only makes records for Warner, but also stars in Warner movies, airs her videos on its cable television services, features on the cover of *People* magazine and is merchandised through Time's direct marketing division. Some elements of these profit-generating interactions also apply, of course, to Sony Entertainment Pictures and MCA/Universal, but for companies like Sony and Matsushita, synergy essentially means the fit between hardware and software. Sony Chairman Morita has said, 'Betamax had the technology, but the lack of software support is what made the difference in the end. Hardware and software synergy is fundamental – believe me, I know it now.' There is a lesson in this for the next generation of technical innovation: Sony has established a HDTV laboratory at Columbia (now Sony) studios, and Time Warner's deal with Toshiba offers it, too, an HDTV hardware-software link. HDTV offers the prospect of theatrical distribution by satellite instead of the current physical distribution of film prints. Toshiba, which also makes computers, could allow Time Warner to anticipate the next phase of industrial integration, which is likely to merge television entertainment with computers and the telephone.

Production

All the same, the billion dollar present and future of the multi-media business still depend to an extraordinary degree on the decidedly chancy and unpredictable process of producing entertainment, in particular movies. Certainly, studios now need to juggle complex equations that include domestic and foreign home video sales, cable sales and ancillaries such as video games, but the performance of a movie in the domestic (that is, North American) theatrical market remains the prime focus of attention. Even though foreign box-office and video now consistently return more profit, North American theatrical release is, as *Variety* put it, 'the engine that drives performance in the ancillaries and the foreign markets'. Foreign box-office is now vitally important in most films' profitability, and becoming ever more so, but it takes much longer to establish performance overseas (and much longer for revenues to start coming back). Movies that disappoint on North American release but then do very well overseas *(Gremlins 2*, for example, which grossed $69 million in Europe alone, after $41.5 million at home) rarely recover from the commercial judgment made about them domestically, which has serious consequences for the degree of promotion given to them as they open in other markets. Domestic box-office remains the crucial focus of attention for the industry because it is there, essentially, that a value will be established for the markets that follow.

1989 was a record year at the box-office in North America, breaking the $5 billion barrier for the first time with $5.03 billion. As 1990 proved to be only slightly less profitable, at $5.02 billion, the feeling grew that movies were recession-proof, and the majors increased their production to more than twenty films a year each. But fears of recession are endemic in the movie business, and each new holiday season is anticipated with dread. Through 1991, returns were off and there was foreboding about the possibility of a big recession, even of a repeat of the early 1970s crisis, which still looms large in Hollywood's collective memory. The impending crisis would have the same causes – budgets that were too high, over-supply of product and excessive reliance on markets outside domestic theatrical – and this, the argument went, would result in the failure of several big-budget pictures, the closure of several important but fragile production companies and pressure from banks (and Japanese corporate parents). Although 1991 ended more or less equal with 1990, higher overall revenues (once home video and foreign theatrical were counted in) in 1990 had not meant higher profits, and this was put down to escalating costs in both production and marketing. The average studio picture in 1991 was reckoned to cost about $23.6 million, but the cost of releasing a picture, taking into account prints and advertising, pushed the cost up to around $50 million, three times as much as in 1988. The minimum cost of releasing a picture nationally is now reckoned to be $3 million. Relatively modest films like *The Silence of the Lambs* or *Sleeping with the Enemy*, produced for a little under $20 million, cost an additional $15 million to release. The market has simply not grown enough to sustain such cost inflation: over the 1980s, costs rose 185% while attendances remained pretty much level. The shortfall in profits this implies were met by higher ticket prices – not a strategy that can be continued indefinitely.

The general conclusion has been that the domestic audience is not large enough to sustain the production of almost 200 major movies a year. In the all-important summer season of 1991, for example, some 40 to 50 movies were competing for audiences, but there were only four big hits (*Terminator 2, Robin Hood: Prince of Thieves, City Slickers* and *Naked Gun 2½*, all except the last independently made and therefore less profitable to the studios) and two significant money-makers in terms of profit on outlay (*Boyz N the Hood* and the reissue of *101 Dalmatians*). *Variety* analysed the figures on three typical movies, none of them with particularly large budgets: *Look Who's Talking* (Columbia's most profitable film) cost $11 million to produce, and total costs (including interest, worldwide releasing and participation in profits) were $71 million, against total revenues worldwide of about $182 million, giving $111 million profit. Disney's *The Rocketeer* cost $40 million to make, but total costs were $76.5 million and total revenues about $76 million, leaving zero profit. *Dutch* had production costs of $20 million and total costs of $41.5 million, but total revenues were only $17.5 million, leaving it with a loss of $24 million.

Further pressure on companies to scale down both production costs and the number of releases has come from changes in the ancillary markets: pay cable and network television prices are paying less for rights to films, fluctuations in the value of the dollar have eroded foreign revenues and, most important, developments in the home video market have removed the certainty of recouping production costs from release on video. The effects of cost escalation can be seen at Disney, which had made its 1980s reputation on the basis of modestly budgeted but 'high concept' movies like *Three Men and a Baby* and *Ruthless People*, and had continued this trend in 1990 with *Pretty Woman*, which cost $18 million to make and release and made $82 million in domestic box-office. But in 1990-91, many of Disney's budgets moved upwards, on productions such as *Dick Tracy, The Rocketeer, Scenes from a Mall* and *Billy Bathgate*, with only very middling results. Elsewhere, 1990 showed that cheap films could be highly profitable: Fox's *Home Alone* cost $18 million but brought in $120 million in domestic box office; Paramount's *Ghost* cost $28 million and grossed $95 million; *Driving Miss Daisy* cost Warner $8 million but earned $50 million. All went on to do extraordinarily well in foreign markets and on home video.

Some big-budget movies also did well in box-office grosses – *Total Recall* and *Die Hard 2* both earned over $65 million, but both cost over $60 million in total, while other big-budget movies, among them *Another 48 HRS, Days of Thunder, The Two Jakes* and *Havana*, flopped.

Looking at such results, studios drew the obvious conclusions: costs for most movies must come down. Disney's production chief Jeffrey Katzenberg concluded, 'We should now look long and hard at the blockbuster business and get out of it.' In a now famous memo, he condemned the 'tidal wave of runaway costs and mindless competition' in a 'period of great danger and great uncertainty'. Notwithstanding its first-place market share in 1990, Disney's profits from movies were at their lowest for three years. Katzenberg saw the main offenders as variously, the 'blockbuster mentality, 'home-run thinking' and 'star-driven packages'.

Several studio heads began to imply in 1991 that a few high-budget movies and many more lower-budget ones would become the rule, with middling budgets most likely to be cut. Every studio would probably go on making one or two big budget pictures positioned for summer or Christmas release – 'event movies', 'hold-your-breath' movies or 'must-see' movies – with bankable stars like Arnold Schwarzenegger or Kevin Costner (insofar as such exist, other sure-thing box-office talents like Tom

Cruise, Bruce Willis and Julia Roberts having flopped respectively in *Days of Thunder*, *Hudson Hawk* and *Dying Young*.) *Terminator 2* and *Robin Hood: Prince of Thieves* are both what the industry calls 'tent-poles', because they are going to hold the edifice up: their success seemed to prove the absolute value of event movies. At the other end of the scale of studio pictures, whether made in-house or by big independents, it was low or moderately budgeted pictures – 'high concept' or genre movies – that were seen to offer the best chance of good returns. Most likely to suffer, then, would be movies with budgets in the middle range ($25-30 million) and talent which, though expensive, was unable to guarantee profits. *Variety* quoted a senior production executive at Sony: 'No way I'm falling into the mid-range trap. It'll be big event pictures and maybe an ocasional low-budget project with non-stars and first-time-out directors. Nothing in the middle.' It is not at all clear that the evidence sustains this view: the middle seems to be where some of 1991's big hits, like *The Silence of the Lambs* and *Sleeping with the Enemy*, came from.

There is certainly no agreement on how event movies work, and *Variety* quotes two senior executives with opposing views. '*Hook* is an event movie. If it's good, it will make people want to see other movies. If they don't like it, it's bad for business, because when event movies don't work, audience expectations are dashed.' The other argument is: 'Event movies bring out the occasional filmgoer, but they do not truly expand the audience. Events distort the marketplace. We need fewer great movies and more good movies.' There is a strong sense, then, that the studios recognise the need to make movies for the regular audience as well as event movies for those who go just a few times a year. The problem here is that an emphasis on event movies changes the status of non-event movies. It is not at all clear that the lesson of frugality will be learned. Anxious memories of the early 1970s recession may also be reminders that big pictures seem to have led the way out of that recession; the industry remains inordinately impressed by pictures that earn over $100 million in domestic box-office gross, almost regardless of what they cost. This has lent a special magic to the name of Steven Spielberg, and even though he had generated no really big hits for some years, *Hook* was being looked to on its Christmas release as the saviour of the 1991 box-office. However, its break-even point on domestic gross was reckoned to be around $400 million, given that some 47 per cent of its domestic earnings would go to Spielberg, Robin Williams and Dustin Hoffman.

On a different front, the failure of several sequels in 1990-91 had many executives complaining about 'sequelitis' and claiming that sequels, which for many years had been so central to sure-fire box-office success, were dead. At the time, *Lethal Weapon 3*, *Batman 2*, *Alien 3*, *Home Alone Again* and *Honey, I Blew Up the Baby* were all in production for 1992 release, while *Terminator 2*, *Naked Gun 2½* and, down the budget scale, *Problem Child 2* all did well on release in 1991. It has been argued that in a recession, when people may be more selective about how they spend their income, sequels seem to offer proven value. In the longer term, sequels do not really solve the problem of what audiences want to see: you cannot have sequels without originals. Sequels and remakes, with their evident dearth of ideas, only point to timidity, the reluctance to take risks that is so prevalent in the industry.

Audiences

The arguments about event movies, sequels and so on show very clearly that, despite the promotional power the industry can wield, it is impossible to generalise about what will succeed. The industry is on the whole very short-term in its thinking and tends to ricochet around trying to repeat successes. Thus, having assumed that what will succeed is action and/or star-oriented pictures, it is then faced by the failure of *Hudson Hawk*, *Days of Thunder* and *Another 48 HRS* alongside the success of much cheaper pictures like *Pretty Woman* and *Ghost*. So the adult female audience is 'rediscovered' and played to, until the failure of *For the Boys* implies that perhaps it is not out there after all, before, that is, *The Prince of Tides* becomes a hit and implies, on the contrary, that perhaps it is . . . To this day, Hollywood gives the impression of being very unsure as to who its audience, or audiences, are. Studios that believe they should spend most on action pictures for a young male audience seem surprised by the runaway successes of *Ghost* or *Driving Miss Daisy* or *Home Alone*.

In fact, the image of the average moviegoer as a teenager that has been around since the 1960s no longer holds true. In 1990, 31 per cent of the American audience was in the 12-20 year age bracket (which makes up 15 per cent of the population), and 25 per cent were aged 21-29, making 56 per cent of the audience under 30. This leaves those over 30 responsible for 44 per cent of ticket sales (30-39 year olds accounting for 20 per cent of admissions and over-40s for 24 per cent. While the proportion of under-30s in the audience has slipped from 67 per cent in 1984 to 56 per cent in 1990, that of the over-40s increased from 15 per cent to 24 per cent. The greying of the movie-going audience (which reflects that of the population at large) will undoubtedly begin to have its effects on the movies being made.

But doubts remain. For Brandon Tartikoff, chairman of Paramount in 1991-92, for example: 'While there is a place for the adult film, or for pictures that don't necessarily have to be made for the most frequent moviegoers – 25 and under – you don't want an abundance of pictures clearly tilted to viewers 25 and up. In a recession, the people most affected will be the least frequent moviegoers, the older audience'. Others, like Fox production chief Roger Birnbaum, argue that the female audience has become more important: 'The demographic on women, today, is very strong, and it makes it exciting that a studio can develop a slate of pictures that doesn't just cater to one demographic. It used to be that we only made pictures for teenage boys. Now, all the demographics are broader and deeper than that.'

Marketing costs have escalated partly because saturation booking and advertising, strategies that used to be more characteristic of exploitation films, have become common for most movies. In this context, audience targeting – in other words, identifying the audience for a picture and 'narrowcasting' to them – has become fashionable, since it is cheaper than blanket advertising. The danger of it is that a film might find its target audience – families for *The Rocketeer*, or women for *Dying Young* – but fail to achieve the cross-over to other audiences that can turn a film into a big hit. On *Dick Tracy*, Disney took targeted approaches to the film's different audiences. According to marketing chief Bob Levin: 'With young males we took an action approach; with young females we focused on the music and Madonna; with families we spotlighted the relationship between Dick Tracy and the Kid; and for older females we used the romantic triangle with Tracy, Breathless and Tess.'

Certainly, the impression of the industry as a whole, in Jonathan Kaplan's phrase, 'pandering to the teenage market' is not quite as strong as it was in the 1970s and 1980s. It is not just older women who have been rediscovered as an audience – there is a wide awareness, prompted by the success of, for example, *Home Alone* and *Beauty and the Beast*, that family entertainment may be more important in the 1990s, in the theatres as well as in the home. Nowhere is this clearer than in the success of animated features like *Beauty and the Beast* and the very profitable re-issue of *The Jungle Book* and *Fantasia*. 80 per cent of animated features showed net profits in the second half of the 1980s – a much better percentage than for live action films – and home video is a particularly effective safety net for this type of film. Ten to fifteen animated features are due for release in 1993.

Merchandising

Merchandising offers an important source of revenue, particularly for big-budget event movies, sequels and children's or family films. *Variety* reported a high Warner source describing the forthcoming *Batman* sequel: 'More than a movie, it's an industry, with a great deal of Catwoman and Penguin merchandising already in place and a deal with Fox Television for 65 animated half-hours.' A series like *Star Trek* can generate a minor industry: Paramount licenses 35 companies to make *Trek* items, and it is estimated that around $500 million has so far been spent on them, while in 1991 alone Simon & Schuster's Pocket Books (a part of Paramount Communications) has sold four million copies of book titles associated with the series. It is a sign of the continuing vigour of some of the straight-to-video market that, at the lower end of the budget scale, Full Moon was planning to produce 10,000 models based on its *Puppetmaster* films *(Puppetmaster II* shipped 45,000 rental copies on video).

A vast and still evolving area of the ancillary market is electronic video games, which find their main market among eight- to fifteen-year-old males. The snag has been that game cartridges can take so long to develop that they reach the market too late to take full advantage of a film's visibility. *Dick Tracy*, for example, opened theatrically in June 1990 and was released on video in December 1990, but Sega's *Dick Tracy* game was not on sale until February 1991; disappointing sales were put down to this delay. Sega now insists on becoming involved in film projects twelve to eighteen months before a film is due for release. Now that new CD-ROM technology can incorporate live action footage into games, there is every reason for studios to bring in game designers early. The logic of synergy is clear at Sony, where the production of *Hook* was accompanied by the development of a CD-ROM *Hook* game for Sony's new Play Station format and a separate game for Nintendo (the game market leader with 25 million 8-byte players in the United States, against Sega's 2 million); the expectation is that the games will be become available within two months of *Hook* opening. Similarly, Acclaim Entertainment's *Terminator 2* game – Acclaim is reputed to have paid $2 million for the right to develop and market it – started with Carolco's initial treatment for the film, and release of the game was expected within a month of the release of the film on home video. Other majors are also involved in interactive game production, and the profits to be made, whether in-house or by selling rights, can be significant: Acclaim's game based on Fox Television's *The Simpsons* show, *Bart vs. The Space Mutants*, has sold over one million copies at $40 each, and royalties on games costing $20 to $79 vary between 35 cents and $1·25 per unit. In a piquant reversal of the usual pattern, Nintendo's most successful game, Super Mario, is being turned into a movie, *The Super Mario Brothers.*

Foreign Markets

With domestic box-office now regularly accounting for only 20 per cent of a film's total revenue, foreign theatrical revenues, averaging 15 per cent of the total, and often much more, can frequently exceed the domestic box-office. *Rocky V*, *Pretty Woman* and *The Little Mermaid* all had higher grosses in Europe alone than in North America, while *Gremlins 2* took $69 million in Europe but only $46·4 million domestically, and *Look Who's Talking Too* took $70 million in Europe and $46·4 million domestically. Revenue from Europe increased from $403·3 million in 1985 to $983·3 million in 1989, accounting for over half of all foreign earnings, and the market shares for American movies have increased still further (85 per cent in Spain and Germany, 70 per cent in Italy, around 80 per cent in Britain). American interest in European co-production was fuelled by rumours that the European Community was considering a quota system (it was also rumoured that Margaret Thatcher had promised a veto, following a call from Ronald Reagan, who had himself been called by MPAA head Jack Valenti).

As North American theatre admission declined in 1991, and video, cable and television revenue has been flat since 1989, growth in the foreign market has been a vital factor in continued profitability. Theatrical takings have gone up partly because of an increase in multiplex construction, in which the potential for growth remains higher in Europe (apart from Britain, where it has already peaked) than in the United States, while the rapid introduction of privatised television and of new cable and satellite outlets in Europe have greatly expanded the ancillary markets. Hollywood has been remarkably agile, too, in responding to the opening up of Eastern Europe: Columbia-TriStar and other majors made deals with the USSR, Hungary, Poland, Czechoslovakia, Bulgaria and Romania in 1990-91, usually with the previous state monopoly companies. Hence, perhaps, the *Variety* headline for 22nd August 1991: 'Hollywood Shaken by Soviet Coup.' The effect of American penetration was that in Hungary, for example, the majors were left in virtual control of distribution and exhibition.

The increasing importance of foreign markets and of home video, has encouraged shifts in the way the majors conduct their distribution business abroad. In the past, the majors had looked to each other for alliances in order to share the risks of distributing abroad. Now, some are looking to control their own foreign distribution in order to maximise returns in view of the rising cost of marketing hit movies in the United States. Thus, for example, Paramount and Universal, working together in United International Pictures, want to integrate theatrical distribution (UIP), home video (CIC) and exhibition (United Cinema International), although European Community rules on competition may provide obstacles. In other cases, co-financing deals with European companies, such as Canal Plus or Penta, result in the European companies retaining distribution rights to theatrical or video, or both.

Home Video

In combination with television and foreign sales, video and cable have had the effect of increasing the proportion of pictures breaking even or making a profit from two in ten to perhaps seven in ten (a situation that may be changing again). The current industry rule-of-thumb is that if a film can earn its negative cost in domestic theatrical release, then other sales will cover release costs and push it into profit; previously a film needed to gross two or even three times its negative cost at the box office to break even. Video-cassette sales, though no longer growing as fast as in the mid 1980s, remain the most predictable source of ancillary income for a film, and worldwide video revenue can amount to as much as eight times the negative cost. Even theatrical flops, in the recent past at least, have regularly shipped 100,000 rental video units, worth $5 million in gross receipts, while a hit film can generate over $10 million worldwide in profits. Overall, in North America, consumers spent $9 billion renting home video tapes in 1990 (13 per cent up on 1989), nearly twice the $5 billion they paid to see new releases in the theatres.

Although home video was introduced in the United States in the mid 1970s – Sony's Betamax in 1976, Matsushita's VHS in 1977 – VCR ownership really took off only in the mid 1980s. This slow growth was due to some initial uncertainty about precisely how the new apparatus was to be used – for time-shifting, for establishing permanent 'libraries' or for showing pre-recorded tapes – and to Sony's consequent battles with MCA and Disney over copyright infringement. By 1986, VCR ownership had reached half the homes in America, and gross revenues from home video for the first time equalled those from theatrical exhibition. The majors soon developed the now familiar two-tier pricing policy for videos: expensive for the first six months and aiming primarily at the rental market, then cheaper, to attract home sales. The alternative strategy of 'sell-through' or 'retail premiere', where a film went out on video at a relatively low price from the outset (though still available for rental purposes), was also used quite early on: Paramount released *Star Trek II: The Wrath of Khan* in 1982 at $39.95 a copy (and by 1991 had sold 10 million copies). Sell-through is normally reserved for popular titles where high volume sales are expected – without exception films from the majors, who earn higher profit margins from sell-through than from rental.

In the early and mid 1980s, the explosion in VCR ownership and the home-video rental market coincided with cut-backs in production by the majors, a combination that afforded tremendous opportunities for independent producers, especially at the low-budget end – this was the period of rapid expansion for companies like Vestron, New World and Cannon. Made-for-home-video productions prospered; Vestron, for example, was releasing eight made-for-video features a month. Towards the end of the 1980s, market conditions began to change rapidly as the majors upped production and focused ever more strongly on the home video market, and as consumers in the growing recession just rented hit titles rather than the wider range they had previously gone for. By 1991, the majors were taking 82 per cent of video rentals, which followed the theatrical market in being increasingly hit-driven, a trend that inevitably favoured the majors. In 1990-91, the record for the number of copies of hit video titles being shipped to retailers was constantly being broken: *Three Men and a Baby* sold 455,000 units, only to be beaten by 477,000 for *Dick Tracy* and 510,000 for *Die Hard 2*, but then *Ghost* set a new record of 642,000 (worth $42 million in wholesale revenues to Paramount Home Video), exceeded again by 655,000 for *Dances with Wolves*; *Terminator 2* is expected to top 700,000 units (excluding an additional 135,000 copies on laser disc). In a very short time, the minimum sales for a hit on video had reached around 400,000 units. Middle-range films could expect to ship, typically, 250,000 rental units (*New Jack City*) to 340,000 (*GoodFellas*). In the sell-through category – though this has been more affected by recession than the rental market – *Home Alone* shipped over nine million units in North America alone, at a retail value of $225 million, on which the wholesale return to Fox will be $124 million and its profit after deduction of marketing, manufacture and distribution costs will be about $40 million.

However, in escalating costs of marketing, as in other things, home video has followed the pattern of theatrical releasing. Sell-through, which depends on volume sales, relies very heavily on television advertising, generally in a two-phase campaign: a launch in the summer/back-to-school period, then a follow-up in December for the Christmas period; budgets of $3-4 million are common. Though hits like *Home Alone* or *Teenage Mutant Ninja Turtles II* were by definition already well known, their marketing blitzes were estimated to have cost $25 and $20 million respectively, and about half the budget for each was contributed by promotional sponsors, respectively MacDonalds and Burger King.

The increasing emphasis on major hits, and A titles generally, has clearly restricted the possibilities for low-budget film-makers, but the remaining independents can still find some opportunities in the inevitable variations in theatrical box-office, where a downturn translates six months later to a dearth of A features for video, making video retailers buy a wider variety of titles. Very low-budget films – the stock-in-trade of video shops in the early 1980s – have pretty much disappeared. Roger Corman, for example, has stopped making films with $1/2 million budgets, but there is still reckoned to be a straight-to-video market for well-made action films and thrillers, especially erotic ones, in the $2-3 million budget range. Corman's Concorde works largely in this area, as do Vidmark, Full Moon and others. It is said that to benefit significantly from the video market, such companies need to boost the profile of their product by aiming first for theatrical release, as Vidmark (through Trimark) has done. It no longer works to promote such films as 'made-for-video', though, of course, they still go straight there if they fail to find theatrical openings.

The overall pattern of developments in the video market over the past decade amounts to the majors organising themselves to dominate what initially looked like a real space for a thriving independent production sector.

Pay Television

Time Inc.'s Home Box Office was the first 'premium services' cable channel which charged a monthly fee for recent, uncut films and exclusive sports events without commercial breaks. At first, it lost a lot of money, but in 1975 it leased satellite space, then challenged the Federal Communications Commission (FCC) on both receiving-dish regulations and its right to show features of any age – FCC regulations worked, in effect, to protect network television. By 1978, HBO was feeding over 700 cable systems and had two million subscribers; it also had competitors. At present, about half of all homes with television subscribe to cable and about a third of these receive at least one pay cable service. Time's merger with Warner in 1989 brought to Time Inc. not only Warner's diversified entertainment activities but also Warner Cable Communications, the fifth largest cable operator, with a million and a half subscribers. By then, HBO was being sold to 7,000 cable systems and Cinemax, also operated by Time/HBO, to 5,000 cable systems. HBO's main competitor is Viacom, with the Showtime channel (second to HBO in size) and The Movie Channel (fourth in size after Cinemax). Viacom's combined market share is about 25 per cent compared with HBO's 58 per cent. Both HBO and Viacom have extensive cable interests beyond the four main channels, with Viacom, for example, generating significant revenues from its advertising-based basic cable networks like MTV and Nickleodeon. The owner of Viacom, Summer Redstone, built his fortune with the eighth largest American theatre chain and moved into pay cable – as well as syndication and television production (such as *Roseanne*) – on the perception that entertainment would be centred increasingly on the home.

The first priority of the new cable systems was to ensure a supply of new product, and first and foremost this meant access to movies. Since the majors produced only about 120 films a year, other sources were necessary, but even the independent producers whose product was considered suitable for cable showing could not meet the demand. As well as financing independent pictures and taking stakes in Tri-Star and Orion, HBO also began to put finance into movies being made by the majors as a way of securing cable rights. HBO became, in fact, Hollywood's largest financer of movies, and the boom in independent production in the early and mid 1980s had as much to do with finance from the cable companies as with the growth of home video. HBO and Viacom were, in a sense, vertically integrated in the manner of the old studios, financing and distributing programmes or movies but also having guaranteed access to their own cable outlets. HBO, with its dominant market share, was particularly able to pressure film suppliers. As a result, the majors attempted to become directly involved in pay cable themselves, but they came up against legal bars to integrating vertically in this way and had to find other ways to counter HBO's influence or at least to assimilate it, as in the formation of Tri-Star by Columbia Pictures, HBO and the CBS network. During the 1980s, the rapid development of home video, and particularly the majors' growing domination of that market, had the effect of reducing HBO's and Viacom's advantage of being able to transmit recent theatrical features, uncut and uninterrupted by commercials, into the home. Warner's merger with Time also implied different relation-ships between cable and the majors in the future.

Among technological developments, pay-per-view promises much for the future; it is clear that movies will be the bedrock of this new business, the technology for which depends on the expansion of channel capacity by the compression of network signals. All the majors have invested in exploring these possibilities. With pay-to-view, viewers will be able to select from three or four current hit movies, each of which will be running continuously on as many as eight different channels (so that waiting time for any film to begin again will be minimal), and they will be billed only for what they choose (instead of cable's current fixed monthly subscription). Time Warner are already exploring the possibilities of this new technology with their Quantum pilot scheme in the New York borough of Queens, using 150 channels based on fibre optics. The great advantage to the studios is that a much higher proportion of what viewers pay goes to them than is the case with either pay cable or home video.

In future, premium cable services like HBO's and Viacom's may be squeezed by these developments (although, in HBO's case, revenues simply get diverted to another division of the same media empire). For the present, though, they remain vital ingredients of the movie-making scene. HBO and Viacom's Showtime have been producing their own films for some years, partly because of the decline in independent production in the late 1980s. Viacom is working towards a strategy in which it will produce twelve features a year by 1993, adult in appeal, with guaranteed cable exposure on Showtime and The Movie Channel and domestic television syndication; these features are also available for foreign theatrical distribution, where they can help fill the middle ground between features from the majors and low-budget independent product. Viacom is working to budgets of around $5 million (which it calculates is equivalent to $7-8 million on a theatrical feature): if the budgets were higher, it would have to seek American theatrical release to recoup costs, but the economics of this would fall down over expenditure on prints and advertising.

HBO, working on roughly the same budgets, has acquired the reputation of offering relative creative freedom to well-known talent on projects that the majors would not consider commercial enough, with the additional advantage, compared to network television, of considerably less restriction over sex and violence (since there are no advertisers to offend). Thus, HBO has attracted directors like Jonathan Demme, Ken Russell and Mike Figgis and actors such as Melanie Griffith, Matt Dillon and Ray Liotta to work for a fraction of their normal fees on thirty-minute adaptations of famous American short stories for two prestigious *Women and Men* movies, and Donna Deitch, Joan Micklin Silver and Penelope Spheeris to direct thirty-minute segments for *Prison Stories: Women on the Inside*. Through the cable companies, the often rigid line between production for theatrical release and production for television may be beginning to break down.

Network Television
The main loser from the rapid development of cable and home video in the 1970s and 1980s has been network television, which no longer dominates the delivery of entertainment to the home. Over the 1980s, the networks' share of the audience shrank from around 90 per cent to around 60 per cent. It was not only cable (advertising-supported basic cable as well as pay television premium services) and home video that challenged network dominance: the main competition came initially from 'superstations', starting in 1976 when Ted Turner began to distribute his local Atlanta WTBS service nationally over satellite and local cable systems on a subscription basis, reaching 38 million homes by the end of the decade. His main competitors were WGN Chicago (22 million subscribers) and the MCA-owned WOR New York (9 million subscribers). Independent stations also grew in number; in launching Fox Broadcasting as a fourth 'network' in 1987, Rupert Murdoch was able to put together over a hundred independent stations (capable of reaching 83 per cent of all American homes with television), adding distribution by satellite. Fox took some years to become profitable and, with its very small staff, showed that austerity of operation was not just viable but essential.

The developments of the 1980s inevitably had serious effects on network television as the prime market for feature films: the ratings for theatrical features on network television declined rapidly as the newer forms of home delivery of features spread. Features ceased to be the essential prime-time programming they had been in the 1960s and 1970s, although there is still a good syndication market for features four to five years after theatrical release, when they have been through home video and pay-per-view, cable television and network television.

While theatrical features became less crucial to network television in the 1980s, made-for-television movies (single features and, increasingly, mini-series, like the 1977 *Roots*), which had begun in earnest in the 1960s, gained in importance. Since they were made inexpensively (in comparison with theatrical features), their production costs often amounted to less than the licensing fee for quite ordinary theatrical features. Although they could attract enormous numbers of viewers (100 million for *The Day*

After, 1983, and over 70 million for *Something About Amelia*, 1984), audience size affected profitability only in raising a film's profile and thus the amount that could be charged for domestic and foreign syndication rights. Increasingly, in the 1970s and 1980s, made-for-television features have been made for the networks by independent producers, to whom the relatively small profits available were more significant than they would be to the majors. Between them, the networks continue to finance more made-for-television features each year than the major studios produce as theatrical features.

Although they have been heavily involved in television production since the 1950s, the majors have preferred to concentrate their energies on series television programming, supplying over half of prime-time shows (the rest being supplied by independents). In the 1980s, revenues from television production began to be outpaced by those from cable and home video, but they nevertheless remain important. MCA/Universal, for example, with major hits in the 1980s like *Kojak*, *The Rockford Files*, *Magnum* and *Miami Vice*, still produces a slate of successful shows like *Major Dad*, *Quantum Leap*, *Law and Order* and *Coach*. Production companies do not make any initial profit on television shows, since licensing fees from the networks, as with made-for-television features, are always significantly less than the costs of development and production. Disney's live action shows, for example, are said to incur a deficit of about $200,000 per episode, but if a show becomes a hit and runs for at least four full seasons (about 88 episodes), then there is considerable profit potential in off-network syndication and foreign sales. In the mid 1980s, *Magnum* episodes sold to the syndication market for almost $2 million an episode, and *The Cosby Show*, syndicated since 1988, is the most profitable yet, selling for $3-4 million per episode.

Under FCC regulations, the networks are prohibited from taking part in the production of programmes, or from having any financial interest in their syndication. In the early 1990s, with the networks' power slipping, these rules have been hotly contested. Deregulation seems likely, not least because of anxieties over the foreign acquisitions of Columbia-TriStar, MCA/Universal and Fox, but also because of the continued erosion by cable of the network audiences. Deregulation would allow mergers between networks and major studios – there have been persistent rumours of Disney's desire to own a network and of Paramount's interest in NBC (or, at least, its entertainment division). More recently, Bill Cosby, the wealthiest entertainer in the United States, has been negotiating to buy NBC. Certainly, the networks are in flux, and the future is expected to involve consolidation and mergers resulting in movie, cable and television interests all belonging to the same media conglomerates.

Meanwhile, cost-cutting has encouraged networks to commission programming from their supposed arch-enemies, the cable companies, at very competitive prices compared with those expected by its normal Hollywood suppliers (for example, ABC's *Hi Honey, I'm Home* series is commissioned from Nickelodeon). Columbia Pictures Television has discussed sharing production costs on prime-time shows with major advertisers like General Motors, in a return to 1950s-style corporate sponsorship of shows, while Procter & Gamble, long involved in sponsoring daytime soaps, has made a similar deal with Universal Television on CBS's *Northern Exposure*, benefitting from reduced advertising rates and a share of any profits.

In the 1960s, the ill-health of the majors and the dramatic rise in power of the television networks gave an overwhelming sense that the movies were dying and that television was taking over. In the 1990s, the feeling is the opposite: the networks seem to be in deep trouble, and the power of the majors has been enhanced by home video, pay cable and pay-per-view, all closely tied to feature production and movie-going, and generally thought, on the experience of the 1980s, to feed back into increased attendance in the theatres.

STARTING OUT IN EXPLOITATION

The dramatic changes in the American film industry at the end of the 1960s, and the atmosphere of uncertainty, even desperation, that they generated provided opportunities for film-making that had hardly existed before. The crisis in the majors can be traced in part to their surprising reluctance to realise that the mass family audience, going regularly to the movies, had greatly diminished. By the 1970s, the 12-29 age group, only 40 per cent of the total population of the United States, accounted for some 75 per cent of ticket sales. For various fairly obvious social reasons, this was the only age group for which going to the movies was still a regular activity rather than a special event.

In the 1960s and 1970s the majors had not yet worked out how best to cater for this audience. It was this uncertainty that enabled a production company like BBS (the initials are from its three main figures, Bert Schneider, Bob Rafelson, Steve Blauner) to operate, for the relatively short period from 1968 to 1973, under the aegis of a major studio, Columbia Pictures. It used mainly young and untried directors, aiming their films essentially at youthful audiences and working with budgets that by Hollywood standards were very low. Its major success, *Easy Rider* (1969), was crucial to its subsequent history since, as the writer Joan Didion put it, 'every studio in town was narcotised by *Easy Rider*'s grosses.' Of BBS's other seven pictures, only two, Rafelson's *Five Easy Pieces*

Still: Dennis Hopper and Peter Fonda in Easy Rider.

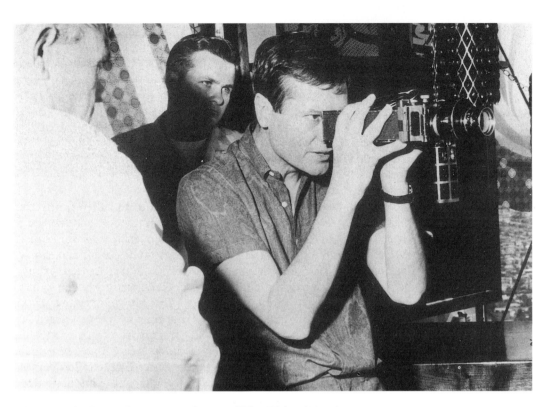

Photograph: Roger Corman on the set of The Trip *(1967)*.

(1970) and Peter Bogdanovich's *The Last Picture Show* (1971), returned a profit, and BBS's production programme did not survive very long; other comparable initiatives in giving chances to young directors within the ambit of the majors suffered the same fate.

The uncertainty that nurtured BBS also provided a space into which independent production companies could move and where they could thrive with a product aimed directly at the youth market. (Later, in the late 1970s and the 1980s, the home-video boom provided similar opportunities for independent film-makers, and, throughout these periods, there was a vast growth of cinema below the level of commercial visibility – in particular, porno movies). Onc youth-oriented company was Roger Corman's New World Pictures, which also gave young film-makers their chance at making movies. Well before the crisis of the late 1960s, Roger Corman, either with independents like Samuel Z. Arkoff and James H. Nicholson's American International Pictures (AIP) or with his own companies, made many extremely low-budget movies – horror movies like *Bucket of Blood* and *I Was a Teenage Werewolf,* teenage action pictures like *Hot Rod Girl* and *Teenage Caveman,* beach movies like *Beach Party* – all aimed at a clearly targeted youth audience. Corman became closely identified, as both producer and director, with these so-called exploitation pictures, making some of the best known AIP pictures (among others, the slightly higher budgeted series based on Edgar Allan Poe's stories, including *The Fall of the House of Usher,* 1960, *The Pit and the Pendulum,* 1961, and *The Premature Burial,* 1962) and directing some pictures in circumstances that have become the stuff of legend – *Bucket of Blood* was shot in two days, over a weekend. As a producer, Corman offered directorial opportunities to film-makers who later acquired far higher status, including Francis Ford Coppola *(Dementia 13,* 1962), Monte Hellman *(Beast from Haunted Cave,* 1959) and Peter Bogdanovich *(Targets,* 1967).

In 1970, Corman, dissatisfied with AIP over the handling of his film *Gas-s-s-s . . .,* founded his own production and distribution company, New World Pictures, with his brother Gene Corman and Larry Woolner. Throughout the 1970s, New World produced and distributed movies for the youth market, making them cheaply and very quickly, thus being able, like AIP before it, to respond to changing tastes much faster than any major studio could. And, like AIP, New World offered chances to many young film-makers to get into the business. Corman also went on producing movies for AIP, among them Martin Scorsese's first 'commercial' picture, *Boxcar Bertha* (1972). AIP itself continued, often very successfully, into the 1970s, but with generally higher budgets than before, more obviously competing against the majors with movies like *Walking Tall Part 2* (1975) and its biggest commercial success, *The Amityville Horror* (1979).

Exploitation pictures have often been compared to the B movies that made up the bottom half of double bills from the 1930s to the 1950s. But while B movies and exploitation pictures both offered work to relatively untried film-makers, they were otherwise very different. B movies were essentially second feature fodder for the majors; they were made cheaply, often by the majors themselves, and sold 'by the yard' (i.e. for a flat fee) rather than for a percentage of the box office gross. They were thus very much a part of the production, distribution and exhibition system dominated by the majors.

Movies made by independent exploitation companies like AIP, and certainly those produced by New World and others in the 1970s, were not B pictures in this sense. They were distributed independently of the majors and were usually marketed as equal-value double bills, aimed not at a general audience but rather at the youth market that the majors, particularly in the 1960s and 1970s, were failing to cater for. Often, at least in the North American market, they were for showing at drive-ins. Long considered by the majors as outlets of only secondary importance, the drive-ins were crucial to the release patterns of movies from companies like New World, which would open its films in the spring in the warmer areas of the south and south-west, then move them north as the drive-in summer season came on.

By the 1970s, other changes provided outlets for exploitation pictures: as large hard-top theatres continued to decline in number, the multi-screen complexes that increasingly replaced them were designed in part to target sectional audiences more effectively. And, increasingly, as shopping mall multi-screen complexes became (as they are today) the prime theatre sites in the United States, the remaining downtown movie houses, which attracted a predominantly male, working-class audience, also came to be considered suitable outlets for exploitation films (and even more commonly for X-rated sex films). Everywhere, the general shortage of product from the majors helped smaller independent companies like AIP and New World to make an impact.

Exploitation films, especially from Corman's New World, have attracted a good deal of critical attention. This has to do with the reputation of Corman himself, already established before the 1970s as an almost legendary figure, the King of Schlock. It also comes out of Corman's skill at hiring talented young film-makers, many of whom went on to greater things but always felt they owed their start to Corman.

The term 'exploitation' differentiates a certain kind of overtly exploitative product from the supposedly non-exploitative product of the majors, and implies that movies thus labelled take advantage of their audiences, for example by promising more than they deliver – in effect, by cheating. Certainly, the impact of New World pictures was based essentially on going for saturation local advertising and playing, then moving quickly to new play locations. The films were sold on lurid titles and advertising material, in contrast to the majors' more extended pattern of press screenings and critical notices (also, of course, accompanied by advertising). As New World's sales manager in the early 1970s, Frank Moreno, put it, 'Sixty to seventy per cent of any exploiter's initial biz lies in the title and the campaign.' It was not uncommon at New World for the title and poster, and even the preview or trailer, to be in existence before the movie itself was actually begun. Joseph Ruben, having just sold his first film to another independent exploitation company, Crown International, was told by Crown that it had a title – *The Pom Pom Girls* – that distributors loved and were eager to show, but no movie, and

Stills. Left: The Hot Box – *captured American nurses in the Philippines become freedom fighters. Right: Pamela Sue Martin in* The Lady in Red.

would he write a script, which he did, in three weeks, and shoot the picture, which he also did; it made Crown a lot of money.

If one title failed to work, a new one that might work better could be tried out somewhere else: before it became *The Lady in Red,* Lewis Teague's 1979 movie, scripted by John Sayles, had been known as both *Dillinger's Mistress* and *Guns, Sin and Bathtub Gin.* As well as promising more than they delivered, exploitation films could be said to have exploited their audiences' baser, more vulgar tastes, primarily, of course, for sex and/or violence – which were no less central to many films made by the majors, though less blatantly so. Their product may have been changing, but the majors still tended to nurse a more respectable, even a family image.

New World's first successful series of movies came out of an idea by one of its founding partners: Larry Woolner suggested a film to be called *Student Nurses,* based on his recollection of what had been considered 'hot' in his youth, and on what he was sure would sell. New World exploited its commercial success with follow-ups like *Night Call Nurses, Private Duty Nurses* and *Candy Stripe Nurses.* Similarly, a women-in-prison cycle – *Big Doll House, The Hot Box, Caged Heat* – seemed to promise sex and violence. Whatever New World thought would sell was promised. But what would sell, or sell best, could change. As Corman put it in 1977, 'The last couple of years, I thought that a large proportion of the American public wanted to see blood or breasts. Now I think they want to see cars. Our biggest film to date, *Eat My Dust!,* just piles up one car after another.'

In industry parlance, exploitation is a relatively neutral term to describe finding or opening up an audience or market. The more pejorative connotations of exploitation films also go along with this more neutral meaning of seeking very specific markets, in this case the youth audience. The less pejorative meaning of exploitation is also contained in another term coined at the time, blaxploitation, for movies designed to appeal to young, urban, black audiences. (This was an area not catered for at all by the majors until the 1970s when the move was spearheaded, ironically enough, by Roger Corman's brother Gene, with his unit at MGM making movies like *Cool Breeze,* directed by Barry Pollack, 1972, and *The Slams,* directed by New World graduate Jonathan Kaplan, 1973, in the wake of the success of the much more expensive *Shaft* in 1971.) Later, the pejorative connotations of exploitation also extended to the idea of the independent companies ripping off the successes of the majors. Joe Dante's 1978 New World movie *Piranha* and Lewis Teague's 1980 *Alligator,* both from John Sayles scripts, were among several movies that exploited the vast success of Steven Spielberg's *Jaws* (Universal, 1975). The success of *Star Wars* (1977) similarly set off a long chain of cheaper imitations, not least New World's *Battle Beyond the Stars* (1980). Such imitations obviously threatened

Still: biker movie - Angels Hard as They Come.

to undermine a strategy being learned by the majors around this time: that they could do pretty well by exploiting their own successes with 'official' sequels, such as *Jaws 2* (1978).

One of the most important meanings of the term exploitation was certainly exploitation of the film-makers themselves. In an industry in which high unemployment had become endemic and large numbers of professionals were always seeking work – and, of course, an industry to which newcomers were constantly seeking to gain entry – it was always relatively easy, despite the craft unions, for independent production companies to pay less than union rates of pay and/or hire non-union workers, certainly to work with smaller crews than those stipulated by union rules. Union staffing and pay rate regulations are among the key reasons why films made by or for the majors are so expensive. Evading the regulations enabled companies like New World, as well as much more respectable companies, to make movies far more cheaply. New World budgets were typically in the $125,000-200,000 range in the early 1970s, rising to an average of $1 million by the end of the decade, when the company was more openly in competition with the majors; costs on the majors' pictures would typically be five to ten times higher.

To find directors, Corman would generally look to young people who had worked for him in some minor production capacity or to eager new talent coming out of the film schools. As Coppola recalled, 'He would tell his secretary, "Ring up UCLA. Get some film student who'll work cheap." ' Although this was not quite the way things worked in the 1960s with Coppola himself or later with Scorsese, on *Boxcar Bertha*, some new film-makers in the 1970s – among them Jonathan Kaplan, Stephanie Rothman and Amy Jones – did arrive by this film school route. Kaplan had been recommended to Corman by Scorsese, who had known him when he was teaching at New York University. Joe Dante, hired initially to cut trailers at New World, had made a student film but had not really been at film school (the concept of which as a direct preparation for the industry was still relatively new), and edited for some time before being given the chance to direct *Hollywood Boulevard* (1976) with Allan Arkush.

Jonathan Demme had been a critic and publicist, and had worked for Corman on *Von Richthofen and Brown* before being invited to script a biker movie for New World. He scripted and produced several movies for Corman (including *Angels Hard as They Come*, 1971, and *The Hot Box*, 1972, both directed and co-scripted by Joe Viola) before getting to direct *Caged Heat* (1974). Ron Howard, who was already well known as a child actor (for example in Vincente Minnelli's *The Courtship of Eddie's Father*, 1963) and young male star on television (notably in the series *Happy Days)*, agreed to star in New World's *Eat My Dust!* (1976) in return for the chance to write and direct (and star) for Corman, which he did with *Grand Theft Auto* in 1977. John Sayles was a budding short story writer and novelist before writing scripts for Corman. At least in more or less official statements of his position, Corman has always been very clear, and apparently very reasonable, about the relationship involved in hiring cheap and relatively untried young film-makers, as he explained in his statement to the *Journal of the Producers' Guild of America*:

'From the beginning it is understood between us that I as a producer . . . am in the business of making feature films which are marketable within a highly competitive industry, and which are oriented towards the young film-going audience that, as analyses of the ticket-buying public continue to show us, still goes more frequently and regularly to the movies than any other age group. I believe that there is a definite advantage in hiring a young director to make a film to appeal to that audience. He [*sic*] is more in touch with their language and their aspirations, and particularly with their humor. On the other hand, however creative and hip he may be, the element of risk in hiring a new young director making his first film is always present. Conservative arguments can always be found for preferring a man who has already shown that he can shoot a film which cuts together, that he can handle an action scene, and so on. Consequently, I do expect that a first-time director will be willing to work for a lesser fee than he will subsequently command if he proves his competence. In the light of my foregoing remarks on the difficulty of securing that initial opportunity (largely because of the financial hazards involved if the producer's faith proves to be misplaced), it is not surprising that

Still: action, humour and sex in Caged Heat.

usually the would-be young director is happy to have the chance to make his first feature, even without the added expectation of making a lot of money from the undertaking. On this basis I give a new young director the opportunity to direct a film on a subject and with a script approved by me as having good commercial potential, and to bring in as good a film as he can make within a firm budget and shooting schedule.'

This is the official version and whether the relationship worked out quite this way in practice is not so generally agreed, although, as Scorsese remembers, 'Corman did leave you alone, provided you played it within the genre and didn't get too crazy.' Jonathan Demme agrees: 'If you buy his concept – that pictures that audiences like contain these three elements: action, humour and sex – and if you really buy it and you commit yourself to get as much of that stuff as possible in them, and if you also want to make a good picture and tell a good story, then the best of both worlds happens – he gets a movie that contains these things and he's confident in releasing it, and you get a chance to make a picture very much the way you want to make it.'

Film-makers do not always agree in their recollection of Corman's creative or nurturing role with his untried young directors. Sometimes, it seems to have been extremely limited, though perhaps nonetheless valuable. Jonathan Kaplan recalled that his first meeting with Corman after being hired to direct *Night Call Nurses* in 1972 lasted about ten minutes, during which Corman laid out the requirements of the nurse film genre – exploitation of male sexual fantasy, a comedic subplot, action and violence, and a slightly-to-the-left-of-centre subplot. Kaplan remembers the conversation ending like this: 'The film is called *Night Call Nurses*. At present we don't have "night call nurses" in the dialogue. I want you to work it in. I want frontal nudity from the waist up. Total nudity from behind. No pubic hair. This is my wife, Julie [who was to produce the film]. Go off and rewrite the script. Goodbye.'

John Sayles, who was hired to rewrite *Piranha*, felt that although there were severe restrictions placed upon him, he was nevertheless able to retain some essential freedoms. It was made very clear what was expected of him, and yet room was left for his own creative input: 'They said, "You're going to rewrite *Piranha*. Make sure you keep the main idea, the idea of piranhas being loose in North American waters." I said, "Okay, how often do you want an attack? About every fifteen minutes?" They said, "Yeah, but it doesn't have to be an attack. Maybe just the threat of an attack – but some sort of action sequence about that often to keep the energy going." I said, "Anything else?" They said, "Yeah. Keep it fun." And that's a story conference at New World. It takes

Stills: 'keep it fun' – Piranha.

about twenty minutes. After that, you're on your own. You can come up with any story, any location, so long as you fulfil what was agreed upon: keep the fish in the country and keep it fun.' Joe Dante, the film's director, adds that as part of the fun, 'we invented a whole summer camp full of kids and we thought, well, nobody will ever think that we'll kill them off, so we'll kill them all – we were very cavalier in those days.'

Scripting *Alligator*, for another exploitation company, Sayles had a similar experience: 'Often I'm just a hired hand – a carpenter for someone else . . . But even as a carpenter I have quite a lot of freedom now. Take *Alligator*, for instance. It was originally a script where they decided that the alligator had got to be a giant one because it lived in the sewers of Milwaukee and the suds from the spill-over in the local breweries [were] making it bigger and bigger. So I asked why the people of Milwaukee weren't that big since they drank even more of the beer. That made them think, and in the end they just said, "Keep the name *Alligator*, keep the idea of alligators in the sewers and do what you damn well like." ' So Sayles was able to give a political twist to the story by featuring an alligator grown to giant proportions from eating animals dumped in the sewers after dying from illegal growth drug experiments.

Demme, on the other hand, recalled that 'the most important thing Roger did for me was to sit down with me before I directed *Caged Heat* and run down just how to do a job of moviemaking. He hit everything: have something interesting in the foreground of the shot; have something interesting happening in the background of the shot; try to find good motivation to move the camera, because it's more stimulating to the eyes; if you're shooting the scene in a small room where you can't move the camera, try to get different angles, because cuts equal movement; respect the characters and try to like them, and translate that into the audience liking and respecting the characters. To me, those are the fundamentals.'

Certainly, almost all the directors who began with Corman at New World talk of there being the atmosphere of a film school, with everybody learning about all stages of the process of film-making. Dante recalls that 'it was sink or swim . . . you feel after you've gone through that, that if you get past that point of your initial entry to working for Roger, you'll never be thrown anything you can't handle, because you're *really* alone then, and you're never as alone again – there are always people around you.'

Corman was certainly cheese-paring. Having co-directed *Hollywood Boulevard* (a spoof on exploitation film-making, featuring a production company called Miracle Films with the motto: 'If it's a good film, it's got to be a miracle'), then gone back to editing for Corman (on Ron Howard's *Grand Theft Auto)*, Dante was finally offered *Piranha* to direct (while his co-director on *Hollywood Boulevard* was given what became *Rock 'n' Roll High School)*. Was it a reward for services rendered? 'One might even call it a punishment.' Dante had by this time acquired an agent, who said he would negotiate the fee. When Corman offered Dante $8,000 to co-write, direct and edit the film, Dante said he had an agent and Corman replied, 'That's fine, and he'll represent you in every deal except mine.' In a take-it-or-leave-it situation, Dante accepted.

After editing *Hollywood Boulevard*, Amy Jones was lucky enough to get into the editors' craft union and edited some mainstream features (such as *Corvette Summer)*, but she realised that she wanted to direct rather than edit, and New World seemed 'the logical place to direct'. Having only a documentary from film school to show as evidence of her talent, she needed to prove herself at directing fiction. Corman's story editor, Frances Doel, gave her some New World scripts to read, and Jones decided she would shoot the seven-minute prologue (modelled on the *Halloween* prologue) of a script by Rita Mae Brown, figuring that an action horror sequence would convince Corman. With the help of friends, she shot the sequence, and Dante told Corman he should look at it. Corman did and then called Jones, who had handed him, for nothing, seven minutes of colour, 35mm film from a script that he owned. Jones recalls the conversation: 'Well, Amy, this is very interesting. How much did it cost?' She replied that it cost

Still: Alligator – *'eating its way through the whole socio-economic system'.*

about $1,000, and Corman said, 'You have a future in the business.' On the spot, Corman asked her how much it would cost to do the rest of the film. Jones had never budgeted a feature, but thought quickly and said $250,000. 'Well, you're going to do it.' Jones then rewrote for a month and shot what became *Slumber Party Massacre* (1982), one of Corman's biggest, and much sequelled, hits. It was lucky for all concerned that the people who worked for Corman were not yet used to high salaries. Sayles recalled that his first novel earned him $2,500 and his second, a year in the writing, $10,000, the same as he got for five weeks' work on *Piranha.*

What many of these film-makers valued most in the Corman experience, certainly in retrospect, when they had experienced mainstream Hollywood, was that movies actually got made and shown. Sayles: 'All those genre pictures were fun to write because Roger and the other two companies I worked for on *The Howling* and *Alligator* were people who were *making movies.* They didn't *talk* about twenty pictures and just make *one.* If they were paying a writer, they already had shooting scheduled. That takes away the annoying wish-washiness of working for a big studio. It was a lot of fun because you knew a movie was going to come *out.'* And Dante agrees: 'For me, this was absolutely the best way to get into the business, the best schooling you can get, because you're making a real film, you're not working on some student film that's going to be in the closet for the rest of your life. You're very conscious that whatever mistakes you're making, they're going to be disseminated broadly. It was exciting. It was the real thing. We were making movies. And the movies got released. The thing you knew with Roger was, no matter what you did, your movie was going to be released.'

This was perhaps the greatest freedom of working for Corman: the opportunity to learn how to make movies by actually making them. A similar kind of freedom had existed in the now defunct studio system, when a rapid turnover of product, often generic, as at New World, meant that film-makers could learn their craft without the pressure of each individual project having to succeed. Once it had become usual for directors to make only one feature every two or three years, and when a film-maker's future could depend on sustained box-office success, such freedom was harder to come by, but Corman's New World and a few other companies provided it. Jonathan Kaplan made five films in three years (*Night Call Nurses*, 1972, *Student Teachers*, 1973, *The Slams*, 1973, *Truck Turner*, 1974, *White Line Fever*, 1975): 'When I looked at the film-ographies of the directors I admired, I noticed that they made a hell of a lot of movies before they made a good one. And I made the decision, consciously, to make as many movies as I could in as short a period of time as I could.' Jonathan Demme recalls a similar desire to learn by doing the job as directors might have done in the days of the studio system. During the Corman years, he, Joe Viola and George Armitage took as their role model the veteran director Raoul Walsh: 'We'd growl at each other and say, "Just give us an assignment and we'll make something of it. We're professionals!" ' The only comparably intensive training ground available for aspiring directors, despite possible danger to their careers in theatrical features, was television.

There were other freedoms, too, and these, again, appeared all the more attractive and valuable from the vantage point of working on bigger pictures. Despite Corman's generic requirements, directors were able to try out different stylistic strategies and could take some surprising turns with subject matter, especially since Corman was known to like liberal story lines. Sayles's scripts for *Piranha*, *The Lady in Red* and *Alligator* all have subversive elements – government-released piranhas in domestic waters, union-isation and feminism, corporate corruption and pollution ('My original idea was that the alligator eats its way through the whole socio-economic system') – but this is perhaps not surprising in the light of Sayles's later films such as *Matewan* and *City of Hope*. More surprising, perhaps, is the fact that the nurse pictures ended up with story lines revolving around abortion, ecological issues, black disadvantage and alternative education.

In many ways, freedom was inherent in the way the films were produced. Expectations tended to be low for a number of reasons: the films would have no aspirations to critical acclaim (as a rule, they would not be press shown), the budgets were extremely low, and producers would generally be absent and more concerned with selling the product than with actually making it – Corman, certainly, would generally absent himself from the start of shooting until it was more or less finished. All that was expected at the end of the process was a marketable product, and as long as this was delivered, the writers and directors had a lot of freedom (though Corman was more likely to intervene in the editing and, some have argued, liked to think of himself as stepping in at this stage to save projects).

Naturally, most of the film-makers working for Corman and other similar low-budget exploitation companies saw their time there as a stepping stone to better things and higher budgets, as indeed has been the case for a great many of them. For some, it has been a relatively easy passage, for others, apparently much more difficult. A few, like Stephanie Rothman (*Student Nurses*, 1970, *The Velvet Vampire*, 1971, *Group Marriage*, 1972, *Knucklemen* alias *Terminal Island*, 1973), though very talented, seem to have dis-appeared altogether. On one hand, as Dante remarks, working for Corman prepared them for anything; on the other, however, the experience did not prepare them for working within the system. The energy and freedom which characterised this early work was often simply not there in more expensive projects, and particularly in studio pictures.

But some film-makers seem to have made the transition comfortably. James Cameron, for example, began in special effects at New World at the end of the 1970s, working on *Battle Beyond the Stars*, among other films, before being hired to direct his first movie, *Piranha II: The Spawning*. He then graduated to *The Terminator*, *Aliens*, *The Abyss* and *Terminator 2: Judgement Day*. As the list of Cameron's credits testifies, the fate of exploitation directors when they move to mainstream Hollywood is complicat-ed by the fact that mainstream Hollywood since the 1970s has become increasingly com-mitted to making its own exploitation movies, with the difference that very large sums of money are spent on them, so that they tend not to *look* like exploitation movies. As an anonymous Universal executive commented, 'What was *Jaws*, but an old Corman monster-from-the-deep flick – plus about $12 million for production and advertising?'

Similarly, recalling his lesson in movie-making from Corman, Jonathan Demme speculated, 'I don't know if Roger had a similar lunch with Coppola, but look at *The Godfather*. It's a classical Roger Corman movie. All the Corman moves are there – a little sex, a little violence, a little social comment. Also, "make the audience like the characters even if they're mafiosi." '

Corman himself was very conscious that the majors were moving in on his territory and making up-market exploitation pictures. He recognised, for example, that Universal's very successful *Smokey and the Bandit* (1977) was closely modelled on movies like New World's comic car crash picture *Eat My Dust!* (1976) and he, too, saw *Jaws* as a throwback to his own earlier movies. Even if he did not want to compete with the majors, he conceded that they could cover the same market more effectively.

This was one reason why, by the end of the 1970s, New World had been more or less forced to compete with the majors on their own territory, mirroring the general industry tendency towards fewer films and bigger budgets. Thus, New World's disaster movie, *Avalanche* (1978, with Rock Hudson and Mia Farrow) cost around $2 million and *Battle Beyond the Stars* (1980, with Robert Vaughn, John Saxon and George Peppard) over $3 million, a lot of money by New World's earlier standards. And these bigger pictures were typically co-produced with the majors: United Artists put up half the budget for *Piranha* in return for overseas distribution rights, and the same ex-United Artists executives in their new guise as Orion made a similar deal on *Battle Beyond the Stars*, benefitting from Corman's cheap, non-union production methods. Collaboration of this sort was not totally novel at New World; in the mid 1970s, the company had produced a series of action pictures for Twentieth Century-Fox, cheaply made features to fill out Fox's distribution schedule. *Capone* (1975), *Fighting Mad* (directed by Demme, 1976), *Moving Violation* (also 1976), and *Thunder and Lightning* (1977) were made on budgets of around $1 million – very low by Fox standards, but high by New World's – which made possible better production values and slightly bigger stars such as Ben Gazzara in *Capone*, Peter Fonda in *Fighting Mad*, and Angie Dickinson in *Big Bad Mama*.

Other industrial factors were at work in New World's new strategies. The majors were increasingly targeting drive-ins, the staple outlet for exploitation material, for the first runs of their own youth-oriented product. As *Variety* reported in 1978: 'The areas hardest hit will probably be the indie distributors. Drive-ins have been the one area where the indie was almost guaranteed a play date and seldom competed with the majors for runs'. At the same time, television had become established as a lucrative market for features and, indeed, as an essential component of most films' profit potential. However, the networks (cable and home video were not yet real market forces) had rigid requirements about screening sex and violence – New World's original stock-in-trade – and demanded a certain level of production values, which had not been of much importance to New World at the start. To benefit from sales to network television, New World needed to change the nature of its product and spend more on it. If an extra $200,000 on a budget might secure a $1 million television sale, it was obviously an investment worth considering. Television was also in the ascendant as a source of production finance for independents, and New World had entered the made-for-television market with two CBS Movies of the Week features, *Outside Chance* (1978), a reprise by Michael Miller of his powerful 1976 New World picture *Jackson County Jail*, and *The Georgia Peaches* (1980).

It may be that personnel changes at New World also had some effect. From the mid 1970s, Barbara Boyle and Bob Rehme continued the earlier diversification initiated by Frank Moreno by distributing European 'art movies' (including Ingmar Bergman's *Cries and Whispers*, Federico Fellini's *Amarcord*, Volker Schlondorff and Margarethe von Trotta's *The Lost Honor of Katharina Blum*, which was equipped with the definitely New World ad line, 'She spent one night with the wrong man – *and the rest of her life in hell!')* The company also handled picked-up independent productions more like its own pictures, and also found the outside financing that would make bigger budgets possible. Rehme left New World in 1978 for Avco Embassy Pictures, where he became president in 1979, establishing a reputation for lowish budget action pictures like Joe Dante's *The Howling* (1980)and John Carpenter's *Escape from New York* (1981). Rehme subsequently turned up as the driving force behind New World after Corman sold it (for $16.5 million) in 1983, expanding the company's activities significantly in the home-video-fed boom of the mid 1980s.

After his adventure of competition with the majors, Corman formed a new production company, Millenium, which, under the terms of the sale, would distribute through New World. This arrangement did not work out, and Corman started a new distribution company, Concorde Films ('I had read a book that said hard C's were the most significant sound to sell products – like Kodak, or Coca-Cola'), which continues as Corman's main production and distribution banner. In 1987 and 1988, Concorde made 44 features – as Corman proudly claims, more than any major studio in that period – most of them typical exploitation titles. These were usually pre-sold to home video and shown theatrically only for short periods (if at all) and then mainly as promotion for the home-video release.

Still: Kevin McCarthy, Bradford Dillman and Heather Menzies – up-market stars in Piranha, *a New World picture for which United Artists put up half the budget.*

MOVING UP

New World was in many ways a very good place to start a career in Hollywood. Joe Dante observes that if he had gone to a major studio as a whizz kid with a good student film ('that's the ticket now to get into a big studio') and been put on a sound stage with a big union crew wondering who the hell he was, 'I'm sure I would have been much more intimidated about directing than in what was obviously a film school atmosphere, where all the people were young and none of us knew what we were doing.' For one thing, everyone learned how to do art direction, lighting and sound 'in a way that's not compartmentalised as it is if you get plunked down in a big studio . . . I got into things as I was able to do them.' Joe Ruben also started out in low-budget exploitation and counts himself lucky not to have jumped straight into major movies: 'There are guys who do their first movie for $15 million for a major studio – that I don't understand, that to me is amazing. To do a $50,000 movie makes sense to me. I can remember that first day. We had set up the first shot, and I pulled the cameraman aside and said, "Now what do I say, when do I say it, what's the procedure here?" He took me through it and I said "OK, great," and we went back into the room and did it. I learned more in that movie than I've learned since.'

It is very common to hear directors who began in low-budget work, especially with Corman, waxing nostalgic about it once they have experienced the system at other levels. Dante again: 'In a non-union film you're groping along, especially when you're starting out. Even after you've made a number of films, there's a very off-the-cuff feeling about non-union films which, now that I've gone back and made them after making studio films, I find very refreshing. At the time we all thought, gosh, we can't wait to stop making these cheap pictures and make real movies, whereas in fact, once you get to make "real" movies you start to get nostalgic for the freedom you had in making low-budget films,' because, although Corman had to be presented with the elements he thought would sell the movie, directors could try different methods of shooting and editing. 'You could do literally whatever you wanted, short of turning in upside-down footage, and nobody came and said "This doesn't look right." '

Dante progressed at New World from cutting trailers to co-directing *Hollywood Boulevard* (1976), which was shot in ten days for $60,000. He then went back to working on trailers, at the same time learning a lot from editing Ron Howard's *Grand Theft Auto* (1977), and eventually directed *Piranha* on the elevated budget (for Corman) of $600,000. Dante describes himself as both surprised and pleased that it turned out so well. It led to his first work away from Corman and New World, *The Howling* (1980), made for the growing and ambitious independent Avco Embassy with a budget of $1.8 million. The relative commercial success (for an independent picture) of *The Howling* meant that Dante was soon being offered better projects, including some from the major studios.

Amy Jones studied still photography and film at MIT and tried, unsuccessfully, to make a career in documentary (working in 1974-75 on an Ed Pincus project). Before that, she had made a documentary, *A Weekend at Home,* which won first prize in a student film festival where Martin Scorsese had been one of the judges; Jones wrote to him, they met, and he took her on as an assistant on *Taxi Driver,* which made up her total education in features. She then quickly established herself as a first-rate editor, graduating from *Hollywood Boulevard* at New World to Scorsese's *American Boy* (1977) and to her first union feature, *Corvette Summer* (1978), part of which was cut at Lucas Film, where she met George Lucas and Steven Spielberg, who offered her various films to edit. She subsequently spent eighteen months working as an editor on Hal Ashby's *Second Hand Hearts,* and learned a great deal from Ashby, who had been an Oscar-winning editor. This rapid success as an editor was very seductive, not least in terms of what she could earn, but she realised that she wanted to direct, not edit, and she didn't think she could write.

After dropping out for six months and having her first child, Jones went back to Corman as 'the logical place to direct' and became involved in *Slumber Party Massacre.* Then she waited for offers, but none came, even though the film was successful, both artistically in its genre and commercially. So she went back to Corman, but with a different kind of project. As this was at the point in the early 1980s when the video market was beginning to be a major factor for independent producers, Jones suggested a 'quality' film that could both feed Corman's art film exhibition arm and be sold to video. New World was changing hands at this time, and *Love Letters* (1983) became one of the first productions of a new Corman company, Millenium, with a budget of $500,000. Unlike *Slumber Party Massacre,* which she took on and felt she could do something with but to which she had no real commitment, *Love Letters* was a project that she believed in very strongly. It concerns a young woman's (inevitably doomed) affair with a married man with a family, following her discovery, after her mother's death, of some love letters written over a period of years to her mother by a lover.

Jones was lucky in several respects, not least in getting Jamie Lee Curtis for the lead role at considerably less than her usual fee – Curtis was at this time seeking to break out of the horror heroine role into which she had been cast by *Halloween.* But also, Corman's way of working meant that once the script was okayed, they were shooting within two months: 'It just *happens* when you work for Roger – it doesn't happen like that any place else.' Lucky though this was for *Love Letters,* it posed problems for Jones as she progressed to other things. She did not want to work for Corman again, because she wanted bigger budgets and better pay, having earned only about $50,000 for the two pictures. But so far she had only been an editor, a craftsperson; she was also used to working with Corman, who liked and respected her. As she concedes, she had 'no experience of how to play the Hollywood system,' and she had a difficult time on her next projects.

One of the people involved in *Slumber Party Massacre* was Aaron Lipstadt, who was co-producer and production manager (as well as a very short-lived bit part player, as the pizza delivery man). Lipstadt had taken a rather unusual route into New World, starting from a critical and theoretical interest in cinema which developed into a PhD project on New World and the exploitation phenomenon, which in turn got him more interested in the industrial aspects of the subject than in continuing with the thesis. Lipstadt initially wanted to work on the production rather than the creative side of the business, and he was taken on as Corman's assistant when Gale Anne Hurd left the job. At first, this meant answering the telephone, opening mail and reading scripts, but when *Battle Beyond the Stars,* Corman's biggest picture to date, went into production, Lipstadt worked on it, partly as Corman's 'spy' and partly to sort out production problems, in the process learning about scheduling and dealing with a crew, and coming to feel that this was something he could do well.

With *Slumber Party Massacre* going smoothly, Lipstadt felt he was on his way to becoming a producer for hire, but then he was invited to be second-unit director as well as producer on *Mutant* (1982, directed by Alan Holzman and known in Britain as *Forbidden World),* a Corman rip-off of *Alien.* Shooting some additional scenes with actors when

Still: science fiction action in Android.

the production fell behind schedule, Lipstadt began to see the greater rewards of directing and told Corman he wanted to direct. Corman agreed that Lipstadt should shoot *Alien Sex Shocker* – Lipstadt was not clear whether this was the concept or the working title, or both – about aliens who kidnapped human women for reproductive experiments (which Lipstadt, working on the script, decided should be 'the Patty Hearst story in space'), on the sets left from *Mutant*. While Lipstadt was writing, the sets were struck in error, and he was told he was out of a job. However, Don Opper and James Reigle were also writing a movie to be shot on the sets of *Mutant,* and this, with goods and services contributed by Corman – plus some $100,000 in cash (also from Corman) for the North American theatrical rights – became *Android* (1982), Lipstadt's first feature as director and widely admired as a combination of science-fiction action and humour.

Any first feature is an intimidating prospect, but Lipstadt had seen plenty of mediocre directors at work and had felt as he watched that he would do things differently and better. When he came to watch his own dailies, he was at first satisfied that at least the shots were properly exposed and in focus, and he continued to feel confident as shooting progressed, partly because he had surrounded himself with a crew he knew well and trusted. On a low-budget feature like this – it cost about $500,000 – what is lacking in experience is often more than compensated for by commitment and enthusiasm as well as by self-interest: it was only the second or third feature for the director of photography, and the art director had previously worked only as a set decorator, so both had much to gain by doing a good job. In addition, Lipstadt had more experience as a producer than either of the two producers on the picture, which gave him an edge on them and forced a situation in which they did what he had himself done as a producer – 'give the director as much as possible'.

Android was a critical success but had little luck at the box office in the United States – Corman did not seem to know quite what to do with a film that was in many ways more art movie than exploitation picture. The producers bought the film back from him and sold it to Island Alive, who were more convinced of its potential, but Island Alive never made any money on the film, which probably fell between the recognised slots of exploitation, genre picture and art movie (to this day, Lipstadt maintains it would have done better dubbed in German with English sub-titles). It was sold to video for $50,000, just before the video boom; a year later, it might have sold for $500,000 or even $1 million. Lipstadt had wanted to get a good *Variety* review, which he did, and he assumed he would follow more or less the same path as other ex-Corman film-makers – a $1 or $2 million picture to direct, then up the studio ladder. *Android* did, as Lipstadt puts it, 'make me a director, get me an agent, and get me some meetings'.

After *Android*, Lipstadt and his producers spent a lot of time working on *Slam Dance* but, unable to get it going, began to develop *City Limits* as another picture to make with Corman; the opening of *Android* in Britain brought the possibility of some British money for it. At that point, *City Limits*, which Lipstadt saw as a futuristic three musketeers story, happened very fast, and *Slam Dance* was put on hold. Meanwhile, in a situation quite typical for film-makers, Lipstadt had an offer from Hemdale to direct what was almost a studio picture, *The Return of the Living Dead* (subsequently directed by its writer, Dan O'Bannon, 1984); both Lipstadt and his agents wanted him to take the job and come back to *City Limits* later.

Out of loyalty to his colleagues, however, Lipstadt went with *City Limits*, a decision that was to teach him a lesson about not going into projects which are under-budgeted and before the script is right. *Android* had been scripted so that it could be done well within a twenty-day schedule, nineteen days of which were on a stage. *City Limits* was budgeted at $1.75 million (with British money and video money) and had a thirty-two day schedule, but much of it was night-for-night location shooting, which proved much too ambitious for its schedule and budget. To cap it all, a public sneak preview was arranged to which studio executives were invited, an occasion Lipstadt remembers as

Still: science-fiction humour – Don Opper in Android.

'nightmarish'. Although the film was then rescored and partially reshot, it was a critical and commercial disaster: 'I was dead.' Although *Slam Dance* was eventually set up, Island Alive had had money in *City Limits* and refused to accept Lipstadt as director (it was directed by Wayne Wang and released in 1987). Despite the relatively low stakes involved, one major flop meant that Lipstadt's career would have to start again in television. He has had a good deal of success there, but it is not where he – or, indeed, almost anyone else in television – wants to be. As the stakes in theatrical features are much higher than in television, Lipstadt feels a need to be extremely careful in his choice of material for another theatrical feature, so that if he has another flop, it will at least be with something that he was committed to and that he made on his own terms, rather than being another feature made for the sake of it: 'If I make what's perceived as a bad movie, I'll probably never make movies again.'

Mark Goldblatt was another film-maker whose path led him to New World – and then to various other independent set-ups. Goldblatt had been very active in student film programming in the lively film culture at Madison, Wisconsin in the late 1960s, thereby getting to see lots of European movies as well as the classic American cinema of Orson Welles, Alfred Hitchcock, Josef von Sternberg and so on. Since films were his main interest in life – he had also shot some 8mm film – he decided that he might as well train properly. He chose to do this at the London Film School, partly because it was very cheap compared with American film schools (and he wanted a trade school rather than an academic one), partly because he had promised himself that, if Nixon was elected president, he would leave the United States. In London his film education was expanded, not just by the school, where he was excited to be taught by out-of-work good craftsmen like Wolf Rilla and Val Guest, but by the National Film Theatre, the London Film-Makers' Co-operative, British Film Institute seminars and summer schools; although the school's diploma did not mean very much, he was pleased to have a grounding in a range of technical skills. Failing to find work in documentary in London, and wanting to get back to his roots, Goldblatt returned to the United States and made his way to Los Angeles in 1974.

He did not feel he could offer himself as a director and, since he did not see himself as a writer, he decided to try getting into the business as an editor. Entry into the editors' union was very difficult at that time and, failing to find studio work, he worked on some independent films and pornographic films to earn a living. This proved to be more than he could stand, and one day he walked into New World where he met Jon Davison (later the producer of such hit movies as *Airplane!*, 1980, and *RoboCop*, 1987) and discovered in him, and soon after in Joe Dante as well, very similar tastes in movies; they were members of a 'small sub-culture with eclectic passions for film from Robert Enrico to Abbott and Costello'. Davison offered him work – but with no pay – as an assistant on Dante's and Arkush's *Hollywood Boulevard* and promised to try to get him in on the editing (in which Amy Jones was already assisting Dante). Goldblatt then got paying jobs at New World assisting Dante on the editing of *Eat My Dust!* and *Grand Theft Auto*, all valuable experience, and managed to get himself an assistant editor's union card working on television at Warner.

His big break, as he sees it, was co-editing *Piranha* with Dante, because this led on to other editing jobs, including New World's *Humanoids from the Deep* (1980), in the horror genre for which he was an enthusiast. As a potential director, though, he had nothing to show. He enjoyed editing, but he wanted to be editing bigger and better pictures which would allow him to set his sights more clearly on directing. He jumped at the chance to edit Dante's *The Howling* which, while still an independent production, had a more prestigious budget than New World material. His first union job as editor (although he had not worked the eight – later five – years required for anyone who entered as an assistant) was *Halloween 2* (1981), but he spent a lot of time in the early 1980s editing films for the then rapidly expanding independent company Cannon, including two films directed by Menahem Golan *(Enter the Ninja,* 1981, and *Over the Brooklyn Bridge,* 1983).

After a number of Cannon pictures, Goldblatt was approached by Gale Anne Hurd to edit James Cameron's *The Terminator* (1984); it meant a cut in pay, but he had known Cameron as an art director at New World (Hurd had been Cameron's assistant on *Humanoids),* and they had similar interests in film. This was Goldblatt's biggest step forward, as *The Terminator* – though modestly budgeted – was a major hit. The next big step came rather by chance: Cannon wanted him to edit J. Lee Thompson's 1985 picture, *King Solomon's Mines,* but Goldblatt refused the price he was offered, even though he had no other prospects at the time. He was on vacation when he was called by Andy Vajna, then head of Carolco, who had seen *The Terminator* and had been given a strong recommendation of him by Cameron; Vajna wanted him to take over as editor on *Rambo: First Blood Part II* (George Pan Cosmatos, 1985). Goldblatt remembers being asked how much he wanted and not knowing what to reply, so asking for what he had wanted (but had not got) from Cannon and being subtly told to ask for more. This was Goldblatt's first major studio picture as an editor, and he found himself working with the second unit and having his advice heavily solicited.

Goldblatt was suddenly in the position of having edited two big hits. Offers began pouring in from everywhere. Among them was one from Joel Silver – a producer he had admired – who wanted him to take over the editing of his Fox picture *Commando* (Mark Lester, 1985). When an editor takes over a picture that is thought to be in trouble, and the picture goes on to be a success, the editor gets extra credit. Goldblatt had established himself as an expert fixer, his price was going up and he was in demand. At the same time, he kept saying that he wanted to direct and took an agent to look for directing jobs. Although Joel Silver and Fox talked of finding him a project to direct, Goldblatt was in the same situation as he had been in with Cannon – 'Cut one more picture, then . . .' – when he was approached to direct a horror comedy, *Dead Heat,* for New World Pictures, which was then in full-tilt expansion. While the project was still in development, New World got a new head, and although there was no guarantee that he would finally direct it, Goldblatt decided to commit himself and stop being an editor, although this involved his turning down some big offers. Meanwhile, his old friend from New World, Jon Davison, was producing *RoboCop* and invited him to shoot second-unit. A fan of Paul Verhoeven, Goldblatt would watch him direct and then the next

Stills: Dead Heat – *LAPD detectives Joe Piscopo (left, confronting criminal) and Treat Williams (right, in pool).*

night do mop-up shots. Although he had not before directed anything on this scale, 'there wasn't any time to be intimidated.' The best thing was that he now felt sure that directing was what he wanted to do, and so he returned to direct *Dead Heat* with some enthusiasm. He thinks, however, that he probably tried to do too many things for a first feature and found it 'a sobering experience to be a director and realise I'm no Orson Welles and probably never will be. You always think maybe you are, but it's OK, I can live with that.'

Dead Heat (1988) is a comic horror version of *D.O.A.*, Rudolf Mate's 1950 *film noir* thriller (there was also a straight remake in 1988) in which the dying protagonist seeks to solve his own murder. The transposition to the horror genre finds the protagonist slowly decomposing as the movie progresses. There were problems over exactly what kind of film it should be and who it should be aimed at, both during production and when it was marketed. Goldblatt wanted something that went all the way towards offensive, though comic, *grand guignol*, like Stuart Gordon's 1985 *Re-Animator,* while New World wanted something more mainstream, appealing to a wider audience than just horror fans. Goldblatt went along with the studio to get the picture made, but the same problem came up with the campaign to sell the movie, which was not sold as a horror picture, (though as Goldblatt concedes, a director's constant lament when a picture fails to find an audience is that the campaign was no good). Goldblatt recalls the company executives continually talking about *Lethal Weapon* and himself taking the line that 'if you want to make a *Beverly Hills Cop* rip-off, fine, go ahead, but this is a horror movie about a guy decomposing . . .'

The move from editing to directing is not particularly common – much less so than from writing to directing, but neither Goldblatt nor Dante saw himself as a writer. Both saw editing as a way in as well as a way of learning. According to Dante, 'in the process of learning how to edit comes an understanding of how films are made' – particularly when you are editing a fifteen-day picture shot in the Philippines and you are seeing how corners were cut and how certain angles that were shot were not really necessary. But Goldblatt reckons that his film aesthetic would somehow be 'purer' if he had not edited so many big Hollywood pictures. Now, when he shoots, he knows very well what

Photograph (opposite): Mark Goldblatt directing Dolph Lundgren on the set of The Punisher. *Still (right): The Punisher in action.*

he needs in order to be able to do certain things in the editing, and so he likes lots of coverage. Dante describes editing as essentially solitary, and Goldblatt sees it as sedentary and cerebral. Becoming directors, both were struck by how many balls there were to juggle and how 'social' a director needed to be to work with crew and actors – Goldblatt recalls the challenge of working with actors like Treat Williams, Joe Piscopo and Vincent Price on *Dead Heat* with very little time for any rehearsal.

Impressed by Goldblatt's dailies on *Dead Heat,* New World offered him other projects, among which was *The Punisher.* A Marvel Comics creation of the 1980s, 'The Punisher' was a renegade cop avenging the death of his family by waging a private war against the underworld – just like Glenn Ford in *The Big Heat,* in fact, and very different from Marvel's rather liberal 1960s and 1970s heroes like Spider Man or the Incredible Hulk. In the movie, this urban vigilante is dressed in black leather, rides an armoured motorcycle and is armed with machine guns. Goldblatt likes comics, though he had not known 'The Punisher' before the project came up. He sees himself as a fantasist, attracted to horror and action and preferring a blatantly unrealistic, stylised universe to a realistic one. The project was therefore attractive to him, not least the 'anti-hero, borderline psychotic' main character; and he felt he could make a stylised action picture as well as something 'darkly humorous'. Goldblatt confesses that if the *Time Out* judgment of the picture – 'destructive, reprehensible and marvellous fun' – is accurate, then he succeeded in precisely what he had set out to achieve.

One aspect of New World's expansion in the mid 1980s was the establishment of foreign subsidiaries to make films abroad more cheaply, and this was how *The Punisher* (1989) came to be made by New World (Australia). Seattle had been considered as a location, but the production would get a larger budget – $9.5 million – if it were to be made in Australia, where New World had funds and costs were lower. First, though, Sydney was checked out as generically able to pass as an American city – Goldblatt would have liked to shoot in the streets of New York, and he feels that the streets still

Still: Arnold Schwarzenegger in Terminator 2.

do not look quite as he would have liked. Despite the enhanced budget and talented Australian crews, shooting in Australia (post-production was done in Los Angeles) posed a range of problems: Australian Equity rules meant only a few non-Australian actors (Dolph Lundgren, Lou Gossett, Jeroen Krabbe), with other parts played by Australians able to do American accents; it was much harder than in the United States to get streets closed off while they shot; the sound stages were 'archaic'. Worst for Goldblatt was the Australian ten-hour day – he was used to seventeen-hour days. 'You just get going and it's time to go home' (overtime was a possibility, but the crew had to vote on it).

Despite the problems, Goldblatt stands by the film which should have led on to new projects, had it not coincided with the end of the 1980s, when many of the decade's big independent companies were in trouble. While *The Punisher* was in post-production, New World was sold and got out of the feature film business. All its unreleased features were shelved. *The Punisher* still remains unreleased in the United States and, despite the film's relative success in foreign theatrical markets and its big success on video, this means that its visibility in the industry is very low; it remains a calling card for Goldblatt, but one that does not have the all-important theatrical success attached to it. As a result, he feels that his directing career lost some of its momentum.

He continues to try setting up new movies to direct, and is being offered some in the $9-10 million budget range, but he also goes on earning a living by editing high-profile features like *Predator 2* (Stephen Hopkins, 1991), *Terminator 2* (James Cameron, 1991) and *The Last Boy Scout* (Tony Scott, 1992) and enhancing his reputation as a fixer (he was, for example, brought in to recut Martin Barker's *Nightbreed,* 1990). Earning a good living, and continuing to learn, while waiting for the right directing project to come up is not quite as convenient as it sounds. Goldblatt spent nine months working on *Predator 2,* and breaking his commitment to it to go off and direct would have severely disadvantaged the producer and the director. The same applied to his very intense six months on *Terminator 2,* even though there he had an escape clause that would have allowed him to bale out had he got a directing offer he wanted to take up. He accepts that he will not be offered the best scripts around – 'I'm not the hottest property' – but while other directors might be just grateful for a job, he would rather be editing until he finds a project to which he can commit himself fully. Certainly, editing features enables him, for example, to avoid having to work as a director in television. A film like *Predator 2,* for example, may not be exactly what he wants to be working on, but he recognises that being an editor in demand gives him some freedom of choice over the projects he takes on, whether as editor or director, though he feels he is more likely to make compromises on what he edits, when he is just a contributing technician, albeit an important one, than on something to direct.

A much more usual career route for directors is from writing, but even here, as Tim Hunter puts it, 'It's all timing, and a lot of it is luck'. Hunter, son of British actor Ian Hunter, had planned from the age of ten to work in the movie industry. A large part of his student days at Harvard were devoted to writing criticism and making ambitious student films (including adaptations of Nathaniel Hawthorne and Edgar Allan Poe), several of them for Boston television. When Hunter was in the first year of the American Film Institute's prestigious directing class and while finishing his AFI film, *Devil's Bargain* (shown at the Edinburgh Film Festival in 1971), he taught critical classes in film at the university in Santa Cruz. As befits a contributor to the Edinburgh Film Festival 1972 book on Douglas Sirk, for which he wrote on Sirk's *Summer Storm,* Hunter's classes reflected an awareness of what was happening in film criticism at the time – he taught courses on Fritz Lang, Otto Preminger, Alfred Hitchcock, *film noir,* melodrama and the western. Part of the reason for teaching was that it allowed him time to work on his screenwriting. The most important outcome of this period was that Hunter linked up with Charlie Haas, then working as a publicist, to come up with a book and screenplay, sold in 1977, about disenfranchised kids in a suburban housing development who finally burn down their school – all based on actual events in Foster City, outside San Francisco. *Over the Edge,* released in 1979, was bought by George Litto, an independent producer and agent who had represented Hunter's father as well as black-listed artists.

Still: Michael Kramer, Matt Dillon and Harry Northrup in Over the Edge.

Litto set it up as a production for Orion. Hunter and Haas pushed for Jonathan Kaplan to direct, but Kaplan's 1977 *Mr Billion* had been a box-office disaster. It was only the chance of a successful network television premiere of Kaplan's earlier *White Line Fever* that made this possible.

While interviewing teenagers for *Over the Edge*, Hunter and Haas found that among the little that kids read, S.E. Hinton's novels were very popular; the two men looked at *The Outsiders* and *Rumblefish* (both later filmed by Coppola in 1983) but were particularly interested in *Tex*. They put together a package of the book, 16-year-old Matt Dillon (who had had a lead role in *Over the Edge*), Haas and Hunter as writers and – the only unknown quantity – Hunter to direct, and took it to Disney. Timing and luck intervened in two ways. Hunter's brother-in-law, whom he had, years before, encouraged in a career as a studio executive, had now risen to be a vice president at Disney; they submitted the *Tex* project to him and he passed it on. Hunter and Haas knew that Disney in the early 1980s was trying to move away from its purely family film image (most publicly marked by the release of *Splash* in 1984) and felt that Hinton fitted their bill of 'reality-based material that had a harder edge, but not too hard an edge'. Indeed, *Tex* does, with its story of two brothers – Matt Dillon playing the younger – trying to keep together the family farm in difficult circumstances.

Hunter was determined to direct, but refused to show Disney the student films he had directed some eight years earlier. He felt that he might never find another package in which a first-time director represented less risk to a studio: it had a low budget ($5 million), was based on an established novel, and had writers who had proved themselves with teenage material and presented no forseeable production problems.

Hunter did not find the experience of directing *Tex* (1982) too intimidating. He had done a lot of student film-making and had been heavily involved on the $2.3 million *Over the Edge* (he and Haas were on the set, Hunter recalls, 'yelling at Jonathan to do it our way'), which had shown him the differences between 16mm student film-making and

Still: Emilio Estevez, Matt Dillon and Meg Tilly in Tex.

Hollywood. Hunter enjoyed wonderful relations with Disney, which was very supportive and loved what he was doing. He recalls meeting the marketing people, imagining them still in *Absent-Minded Professor* mode and fearing they would want him to soften the material, but not at all: they wanted 'a hard PG' classification. But *Tex* was a small picture for Disney and took the studio into new areas. Hunter feels they did not know how to market it: 'Often you can make a good film and find yourself very frustrated when it comes to watching how the studio distributes it.' Finally, Hunter feels, you just have to reconcile yourself to this and be satisfied with making the movies. *Tex* was a critical success but did not make much impression at the box-office. Hunter insists that critical approval, while not as good as box-office success, is 'the next best thing in terms of maintaining interest on the part of studio people.'

Tex was followed – as far as credits are concerned – by several years of inactivity, which in fact meant a lot of offers of commercial pictures that he turned down, several projects in development with Disney that did not pan out and being hired by Diane Keaton to rewrite a project which also failed to come to anything. A couple of years had passed when producer Ray Stark offered Hunter *Sylvester,* a 'family-oriented horse movie'. Hunter's situation typified that of most directors most of the time: 'I kind of liked it and I felt I could do it, so I did. At that point [the film was made in 1985, three years after *Tex*], I needed to work. After a while, you work and work to try to get the stuff you like off the ground, and you've made either the right or the wrong decisions on the stuff that's been offered to you, but finally you just have to take a deep breath and take a job because you need the money. I remember asking Jonathan [Kaplan] if I should do *Sylvester,* and he said he always believed in the earn-while-you-learn theory.' At $8.5 million, *Sylvester* remains Hunter's biggest project to date. He enjoyed the experience and likes the first half of the film which, with a lot of western elements, was fun to do, but felt it was a step backwards, more like old-fashioned Disney: 'I knew, going in, it was a picture for an audience that really didn't exist any more.' Certainly, it did not find an audience, grossing only $750,000, 'the worst grossing film in Columbia's worst year in its history,' as Hunter puts it, and it was not a critical success either. Hunter believes that the film was not helped by his being forced to take Melissa Gilbert, from television's *Little House on the Prairie,* as the star – audiences had got used to seeing her for free.

'After *Sylvester,* I just assumed I'd have three or four years of unemployment.' It was 'just luck' that *River's Edge* (1986) came up. In the autumn of 1985, Hunter met producers Sarah Pillsbury and Midge Sanford for a general discussion, and they wondered if he would like to read the *River's Edge* script, which was about a group of small-town teenagers who agonise over reporting the apparently motiveless murder by one of them of his girlfriend (like *Over the Edge,* this was based on a real incident in California). The script had been around the majors, none of whom would risk the $5 or 6 million they felt was needed for it on such difficult material; Pillsbury and Sanford had been using it more as an example of what they and its writer, Neal Jimenez, could do. Understandably, Hunter was not anxious to do another teenage picture, but he was knocked out by the script and suggested that they make it independently and on a very low budget – Hunter guessed he could do it for $1 million (it was budgeted at $1.6 million and came in at $1.8 million). With such low costs, there was a lot of interest from independents, among them Hemdale, who read the script in September and put it into production by January. It was 'the fastest thing I've ever been involved in.' *River's Edge* was made non-union which typically means, as in this case, that the Directors' Guild allows productions under $3 million to defer up to half the director's salary until after release – an important consideration on a low-budget picture; other union members, such as assistant directors and actors, would be paid DGA and SAG scale rates. Although such an arrangement could dent the image of a well-established studio director, it is now quite common practice and would present no risk to someone in Hunter's position.

Still: River's Edge – *Dennis Hopper and inflatable doll.*

Hemdale is certainly not unique in having something of a reputation for interfering in productions, but in a very low-budget picture like *River's Edge* interference was likely to be less of a problem. The film was another mid 1980s production that benefitted from the video boom, and Hemdale made its investment back on the video alone: the video shipped over 140,000 rental copies just in the United States. Hunter has always enjoyed cordial relations with his producers and counts this as very important. Together, director and producer are able to present a very strong united front against the studio; if there is rift between them, studios are very quick to move in to divide and conquer. It is more or less the norm now for directors, with the higher status accorded them over the last twenty years, to get first cut on their features. Hunter, among others, likes to be tough on his material in the cutting room: 'I don't like to show anybody anything that's long – I don't see why I should give executives a lot of extra footage to figure out what to do with.'

Low-budget movies by young directors tend not to get terribly experienced actors. When they do, it is often very valuable. Joe Dante remembers how Bradford Dillman was a bit disappointed to find himself in a 'cheesy' movie like *Piranha* but that he was very professional and helped Dante in many subtle ways that he fully understood only when he got to the editing. Hunter enjoyed working with Dennis Hopper on *River's Edge,* though 'he was the last person I wanted to cast in the part,' because Hopper, whose work Hunter greatly admired, had become so typecast. But no other actor that Hunter wanted would touch the complex part of the crazy renegade hermit figure of Feck. Hopper, who in any case likes to associate himself with projects at Hollywood's cutting edge, loved the part and understood immediately that the character's relationship with a sex doll could be touching. Hunter concedes that he was 'the best thing that could have happened to the picture.' Hunter was also touched by Hopper's concern for him as a fellow director: 'a couple of times he'd see me doing something and he'd take me aside or shake his head or roll up his eyes to make me think about what I was doing, though he'd never do it in front of anybody, and he was usually right.'

Despite the critical success and respectable commercial performance of *River's Edge,* Hunter was surprised to find that it did not lead to other offers. It also rather typecast him in producers' eyes: 'It seemed to brand me in town as a 'dark' film-maker.

I still hear it all the time, "Isn't he too dark?" I think it scared a lot of people off.' In the long period of unemployment which followed, he worked on *Judge Dredd* and would have been willing to direct anything as long as he liked it: he wanted to do *The Handmaid's Tale*, but the producer had disapproved of *River's Edge*. In frustration, Hunter said yes to *Paint It Black*, 'a grade C Vestron thriller in the Hitchcock rip-off tradition', which he had already turned down because he did not like the script and which Vestron had begun shooting with another director, who was fired after a couple of weeks.

Hunter was asked to step in at two days' notice, as he already knew the script. He found himself shooting by day and rewriting at night, trying to turn it into something coherent. Though he never thought the film could be good, he did think he had some chance of making it entertaining and (retrospectively at least) he fancied the chance to do a sort of *film maudit*: 'Nowadays, when you don't work as regularly as you did when you were under contract to a studio, doing one or two films a year, and you don't have a chance to do a range of projects, I thought, here's my chance to do a C picture in the great Edgar G. Ulmer/Jacques Tourneur tradition.' Hunter's way of thinking here is common among many directors of the cine-literate generation, with a vast knowledge of movies and an awareness of debates about authorship in commercial American cinema. It was in this spirit that Jonathan Demme, Joe Viola and George Armitage at New World thought of themselves as latter-day Raoul Walshes accepting assignments; Joe Dante says much the same of his work on *Innerspace*: 'I'll be a director for hire, I'll do this picture and it'll be my "assignment movie", it'll be like Michael Curtiz being assigned to do a picture.'

Vestron was a victim of the squeeze on independents who, like New World, rapidly expanded in the 1980s. It went bankrupt while *Paint It Black* was in post-production, and the film went straight to video. Hunter is of the opinion that the decision to make *Paint It Black* did not hurt his reputation, partly because people in the industry know the circumstances in which he took it on; and it did enable him to support his family for a year. Aside from some involvement with television, Hunter was next scheduled as the director of *RoboCop 2*. The producer Jon Davison, who had begun at New World, was a friend and had approached Hunter to do the original *RoboCop*, at a time when he was

Still: River's Edge *with (left to right) Keanu Reeves, Crispin Glover, Roxana Zahl, Josh Richman, Daniel Roebuck and Ione Skye Leitch.*

doing *River's Edge*. Davison now involved him in the sequel, which Hunter found a nightmare, mainly because of pressure from the studio to make it very much the same as the original. After working on it for six months, Hunter made it clear that he did not like the script, and in the end he did not direct it. Didn't *Robocop* look a little odd as a project alongside Hunter's other films? 'Yes, but Jon Davison and I have known each other for many years, and he knows that basically I'm a cash-and-carry melodrama man and that I just fell into teen pictures – though nobody offered me teen pictures after *River's Edge*, they just offered me all the dark, sick shit that was going around town.'

More recently, Hunter has been working on a project for Paramount, *Success*, in the *All About Eve* genre, which 'hinges on relationships and good old-fashioned plotting,' and he has written and directed a critically very well-received thriller for cable, *Lies of the Twins* (1991), with Isabella Rossellini and Aidan Quinn. Hunter's films are notable, among other things, for the complex way in which they situate point-of-view for the spectator and for dealing with characters who are morally ambiguous, and he feels the climate in Hollywood is not particularly accommodating to such an approach: 'I fight actively against projects whose sole aim is to get an audience to identify with how wonderful and sympathetic and appealing a character is, and there's so much of that in Hollywood now.' Had his critical background and his interest in classical Hollywood worked against his possibilities as a film-maker? 'It's always been an obstacle. Who the hell ever got anywhere in modern-day Hollywood being primarily influenced by Otto Preminger? It's suicide, but those are the breaks.'

Where Hunter has worked in both independent and studio – though relatively low-budget – pictures (as well as in television, on occasion), Bobby Roth was more consistently involved in independent production before moving in recent years towards movies for cable; he also worked on several television episodes. Roth, who came out of Berkeley at the start of the 1970s, got into film because he wanted to make political, organising documentaries that would contribute to social change (the strongly politicised climate of the late 1960s/early 1970s no doubt accounts for the fact that quite a few new film-makers in this period began with ideas of working in documentary). Accordingly, he went to UCLA to make documentaries, but his master's film, *Independence Day* (1974) was in fact a 'drama documentary', a 16mm feature made for $27,000, with a $10,000 grant from the AFI, UCLA equipment and some people from New World. With an almost exclusively black cast, it concerned the political struggle of a black couple, and was centred around a strike.

It was no surprise to Roth that 'Howard Koch at Paramount told my father, when he saw the movie, that I had no chance of making a living in this business,' but at that time Roth, arrogantly, as he now says, felt a strong antipathy to most of what Hollywood stood for. He was more in sympathy with European cinema, especially the work of Jean-Luc Godard, and *Independence Day* was shown at festivals all over the world. Despite the critical reputation this earned him, Roth got no offers of work, and so wrote the script for *The Boss's Son* (1978), about a young man who reluctantly goes into his father's carpet business, and used his first film to show to prospective actors. This became a $200,000 35mm feature with professional actors, including Rita Moreno, and a technically adept crew, which made this second film a very different and more pleasant experience. It has probably been Roth's most profitable film too, having had a long life on cable and been sold extensively to overseas television as well as to network television in the United States. It also led to him being signed with Mike Ovitz at CAA.

Money and success beckoned, and Roth expected that he would go on to make bigger independent pictures and probably studio pictures. Even, then, however, Roth had the problem that besets so many directors: he saw himself primarily as a writer-director who would direct his own material, not as a director for hire (though he has directed scripts by others and more recently wanted to direct *White Palace*, which was eventually directed by Luis Mandoki, 1990). Nevertheless, Roth was flattered to be asked to

Still: Peter Coyote and Carol Wayne in Heartbreakers.

direct *Circle of Power* (1983), his first real 'commercial' picture, an Anthony Quinn project with Yvette Mimieux budgeted at $1.4 million. In retrospect, Roth feels it should never have been made: its budget limitations and the fact that he could not cast it satisfactorily meant that he was unable to realise his ideas properly. Despite a few not bad reviews, this was a setback; Roth recalls with a laugh that the *Variety* review was one of the worst he has ever seen – it commented that the film 'looked like it was shot by an Irish setter'.

This experience made Roth think again. He had committed himself fully to *Circle of Power,* so there was no excuse for its failure, but he had made a picture about people he neither understood nor cared about. Deciding that if he had any strength it was in writing from his own vantage point, he wrote *Heartbreakers* (1984): 'I like *Heartbreakers* because I really feel I know those people. They're right out of my own life and my own emotional base.' And *Heartbreakers* does indeed feel like an intensely observed film. It is about a thirty-something artist (played by Roth's favourite actor, Peter Coyote) going through a crisis with his best male friend when his long-time girlfriend leaves. The assurance with which it is written and directed seems to come from absolute confidence in and familiarity with the material. *Heartbreakers* cost $2 million to make – independently, of course – and, though it has taken about $4 million, it is not yet in profit, which causes Roth to speculate about the current state of independent film-making.

People had hoped that independent production would involve so little cash outlay that more movies would be made and there would be more 'accidents' like Bob Rafelson's *Five Easy Pieces* (1970), but Roth feels that the accidents are becoming fewer and fewer, even since 1989, the year of *sex, lies and videotape* and *Drugstore Cowboy.* The main reason is that the costs of marketing and advertising a feature for theatrical release have become so inflated: even if you manage to put together the whole of your production budget, 'if you don't have a p. & a. [prints and advertising] commitment and a US distributor, you don't have anything really, because all the other money – the pay cable money, the video money – falls into place based on theatrical. Video has

Still: L.M. Kit Carson in David Holzman's Diary.

turned out to be this funny monster. We all thought, wow, now they have this downside, they can afford to take risks, but in fact video has become just part of theatrical.' From this point of view, *Heartbreakers* was lucky to be made when it was: the budget was put together through deals between Orion, Vestron and HBO for rights to American theatrical and network television, video, cable and foreign in such a way that, ironically, it was 'such a good deal for everybody involved that there was no incentive to push the movie, so they just dumped it.' The critical success of *Heartbreakers* helped Roth to a deal with producer Ray Stark to do a $10 million dollar studio picture which did not work out but which earned him $250,000, more than he had ever earned before, and for *not* making a picture. Since then, Roth has worked extensively for episodic television and, particularly, for cable, as well as making a feature, *The Man Inside* (1990), in Europe.

Jim McBride began his involvement with film a little before Roth, but was influenced by some of the same cultural factors. He had never thought of making movies, but while taking a film course at New York University, he 'noticed that others in the class were actually planning to make movies. You didn't have to be royalty.' Among those classmates were Martin Scorsese and Michael Wadleigh, later known for the documentary *Woodstock.* McBride's first film, *We Shall Overcome* (1966), a five-minute montage of news broadcasts over still images, reflected the political climate of the time and was made for an FM radio station which was winning awards for its coverage of the counter-culture and for which McBride was doing some film reviews. The 1960s was a period of exciting technical and aesthetic developments in documentary. McBride and colleague L.M. Kit Carson were doing a monograph on *cinéma-vérité* for the American Film Institute, which involved them interviewing film-makers like the Maysles Brothers, Richard Leacock and Donn Alan Pennebaker.

This interest in what Americans preferred to call 'direct cinema' was the dominant influence on McBride's early film-making. *David Holzman's Diary* (1967), made for

$2,500, is almost emblematic of the time: Holzman (played by L.M. Kit Carson) takes up Godard's celebrated pronouncement that 'film is truth 24 times a second' and attempts to get at the truth of his life by recording a week in it. Much of this concerns his relationship with his girlfriend Penny, who becomes so irritated by the process that she breaks off the relationship. A fascinating, ironic exploration of the ethics and aesthetics of *cinéma-vérité*, and particularly the way in which the presence of the film-maker deforms the reality that he/she tries to record – 'it was often mistaken for *cinéma-vérité*, which says something about the nature of the medium' – the film was a great international art film/avant-garde success and established McBride's reputation as an almost experimental – or, in the term used at the time, 'underground' – film-maker.

The films that followed *David Holzman's Diary* picked up on its approach: *My Girlfriend's Wedding* (1968) was made as a short film to go out with the 73-minute *Diary*, using $10,000 from its distributor, and was about McBride's English girlfriend getting married to a man she had never met in order to get her green card. *Pictures from Life's Other Side* (1971) was a kind of sequel to *My Girlfriend's Wedding*, in which McBride and his girlfriend, now pregnant, and her seven-year-old son, move out of New York and, hippie-style, visit communes. It was made with a short-film grant from the AFI. Between these two, however, McBride made his first proper feature, *Glen and Randa* (1971), which was co-written with New York friends Rudolph Wurlitzer and Lorenzo Mans: 'The AFI were sponsoring movies, so we wrote the script for them. They kept it for a year, and it turned out that the studios weren't kicking in any money, so we went out and shot it on our own.' *Glen and Randa* – Wurlitzer has commented that it had 'nothing to do with Hollywood . . . [it] was more an underground thing' – has acquired the status of a cult film. Two teenagers, having survived the nuclear holocaust, and with little knowledge of the old world beyond information they gain from a 'Wonder Woman' comic, travel across a wasteland encountering relics – people and artefacts – of civilisation; their adventures are filmed in long takes, with fades between scenes, and the overall tone of the film is deadpan.

Though the distribution of McBride's early films was, inevitably, minimal, they nevertheless established for him a significant critical reputation as an experimental film-maker. At most times, this was unlikely to identify him as a prospect for Hollywood. But this was in the late 1960s and early 1970s, when Hollywood was in crisis and the usual divisions between commercial and experimental work were not quite as watertight as usual. It was perhaps not so surprising, then, that McBride should get a call out of the blue from Bob Rafelson and BBS. After the success of their very low-budget *Easy Rider* (1969), BBS had set up a deal with Columbia under which BBS hired young, new directors to make features and, provided the budgets did not exceed $1 million (at that time, not as little as it seems now), they did not have to clear projects with the studio. McBride recalls being told, 'We want you to do anything you want.'

The project he came up with and was signed for was *Gone Beaver,* a story of French mountain men in the 1840s, and he was given money to develop the script, which he did before a series of problems ensued and resulted in the film not being made. McBride had been over-ambitious and, when budgeted, the project came out at well over $1 million. The timing was tricky because shooting needed to take place in the fall and winter. BBS had offended the unions, and work permits were denied to Nestor Almendros and Vanessa Redgrave, among others; they needed either to fight the decisions or to find Americans to hire in their place. Finally, BBS decided to move the whole thing to Canada, but by then it was already too late in the season. McBride concedes that the biggest problem was probably himself, 'an arrogant young artiste from the East,' as he puts it, who was not used to answering to other people and failed to make appropriate compromises or fully to understand the pressures at work. Even so, McBride resents the rumours that started about him freaking out on acid, building a reputation that he had to live down when he finally came back to live in Los Angeles.

Greatly disappointed by this abortive first contact with Hollywood, McBride returned to New York thinking he would go on making little independent films, as he had before. In practice, he found himself driving a cab to support a wife and two children and then accepting $5,000 to write, direct, produce and edit a low-budget ($30,000 rising to $50,000) sex comedy, *Hot Times* (1974, originally *A Hard Day for Archie,* as it was based on the 'Archie' comics). 'It had to be about teenagers, and in every scene they had to be doing it or talking about doing it.' McBride calls it a porno movie (although it was originally cut and rated R, because the Supreme Court had ruled against hardcore, it was released with twenty minutes of hardcore material inserted because by then the court's decision had been reversed), but it is also in many respects a send-up of the sex movie, with a plethora of comic inventions in action and dialogue. McBride describes the experience as 'a terrific lot of fun,' mainly because he had not made a movie for several years and was glad to be working.

Between 1974 and 1983 he was still not working, or at least not directing, though during this period he was writing scripts and trying to set up movies. He moved to Los Angeles in 1975, an indication of his resignation to the fact that he would have to 'do it their way . . . ' – until then his whole orientation had been to art films and a very personal approach to film-making. Before, everything he wrote had been with the idea of directing it; now he slowly established a reputation as a writer as it became clear that no-one would hire him as a director. An adaptation of Walker Percy's novel *The Moviegoer,* with L.M. Kit Carson, was a project dating back to the mid 1960s – it involves some of the same concerns as *David Holzman's Diary,* in the movie-goer's obsessive desire to see his life in terms of film. McBride recalls this as a project that almost got made several times – in the late 1970s, it was to star Carson's wife, Karen Black, whose name would have helped raise the finance – and, as is common in Hollywood, where projects rarely die completely, it came up again as a prospect in 1990. McBride also worked on adaptations, to be made by other directors, of Ross McDonald's *The Instant Enemy* and Thomas Berger's *Sneaky People,* neither of which reached production. Such scripts helped McBride to establish himself as a legitimate writer, and a friend at Lorimar got him a job writing the narration for Samuel Fuller's *The Big Red One* (1980), which Fuller had turned over as a four-hour film and refused to cut. The released version, cut by someone else, was confusing and needed narration, which McBride pieced together from the proofs of Fuller's novel: 'I met Fuller a few years later, and he said I'd done a good job.'

One of McBride's projects in the late 1970s was *Breathless,* a remake of Jean-Luc Godard's celebrated *A bout de souffle* (1959). Casting around for projects that would be considered commercial but would still interest him, McBride decided that here was an idea with a certain cachet even though the original was relatively unknown to the general public. Through a friend, he got permission from Godard (though apparently Godard had sold the rights to various different people at different times), found a producer and very quickly, after several years of pitching ideas and getting nowhere, someone at Universal was interested. The project seemed set to take off. 'Little did I know it would take five years to get it made.'

McBride – like Amy Jones at about the same time – took to writing as a way to bigger projects after being a director in a low-budget and rather marginal way. Much more commonly, film-makers will work as writers, consciously – as is usually claimed – or not, with the ultimate aim of becoming directors. This was the case with new directors Mick Garris and Rockne O'Bannon, both of whom remember writing seriously from the ages of ten or twelve.

O'Bannon's progress sounds superficially like the stuff of myth – starting out in the Warner Brothers studio mailroom and ending up a director. In reality, it was quite a tough path for a long time, though both O'Bannon's parents were in the industry (his father had been a gaffer, or lighting director, at Warner, and his mother was a contract dancer at MGM) and it seemed natural that he would end up in the business; indeed

Photograph: Jim McBride (left) with Richard Gere on the set of Breathless.

he never entertained notions of any other career. O'Bannon considered going to film school, but it was even tougher to get into the Warner mailroom, which he considers his 'college' experience. The mailroom staff led the tours round the studio, including the sets of shows like *The Waltons* and *Kung Fu,* and O'Bannon valued the chance to see people in action on set. *The Waltons* was produced by Lorimar, which rented space at Warner and the nineteen-year-old O'Bannon's next job was as production assistant with Lorimar, where, as well as being around sound stages, he discovered what went on among the producers and read scripts constantly, learning about screenplay form and dramatic structure and coming close to being a pest in his desire to talk to writers.

O'Bannon then left Lorimar to spend time writing scripts on spec for television shows, such as *Magnum,* never selling anything or earning any money, but keeping going and trying to build on the advice he got from other writers. After two years selling nothing, he got a job with MGM, first in the publicity department then in the story department, a clerical post, but one that allowed him access to scripts and the comments that readers made on them. He began to see the other side to submitted scripts, feeling finally that his own work was OK but that the system worked against him: spec scripts were just rejected, but scripts from assigned writers, which might not be any better, were worked on. He concluded that if he plugged away, something would happen; in any case, there was nothing else he wanted to do. A new agent, who specialised in television, showed around some scripts for episodes that he had done. It was an opportune time – this was 1984 – as Steven Spielberg's *Amazing Stories* anthology television show had been announced, as well as a revival of *Twilight Zone.* In the same week, both shows expressed interest: 'this was my "Am I dreaming this, or not?" week.' *Twilight Zone* called him in first and bought one of his spec scripts, plus another based on a story outline he pitched them, then decided to bring him in as a staff writer, during which time he adapted a short story for them. He was then made story editor for the show – 'one of those twenty-year overnight success stories.'

Mick Garris's progress was very similar: 'A true Hollywood story – I went from food stamps to writing full-time for Spielberg's *Amazing Stories* – that was the overnight success that took years to get.' Garris started out as a movie publicist. His first job was as receptionist for *Star Wars,* a job that involved writing speeches for producer Gary Kurtz and operating the film's robot, R2D2. From that point, he developed in two directions. He wrote journalistically about the cinema and became a horror/fantasy/science-fiction film fan, going on to do a behind-the-scenes show for television on which he interviewed film-makers like Spielberg, Dante and John Landis. At the same time, he wrote screenplays, working on his first when he was on *Star Wars,* ten years before he sold his first script. Garris already thought of himself as a writer, partly because writing imposed no limits and involved no partners: it was a sort of free zone to operate in.

Though ambitious, he had no plans regarding how to progress. It was always one step at a time – 'it would be fun to write this,' and then 'it would be fun if something I wrote got made . . . if something I wrote got made by someone I admired . . . if I could direct something of my own.' While working as a publicist, he did make a short film, mainly to demonstrate to himself that he could direct: it came close to being developed into a feature, and although it was never made, it did get him an agent and meetings. Steven Spielberg had been among the film-makers profiled and interviewed by Garris on his television show, and had asked Garris to do documentaries on some of his films. He now read one of Garris's spec scripts and subsequently took him on as a story editor of *Amazing Stories* (the one story that Garris later directed was written by O'Bannon). Garris could not have afforded film school: he looked upon his television show as his 'own little film school', while working in television for Spielberg was 'big film school'.

Though television gave Garris the chance to direct, its immediate effect was to raise his profile as a writer. 'I was a writer because [Spielberg] said I was a writer – I was just another ass-hole with a script in my back pocket until someone the industry respected said I was worth hiring'. However much things in the movies depend on fluke, Garris believes that if you are good and persistent, talent will out, if only because so many people are desperate for good scripts. He had come close to selling material before, but had failed to do so. One problem was that executives are so well protected: 'the people who can say yes are really only exposed to the material that climbs its way kicking and screaming through all the other people.' For Garris, his work on the first two drafts of the Spielberg production *Batteries Not Included* (Matthew Robbins, 1987) led to his directing a one-hour television show, *Fuzzbucket,* for Disney, while the episode he directed for *Amazing Stories* became his calling card.

The next step was a theatrical feature, but this took another two years. In the interim, David Cronenberg recommended Garris as writer for *Fly 2,* the only script among the several he worked on in this period that got made (though the resulting film was not much to Garris's liking). Then *Critters 2* (1988) came up. The original *Critters* (1986) had done unexpectedly good theatrical business (about $11 million domestic) for a low-budget movie, but the only reason for a sequel was the booming video market. Garris had felt that 'nobody wants to see a sequel to a low-budget rip-off of *Gremlins*' – and was proved right – but it was the only green-lighted project being offered him. 'I could develop things to death and never get them made, or I could step in and do this and have made a movie.' In any case, Garris enjoyed the script and was able to rewrite at will. It was 'hard to say no to a movie I thought I could have fun with and learn from.' Budgeted at $4 million, with pre-sales to RCA/Columbia Video and to overseas markets, the film was into profit before it was shot; it grossed about $5 million at the box-office in the United States and shipped over 100,000 rental units on home video. Although the video market is vital to the industry, video success is relatively invisible. Videos have increasingly depended on having been shown successfully theatrically. Sequels are the exception: *Critters 3* and *Critters 4* (with which Garris had nothing to do) were made back to back and released only on video, but because *Critters 1 and 2* were shown theatrically, audiences were likely to assume the further sequels had been too. Similarly, further sequels to *The Howling* keep being made (six so far) and these are also an exclusive video phenemonon. Garris's next project was *Psycho 4* (1990), and it must have seemed that he was bidding fair to become king of the sequel, but this came about only by chance, because other projects did not come to production. Unlike the *Critters* series, *Psycho 4* was a cable movie.

While Garris was at the big film school of *Amazing Stories*, Rockne O'Bannon was getting his two years on *Twilight Zone* – 'my greatest education as a director,' even though he did not direct. 'Everyone's ultimate goal is to work in features, but my interest and the extent of my ambition to that point were just to be a viable working writer.' O'Bannon was succeeding in this: the status of *Twilight Zone* (and the fact that its episodes were all separate stories) made him hot (just as *Amazing Stories* made Garris hot).

In summer 1985, he entered into a deal with Columbia and his later partner, producer Richard Kobritz, for a horror script, *Mechanicals,* about a doll that takes on a life of its own (this was before *Child's Play*). Two days later, David Puttnam took over as head of Columbia; *Mechanicals* was not the kind of movie he wanted to make. O'Bannon turned in the script the following year and many at Columbia liked it, but it went immediately into turnaround. O'Bannon's next project – with Kobritz – had originally been one of his spec scripts. This was *Alien Nation* (released 1988). It combined the two genres that specially interested him: science fiction fantasy and police procedural. In it, aliens who had crash-landed in the Mojave Desert some years before have become an established community in California, although they are not accepted by some people, including a cop (a part taken in the film by James Caan) who takes on an inexperienced 'newcomer' – alien – (Mandy Patinkin) to help him find the newcomer gang that killed his partner. Six months after he had sold the script, in a bidding war, to Twentieth Century-Fox, the film was in production – 'quite miraculous' – and fifteen months after the script was finished, the film was in theatres. Since the producer, Kobritz, was O'Bannon's partner in the project he was closely involved in the production process, the nearest he had come to the making of a theatrical feature.

Despite the 'formidable and frightening apparatus' of the studio feature machine, the experience confirmed O'Bannon in his ambition to direct. He saw that the director got much greater respect than in television and was 'the one who really sticks his neck out and creates the film.' The head of Fox at this time had himself come from television (where he had been one of the producers of *Starsky and Hutch),* and it seemed to O'Bannon that his approach was rather television-oriented: he seemed to want a *Starsky*-type product, and the director (Graham Baker) was hired, essentially, as a controllable figure who would 'run the set', but did not have real power. O'Bannon's script had aimed to situate the aliens in a very bright, upbeat Los Angeles – an everyday, familiar milieu – but, as the film came out, the settings were seedier and more *noir,* and the mystery plot was much more dominant than he had intended. Seeing that some of his original ideas had not been realised and that the film overall was more formulaic than he had hoped, he determined to arrange things so that he had maximum control over his future work. With this in mind, he formed a production company with Kobritz, so that studios would have to deal with the company, not directly with the director. On a different scale, this was what Ron Howard was after in setting up Imagine, or Rob Reiner with Castle Rock.

Writing *Alien Nation* made O'Bannon 'legitimate as a feature entity': people were now approaching him, and he took great pleasure in turning down rewriting jobs for large sums of money. He could always go back to feature writing, or to television, but he wanted to direct and wrote the screenplay for *Fear* with this in mind. It thus had to work at a certain budget level, with a smallish cast and no need for big stars. The script was generally well received; O'Bannon and Kobritz could have gone to a major studio, but they felt that though a major might grudgingly have taken O'Bannon on as a director on a 'pay or play' basis to get hold of the script, it would not ultimately have let him direct. (In a pay or play arrangement, the studio gives a commitment that it will use a particular director or star, but that if it does not do so – whether because the project does not go ahead or because someone else is hired instead – it will pay anyway, because giving a commitment has made the director or star unavailable for other work.) Since the main objective for O'Bannon and Kobritz was not to get the bigger budget the majors would provide but to get the opportunity for O'Bannon to direct, they decided to take the script to a mini-major, who would not normally get first look at material of this calibre and would be more likely to be excited. Vestron agreed to do it, on a budget of $6.5 million (rather than their usual $4-5 million), a big budget for a first feature.

Thus, *Fear* (1989) was made, a thriller about a psychic (played by Ally Sheedy) who has a history of helping police to track down serial killers and who has become famous as an author of books about her experiences; she becomes closely and personally involved in one last case, with a psychic killer who feeds off her fear. It is certainly not wholly successful – its intriguing premise is not followed through interestingly enough and its climactic shift of gear is not quite managed – but it is nevertheless a very promising first feature, with a finale that owes a conscious debt to the climax of *Strangers on a Train,* and perhaps also to the climaxes of *The Lady from Shanghai* and *Some Came Running.* O'Bannon felt comfortable in his new role of director, getting anxious only as shooting time ran out and the finale carnival sequence got behind schedule. He and Kobritz had been careful to take on a good crew: 'I knew what I knew and I knew what I didn't know. Even though I wanted to be the commanding presence on the set, I did not let the overriding need for that overpower [my awareness] that if you act as if you know what you're doing and you don't, people will write you off instantly.' O'Bannon recalls his cameraman and assistant saying at the end that what made it easy for them was that he knew what he wanted, but did not necessarily always know how to do it, and was willing to describe what he wanted and let them come up with the means.

While production on *Fear* progressed, Vestron decided to get out of film production, and *Fear* was caught in the same bind as Mark Goldblatt's *The Punisher* for New World – left on the shelf, unreleased. On the positive side, this meant that O'Bannon was left alone while the film was being made; on the negative side, his reputation as a director has not been established in the all-important American theatrical market. Alone among the five or six films Vestron shelved, *Fear* has now been shown on Showtime cable as a Showtime Original (a slot often used for unreleased theatrical titles), and there is little chance now that it will ever be released theatrically. However, the reviews for the cable showing were generally good, and the head of MGM, who happened to watch it at home, felt that MGM should be working with O'Bannon and Kobritz. MGM at this time had just been sold to Pathé and wanted to be back in production in a big way. It was bad luck for O'Bannon that, by the time he had finished his script, the MGM/Pathé debacle was still running and the project (which would have been budgeted at around $12-15 million) was put into turnaround and was being considered by other studios.

The chances of any of the majors offering O'Bannon the opportunity to direct, even with a great script, are remote. Indeed, the better the script, the *less* likely it would be that he would be able to direct. In the recent past, one of the stories most told about Hollywood's way of working, especially by writers wanting to be directors, concerns *Radio Flyer.* In order to get a script they wanted, Columbia paid over $1 million, taking on the writer, David Mickey Evans, as director on a pay or play basis. The production was set up, and the inevitable then happened: after a few days directing, Evans was fired, amid claims of incompetence, and the production was set up again with the experienced, 'safe' Richard Donner as director (at a fee reputedly around $5-6 million); everyone assumes that this was always the studio's plan.

72

O'Bannon is not too disheartened by the fate of *Fear* – he keeps in mind that James Cameron made *Piranha II* before he made *The Terminator,* or John McTiernan *Nomads* before *Predator:* 'everyone's always ready to give you the first one.' O'Bannon wants to remain a writer-director and is trying to put together an HBO or Showtime cable movie based on an idea of his, but he is also interested in directing scripts by other writers, as this would help establish him as a director. Making a cable movie is seen as being very close to making a theatrical feature, and a move to cable would not pose a risk to his industry profile; someone like Roger Spottiswoode, in a career dip, can direct a couple of cable movies and then re-establish himself in theatrical features. Any success beyond cable – such as overseas theatrical release – can be good for a director's reputation, but a flop on cable barely damages it. O'Bannon's latest project is for a Fox network 'Night at the Movies' feature, which will be a television film in the United States and into which Carolco and Indieproduction are putting extra money so that it will be suitable for release overseas as a theatrical feature. An action picture, with a budget of about $5 million, *Alcatraz 2000* will be set in an automated, reopened Alcatraz, and O'Bannon hopes that with a background of similar material to a Cameron or McTiernan – albeit on a tiny budget compared with their work – he will be more palatable to the theatrical feature business. At the same time, if needs be, he can go on working as a writer.

Still: Pruitt Taylor Vince and Ally Sheedy in Fear.

THE BIGGER PICTURE

The distinctions between independently-made pictures and studio pictures are not always clear-cut as far as budget and working conditions are concerned, but most film-makers are nevertheless very conscious of them. This has a lot to do with the weight of the past, now that the Hollywood of the studio system has passed into legend – film-makers are as likely as not to have grown up as movie fans and may have had some acquaintance with critical debates.

Joe Dante's first directorial experience on a big-studio sound stage was directing a segment of *Twilight Zone: The Movie* (1983), a compendium of four remakes of stories from the original television show, produced by Steven Spielberg and John Landis, who each directed one segment (the other segment was directed by George Miller). It was the film on which – in Landis's segment – Vic Morrow had his fatal accident with a helicopter. Dante was rather surprised that production still continued. 'This was Warner Brothers. A grip came up to me and said, "You see that corner over there? Errol Flynn pissed in that corner when we were making *The Sea Hawk*." I thought, "Wow, this is great." I was really thrilled. I went to the set one day and thought, "I guess this is it. I guess you're supposed to say, I've made it." I didn't really feel like I'd made it, but I did have a sense of satisfaction that I had somehow fooled people on all these movies and they hadn't figured out yet that I didn't know anything.'

Mick Garris was also conscious of the past when he was shooting his first studio picture, *Stephen King's Sleepwalkers* (1992), on the old MGM lot at Culver Studios (now owned by Sony/Columbia). All the great MGM movies had been shot there, but Hollywood's present weighed perhaps even more heavily: 'Shooting next door was *Hook*. The three feature directors at work on the lot were Steven [Spielberg], Francis [Coppola] and Mick – very rarefied company.'

Coming to studio pictures after independent pictures almost always means coming from smaller non-union crews to very large union ones (though film-makers who have started in television are already likely to be familiar with union crewing regulations). This can be both a shock and a pleasure. Michael Mann studied film-making in the mid 1960s at the London Film School, preferring it to, say, UCLA as being more art- and less industry-oriented. He then struggled to work in documentary in Britain: he shot some material in Paris in May 1968 and tried to set up a documentary on Mike Halewood, the British motorcycle racer. He also did budgeting and storyboarding at Twentieth Century-Fox's London office and shot some commercials before returning to the United States. There, in 1974, he suddenly and unexpectedly found himself earning a good living writing for television, working on 'classy' shows like *Starsky and Hutch*, *Police Story*, *Police Woman* and *Vegas*. He used the experience to set up an ABC Movie of the Week, *The Jericho Mile* (1979). Mann's first theatrical feature, *Thief* (1981 a.k.a. *Violent Streets*), a cool reflective thriller, self-consciously stylish and stylised, with James Caan as a meticulous jewel robber, was, as he says 'big time', his first experience with a first-rate camera crew and with a big star (he calls Caan 'one of the five greatest actors in America'). It was a little intimidating, but 'as Orson Welles said, there's nothing as good as a first-rate Hollywood crew.'

When Jim McBride made *Breathless* (1983), it was not at all comparable with anything he had done before. 'It was terrifying. I don't think I had ever been on a proper set before in my life. Here I was working with a lot of old pros on the crew, and that scared me as much as working with Richard Gere, the movie star.' He recalls there being a lot of anxiety and distrust during pre-production, when it was still unclear to anyone whether he was going to be able to bring it off, but once shooting began, everything was fine. 'I had been anti-Hollywood not just in terms of theme and style, but in terms of the whole process of how you work. I was from the underground *vérité* school – street film-making, hand-held camera, small crew – and there was some kind of moral imperative in all that that I can't quite remember any more. And suddenly, here I was with 60 or 70 people, the big lights, this gigantic camera. But I found that the whole crew was really great. Everybody really knew how to do what they had to do. And they were very supportive. It's partly this tradition in Hollywood of deference to the director, but I felt this tremendous wave of support from the crew, and it really made it fun.' Big productions naturally surround directors, especially new ones, with a crew that will guarantee a certain level of expertise and competence, 'to cover for you in case you blow it,' as McBride acknowledges.

But it took a long struggle – five years from *Breathless* being first set up to its being realised. Such a time-scale is quite common for studio pictures whereas it would be rather unusual for most independent pictures, like, say, *River's Edge,* which could be shooting just a few months after being set up (while low-budget films like Corman's could be shooting in a matter of weeks or even days). For most of the five years that *Breathless* took to get made, McBride was not its scheduled director. The original agreement to make the picture was with Universal, who wanted to make it if Robert De Niro would play the main part. De Niro took six months to turn it down, by which point they had lost interest. The project languished for a long time and started to circulate. People liked it but 'did they want to do it with Jim McBride, this weird arty guy?'

Still: Valerie Kaprisky and Richard Gere in Breathless.

McBride's agent persuaded him that it was more likely to be made if he backed out as director, and he did. The project was by now with Orion, and McBride was sent to see John Travolta and then Al Pacino as possible leads. McBride did not, however, make a very good impression on them, and the British director Franc Roddam (who had recently made *Quadrophenia*, 1979) was brought in. This helped interest Richard Gere, who was hot from the runaway success of *An Officer and a Gentleman* (1981). Then Roddam went off to make another film (*The Lords of Discipline*, 1982*)*, and Gere brought in Michael Mann (fresh from doing *Thief*), who completely rewrote the script, with results that Orion did not much like. Coincidentally, another of Mann's scripts (*The Keep*, 1983) was taken up and he went off to do that. Now Orion had a script and star it liked, the money, a start date, and a list of directors who were acceptable to Gere – but they could not get one they wanted. Mike Medavoy, head of Orion, who was very supportive of McBride, asked Gere to reconsider him. Finally, Paul Schrader, a friend of McBride's, who had recently directed Gere in *American Gigolo* (1980), asked Gere to meet McBride, and agreement was reached.

Thinking back on this process, and on his career as a whole, McBride concludes that 'it's *all* accident and chance, as far as I can tell. I can't see any logic to my career. I can't see anything I did right or wrong. It's all a total mystery to me, and I honestly think it's a mystery to most of the people in the industry.' Certainly, the on-off process is one that directors (not to mention writers and stars) have to get used to. Joe Dante recalls that after the success of *Gremlins* (1984), he met Peter Guber, who had an idea for a serious spy movie in which the protagonists were miniaturised (Guber did not know about Richard Fleischer's *Fantastic Voyage*, 1966, which was based on just this premise – just as the producer of Dante's *The Howling* had not heard of *The Wolf Man* – 'you'd be surprised,' says Dante, 'how people are really not that connected with what's gone before'). Dante did not find the script very interesting, passed on it and made *Explorers* (1985) instead.

But, after *Explorers*, the script came back to him, now rewritten as a comedy, with the idea that 'Dean Martin is shrunk and injected inside Jerry Lewis.' Dante felt that this was 'irresistible' and would make a very commercial picture (having been told by a friend after *Explorers*, 'You know, you're going to have to stop making movies that are just for you and us'); it became *Innerspace* (1987), the project that Dante looked on as his assignment, although, as it developed, it became 'crazier and more personal'. The project had been offered to Dante by Guber Peters and Warner Brothers, and Warner decided, as the budget was considerable, to see if Steven Spielberg wanted to become involved as producer. Once Spielberg was involved, 'a lot of money goes south' (the budget ended up at around $25 million), and the movie therefore had to make a lot more money. Spielberg read the script and, at a meeting with Dante on some other subject, told him: 'I've got this great script, *Innerspace*, and I'm going to give it to Bob Zemeckis.' 'I figure, "Now wait a minute, how can they give this to Zemeckis? I actually started this picture with Peter Guber."' So Dante went to Warner who told him, 'What can we do? If Spielberg wants to take it to Zemeckis . . .' 'But you offered it to me!' 'Well, yeah, but now Steven's got it . . .' As it turned out, Zemeckis decided against it, and Spielberg went with Dante (although Richard Donner was also dying to do it).

Mick Garris had a not dissimilar experience on *Sleepwalkers*. Columbia had seen Garris's cable movie *Psycho 4*, and Stephen King, whose original script was the basis of the *Sleepwalkers* project and who had director approval, had also liked it. Typically for contemporary Hollywood, Garris, King and the film's producers were all represented by the powerful agency CAA, which could get all the parties together. Columbia liked the way Garris saw the picture and told him 'You're our guy,' but there were other people they had to see as a formality. 'A few days later, they'd hired one of the "formalities",' a director who had come from rock videos and had made a well-received television

Still (left): Joe Dante, left, and John Landis, right, guest actors with Cynthia Garris and Jim Haynie in Sleepwalkers. *Photograph (right): Mick Garris directing.*

movie-of-the-week. He worked for a month or two on the picture. Garris, meanwhile, had moved on to other projects, but it transpired that King and the director were not agreeing – Garris assumes that the director may have been a little embarrassed to be working on a horror picture – and Garris was brought on to the production.

Dante on *Innerspace* and Garris on *Sleepwalkers* were directors for hire, brought in to work on projects that they did not originate. The distinction between the often more personal projects that film-makers have developed themselves – like *Breathless* for McBride – and those for which they are merely hired is commonly made, even though a director may well have significant input on an assignment. Though Garris was a director for hire on *Sleepwalkers,* his primary goal was to direct his own material. One reason for his becoming involved in *Sleepwalkers* – though as Garris concedes, an assignment that happens to be an original screenplay by Stephen King is a bit special – is that a high-profile studio picture that will open in some 1,500 theatres and receive massive publicity will necessarily change things for him: 'it may allow me to get better things offered to me or the likelihood of directing my own screenplays, that so far I've been able to develop at studios but not get made.'

Most writer-directors find themselves in this sort of situation. Tim Hunter, for example, since making *Sylvester* in 1985, has been trying to put together a project based on crime novelist James Crumley's *Dancing Bear.* As part of a development deal with Warner, Hunter and Crumley worked on a script (and also scripted together a project called *The Tunnels of Ku Chi*, which foundered in the glut of Vietnam movies around the time of *Platoon*, 1986, and, more recently, a script based on the *Judge Dredd* comic book). But Warner put the *Dancing Bear* script into turnaround. Hunter still dreams of doing it; old scripts rarely die completely, although they become less likely as time passes.

When a script goes into turnaround, the studio's development costs and the interest that starts to accrue on them become attached to the script. Hunter reckons that about $300,000 is now attached to the *Dancing Bear* script. This makes it very difficult for an interested smaller company to step in on spec and option it for a rewrite. The situation has become even more complicated because, in the meantime, the rights to the novel have reverted to Crumley. This means that if an independent company wanted to make a film of the book, they could buy the rights and write a new screenplay, simply ignoring the existing one (though, Hunter adds, 'they should hire me to direct it anyway'). There are many reasons why scripts do not get made, but Hunter concedes that *Dancing Bear,* a whodunnit in which the killer is a peripheral figure who is introduced very late and the hero takes cocaine and would need to be played by a big star, may be a bit too offbeat for a major studio, yet too big a project for most independents. Even though

Hunter is personally attached to the project, there is no guarantee – as with McBride and *Breathless* – that he will wind up as its director if it ever gets made.

As Mark Frost says, 'it will cost you, eventually' to become too attached to any project, and any project one is involved in needs to be balanced with others: 'it's like numbers in a bingo game – they're all down there, and every once in a while, one of them pops up.' Frost was associated with his first feature, as writer and director, for six years before it was made. Frost's route to being writer-director of *Storyville* (1992), a psychological thriller set in New Orleans, independently made but at a budget estimated to be between $12 and 15 million, started with writing, which he has done since the age of 11. He has been a writer for television, but he claims he *always* saw himself as moving towards directing, 'to have more control over the creative process. The best and quickest way for me to get to the point of being a director working with his own material was to establish myself as a writer. I didn't want to go the route of being a director, because that was not my initial skill. It would have been harder for me to get a job directing commercials, say, than to continue on the path I was on.'

For him, writing meant learning how to direct, though his 'final master's class' was working as associate producer on John Schlesinger's *The Believers* (1987). Frost worked closely with Schlesinger for two years, from the first conceptual meetings to the film's opening. After this experience, he felt ready actively to pursue a directing career. As usual, the vagaries of the system intervened. A project about Marilyn Monroe, which Frost was to write and David Lynch direct, got scripted but then dropped, as perhaps too explosive a subject. A feature jointly written with Lynch, which Frost was to produce, was to be made for Dino De Laurentiis, who had made *Blue Velvet*. It was cast and set to go when, six weeks before shooting was to begin, De Laurentiis joined the ranks of other over-ambitious independents of the 1980s and went bankrupt. And then there was *Twin Peaks*, with Frost producing and writing, as well as directing (he had also directed an episode of *Hill Street Blues* while working as a writer on the show). Lynch and Frost were both very 'hot' when *Twin Peaks* began to be broadcast in 1989.

Though Frost had been involved in the script of *Storyville* since 1986, its producer, David Roe, had been with it as far back as 1983, when he first optioned the Australian novel, *Juryman*, on which it is based. One reason why projects take so long, and their courses are so uncertain, is the complexity of the arrangements by which they are financed, particularly in the case of independent films. *Hollywood Reporter* reckoned that more than 100 people and maybe as many as 200 – producers, lawyers, agents, banks, studios, insurance companies – were involved in negotiating a contract and that eight separate parties had to agree on every aspect of every point in the deal.

Early development funds, which enabled Roe to buy and develop the property, came from a European-Australian joint venture, but it was not until RCA/Columbia Home Video was persuaded to put up some financing that the project began to come together: John Davis, son of the industrialist and former owner of Twentieth Century-Fox, Marvin Davis, brought Davis Entertainment in as a partner. Through a deal with Davis Entertainment, Fox came in for the American distribution (though Davis was to pay for prints and advertising and Fox would get only a distribution fee, without a share in any profits). Next, the independent producer Ed Pressman came in and helped to secure the main star, James Spader, going out on a limb and signing him although the financing was not all in place; Pressman was also involved in bringing in Spelling Films International as the third major partner in the deal. Frost recalls that even when they were already down in New Orleans doing pre-production, the deal had still not finally been signed – a level of suspense and uncertainty that is quite common with independent productions. With the *Twin Peaks* feature, *Fire Walk with Me* (1992), on which he was executive producer, the finance was still in the balance just four or five days before the start of production. Despite all the doubts, the *Storyville* deal is typical in that by the time the film is released, given its video sale and sales to overseas territories, it will have covered its costs, and each of the partners is more or less guaranteed a profit.

While this deal-making was going on, Frost, who had no producing role on the film, was not directly involved and was actively engaged in other projects. Fortunately, the financing came around as he was free to do it, but in many cases the timing will not work so well. Frost was simply 'trotted out for a meeting' every time a new source of money was being explored, and had meetings with actors – like Spader – whose involvement, they believed, would help to get the movie made. Initially, Frost's participation was only as writer, but in 1988 he made it clear to Roe that he would continue working on the script only if he was also to direct it. This was when the *Twin Peaks* series began to be made and broadcast: 'Frankly, *Twin Peaks* helped a lot to get the movie made.' But Frost had, of course, worked to get himself to that position: 'I don't know anybody who could have been more ready to do that particular job than I was, given what I'd done in my life, so I didn't feel overwhelmed by it at all.' But despite having been in the business a long time, and having directed episodes for television, this first feature was nevertheless a very different experience, particularly because of having to shoot over a long period of time: 'Stamina became almost the biggest issue – I had actually *trained* for it for some time.'

In view of the large parts played by luck and chance, and the fact that directors spend much longer periods of time attached to projects (and thus make fewer films) than they did in the studio system, it is not surprising that there should be large gaps in directors' filmographies, as in Jim McBride's apparent inactivity between 1974 and 1983. Although these are not the periods of inactivity that they seem, the gap in the filmography of George Armitage, 1979 to 1990, or – if we exclude *Hot Rod* (1979), a television movie-of-the-week – 1976 to 1990, seems very large. To all intents and purposes, Armitage seemed to have disappeared. After a start very much like Jonathan Demme's or Jonathan Kaplan's, this seemed strange.

Like Demme, Armitage had worked elsewhere in the industry before surfacing with Corman at New World. From film school at UCLA and a job in the Twentieth Century-Fox mailroom, he had worked his way up to become associate producer of the highly successful television series *Peyton Place* and then *Judd for the Defence*, before producing Fox's first television movie-of-the-week, *Panic in the Streets* (a remake of Elia Kazan's 1950 Fox picture), and writing the screenplay for Corman's *Gas-s-s-s . . .* (1970), about a killer gas that wiped out the population of the planet. (The distribution problems that Corman encountered with this film were a contributory factor in his setting up New World Pictures.) Armitage was then well placed to direct his first picture for New World, *Private Duty Nurses* (1972), the follow-up to the very successful *Student Nurses* (Corman claims the title came up when the Private Duty Nurses Association complained that *Student Nurses* did not give an accurate picture of student nurses' lives: 'They have given us the title for the sequel – it's a great title.') Armitage wrote, produced and directed and went on quickly to make a second feature, *Hit Man* (1972), a reworking of the British movie *Get Carter* (1971) in a black setting for MGM's low-budget 'blaxploitation' unit under Corman's brother Gene.

Just as both Demme and Kaplan then moved on to somewhat higher-budgeted action pictures – Demme with *Fighting Mad* (1976), still for Corman, but with Twentieth Century-Fox money, Kaplan with *White Line Fever* (1975) – so Armitage made *Vigilante Force* (1976) for United Artists. As the title implies, it is a vigilante picture – like both Demme's and Kaplan's, though all three try to be critiques of the conventional vigilante film that was so popular at the time. It starred Kris Kristofferson as a Vietnam veteran hired to restore law and order to a small mining town. Even though *Vigilante Force* may not have been very good, it is surprising that Armitage should not then have made a theatrical feature for the next thirteen or fourteen years. This was partly by choice: he was offered other projects, but, in the way of Hollywood, they all tended to be the same kind of action-exploitation material with which he had become associated.

He wanted to be a writer-director, as he had already been, rather than a director for hire, and his own story ideas were more personal and more character-driven than action-oriented. Although Armitage did make the television movie *Hot Rod* in 1979, and had had experience of episodic television as a producer in the 1960s, he did not want to go down that road, which would have been an obvious way of earning a living as a director. Instead, Armitage spent the years writing scripts and trying to set them up. Though he had no success, he nevertheless felt that he was developing and learning all the time, as a writer and even as a director; he never thought that he would not work again. Armitage believes that the theme behind his career is that if you stick at it, if you don't give up – and if you are good in the first place and get better in the wilderness – then the As (as in Armitage) will come round again. This is what happened with *Miami Blues* (1990), which was based on a fine crime novel by Charles Willeford, one of several using the central character of battle-weary police sergeant Hoke Moseley, a combination of hard-boiled cop and soft-centred father (Armitage loves the series and would like to do another, especially *Sideswipe*).

The project came up by way of Armitage's past association with Jonathan Demme. The actor Fred Ward, who had had a small role in Demme's *Swing Shift* (1986), read the novel, and sent it to Demme, who read it and sent it to Armitage, who liked its idiosyncratic mix of crime and quirkiness. The deal that was later made was for a $7-8 million picture with Demme producing and Armitage directing for Orion (which was backing Demme's own pictures over this period). Even so, from Ward reading the novel to the film's release was another five years. For Armitage, the gaps in his directing career have meant that each time he makes a picture it is like the first, exciting but terrifying. *Miami Blues* was not a big hit, but did not lose money. Although commercial success is always the bottom line, critical success, which the film certainly won, can also be valuable for a director. But, in Armitage's view, probably more important than critical success was the fact that the Hollywood community itself liked the film.

After a rather dead period of a year or so after its release, Armitage noticed that his status had changed and that he was getting a different kind of offer from before: good – though not absolutely top-line – studio pictures (several of the projects he turned down have since been made). Armitage has done a quick rewrite on John Mackenzie's *Blue Heat* (1990, originally titled *The Last of the Finest*) and, as of summer 1991, had two projects going, *Pacific Electric* for PentAmerica (funded by Silvio Berlusconi's Italian organisation, which has deals with American majors), an unromantic, *noir*-ish picture set in Los Angeles in wartime, which was on the back burner because Richard Gere, who was interested in it, was otherwise engaged, and *Ernie Popovich,* for Columbia, a romantic comedy about a character rather like Hoke Moseley in *Miami Blues.* Finding himself still attached to the latter project at the third rewrite, Armitage thought that the prospects of its going ahead were good. The Columbia picture would have a budget of about $17-18 million, much more than *Miami Blues,* but Armitage confesses himself interested in bigger budgets only for the prospect of more time, a longer shooting schedule, which is what was most lacking on the pictures he made in the 1970s.

Film-makers deal with career gaps in different ways. Rob Cohen's early career has similarities with Armitage's. As a producer, he initiated made-for-television movies at Fox and then worked for Motown for five years, producing seven films (including *Mahogany,* 1975), before becoming a producer at United Artists. His first feature as a director, *A Small Circle of Friends* (1980), about student protest and the fates of a group of friends involved in it, came about almost by accident, although directing had always been his goal: John Korty was set to direct but dropped out, and Cohen took over. The movie was not a great success, and the early and mid 1980s represented a career low for him and were very difficult for someone who had been so active in producing pictures. A year was spent trying to set up a picture with Richard Gere, and Cohen dissociated himself from producing (stupidly, he now feels) in order to be taken seriously as a director.

He was then invited to direct a writing job he had done for money, 'a mediocre romantic mystery story,' *Scandalous* (1983). The conditions were very difficult: for tax shelter reasons, it was to be made in Britain, where Cohen had no contacts, and it had to be completed in four months. But it was work and money, even if the result was dire. In most people's eyes Cohen was now a failed feature director. His strategy became to diversify and use his considerable energy to learn and to generate pictures in whatever way he could. 'To make it happen, you have to package yourself and put yourself forward: the more activity you generate, the more possibilities there are.' Despite the risk of 'people thinking you're not serious,' Cohen worked for episodic television, made commercials, wrote scripts, worked as a producer on pictures like *The Witches of Eastwick* and, for Taft-Barish, *The Running Man, Light of Day* and *Ironweed* (all four 1987).

In the late 1980s, he went into partnership with the director John Badham as the Badham/Cohen Group, with a deal at Universal under which Badham directed and Cohen produced *Stakeout* (1987), *Bird on a Wire* (1990) and, most recently, *The Hard Way* (1991): 'You have to package yourself and put yourself forward.' Although Cohen has been the producer half of Badham/Cohen, he has directed second unit, and more, on *Bird on a Wire* and *The Hard Way* (so that Universal saw the quality of his, as well as Badham's, dailies), and was also working on scripts and projects. As a result (and as he expected), Cohen has since been able to put together and direct another feature, *Dragon, A Life of Bruce Lee* (1992) for Universal.

As the circumstances surrounding Cohen's *Scandalous* make clear, movies do not always get made for the right reasons. Joe Dante, for example, recalls that his reasons for taking on *The 'burbs* (1988) had everything to do with his particular situation at that time: he had finished an expensive effects movie, *Innerspace* (1987), which had been a box-office disaster, and he wanted to do something different. He spent a year developing *Little Man Tate* (eventually made by Jodie Foster, 1991) as a sort of art movie, first at Warner then at Fox, only to leave over unresolved differences shortly before shooting was due to begin. Meanwhile, Warner had come back to him with *Gremlins 2,* and he was debating with himself whether or not to do it. If he did, as it was another effects movie and would take up the best part of two years, there would be

Still: Alec Baldwin in Miami Blues.

Photographs. Left: Tom Hanks, Carrie Fisher and Joe Dante on the set of The 'burbs.
Right: Jonathan Demme and Goldie Hawn on the set of Swing Shift.

a three-year gap in his filmography. He felt he had to make another movie, and, since a writers' strike was looming, it had to be soon.

At this point, Imagine came up with *The 'burbs* (then titled *Bay Window)* which was in development. It needed a big star, and Tom Hanks wanted to do it. But if you have Tom Hanks, he cannot be killed off at the end, as the script originally specified, and a new ending was needed. Hanks's participating also changed the nature of the project from what Dante had imagined – an Ealing-type comedy – to something much broader, with more slapstick. Inevitably, the studio wanted something more like Hanks's success with *Big* (1988). Since Dante was fitting the picture in before getting to work on *Gremlins 2,* he wanted to make it right away and, instead of shooting it on location, he wanted to do it on the Universal backlot, which is what happened. Dante enjoyed making the movie and it was successful enough for Imagine. Looking back on the experience, though, Dante feels that 'I want to be able to make a picture for the right reasons, not because I'm desperate to work, which is why I made *The 'burbs*.' Even though *The 'burbs* was made quickly, it still took a year.

David Friendly, a production executive at Imagine Films, stresses the 'circumstantial' nature of movie production: 'One of the things that people who don't work in the movie business don't understand, and one of the things the movie business itself doesn't necessarily talk about so freely, is that movies get made for lots of reasons. They're never purely aesthetic, and they're never purely commerce-related – it's usually a blending of the two. For example, on a film that was produced a couple of years ago [Friendly did not feel able to name it], I know the star did it because he was looking for a movie locally. He was building a new house, and he wanted to be in town during the remodelling, and he'd recently been married. There's a perception [from the outside] that the best scripts are done by the best directors and then the actors have their pick of them, so that what comes out [should be] the best movies. It's nothing quite that scientific. Often the script that actually gets shot may be, in the director's mind, not as good as the one that does not get shot, but people forget it's a business, and film-makers have to live and eat and pay mortgages.'

A number of these factors very clearly came together in Amy Jones's career in the mid 1980s. She did not want to work again with Roger Corman after *Love Letters,* not because Corman had treated her badly – quite the contrary – but because she wanted to work with bigger budgets and make a better living. Working with Corman was in many ways a bad preparation for coping with the way the system worked, as Jones soon found out. After *Love Letters,* Jones began working on a script for what was to become *Mystic Pizza,* a women's coming-of-age or rite-of-passage story about three (four in

Jones' original story and script) young women, who work at a restaurant called 'Mystic Pizza', in Mystic, Connecticut. Typically, this was not *all* she was doing: she also had a deal to do a witchcraft horror script for Columbia, which she pulled out of when Columbia had second thoughts about it and changed it after the commercial failure of *Christine* (John Carpenter, 1983). And she was working as a story editor for the independent company Vista. But *Mystic Pizza* was certainly her central concern, the project that was most personal to her; it was to her, she says, as *Diner* (1982) was to Barry Levinson.

The script went around; Universal were interested but wondered if it could be about four boys; Orion were interested and went as far as making budgets for it, but then the success of *The Terminator* pushed them in different directions. The Goldwyn Company wanted to option it, but felt it should be more like *Diner*. Used to Corman's schedules and honesty, and not really knowing how the system worked, Jones hoped to begin the film that summer, 1985, and handed in a new draft script before all the paper-work was done. All kinds of problem ensued, with Goldwyn wanting major changes, hiring and firing other writers, and eventually firing Jones, who spent almost a year and a lot of money trying to get back control of her script. Finally, the Writers' Guild took action and ensured that she was properly paid for the script, even though she lost control of it (Goldwyn kept it and had it rewritten and made in 1987, directed by Daniel Petrie). The experience was heart-breaking for Jones – she almost did not recover from it: 'I just didn't understand how the game was played and, ultimately, I didn't understand that the game *had* to be played, that it wasn't just a matter of making movies.' She realises now that she should have written the experience off immediately, though this was very difficult when other companies were keen to be developing the project, and nothing was happening to it. Although she does not regret it, she also turned down *Teen Wolf* (1985) because she had just finished the *Mystic Pizza* script and was anxious to direct it.

Writer-directors often find themselves in difficulties simply because what Hollywood needs more than anything else – certainly more than particular directors – is a constant supply of good story material, and it will do almost anything to secure it (as with *Radio Flyer*). As Jones says, 'They just wanted control of the script . . . If you care too deeply, you're set up to be hurt.' The sensibilities of writer-directors who are personally attached to their material hardly enter into the way things are done, unless the director is already very well established. With nothing happening on *Mystic Pizza,* Jones had the chance to develop and direct a project at Vista, *Maid to Order* (1987), a comedy about a rich girl sent to work as a maid, which was not at all personal and over which she had very little control. Vista insisted, for example, on the casting, including Beverly D'Angelo, which had consequences for the broadness of the comedy, while the score by Georges Delerue, marvellous though it may have been, was not, in Jones's view, what *Maid to Order* needed: the film was aimed at a teenage audience, and she wanted songs. So, despite a $4 million budget, which seemed a fortune to her compared with her previous budgets (though it was still a non-union film), Jones was working with material that she was not committed to in any personal way. Even then, she had to make compromises that she saw as working against the best interests of the picture, which still grossed about $12 million at the box-office, good by Vista's standards. The *Mystic Pizza* debacle had made Jones aware of how you can lose projects simply by saying that you do not want to do something in a certain way: no matter how reasonable you might be, you can still be removed.

Jones then spent a year with Holly Sloan writing drafts of *It Had To Be Steve*, which she was to direct and Imagine was make, with Ron Howard as executive producer, for Universal. After that, she did nothing for four months while the writer's strike was on. Once the strike was over and lots of movies were beginning, the film became hard to cast: Julia Roberts was to be in it but, despite her success in *Mystic Pizza* and *Steel Magnolias*, Universal would not give her a pay-or-play commitment. Imagine was not able to push Universal forward and, as happens to many pictures, after a year of pre-production and casting, the project just slipped away.

Jones began to reassess her situation: the success of *Mystic Pizza,* and her credit on it, meant that she had gained considerable status as a writer. She decided that writing was a more controllable area than directing, and so began to work more as a writer, and began increasingly to enjoy it. She feels she gets respect in meetings, whereas being allowed to direct seemed like 'a big favour'. *It Had To Be Steve* was initiated as a cable movie for Showtime, but *Sea of Love* (1989) had come out and bore some similarities to it, and this meant a rewrite (the film was later retitled *Indecently).* Mainly, however, Jones has chosen, rather than making cable movies, to write for big features, for example, doing a rewrite on John Hughes's *Beethoven* (1992), as well as writing *Indecent Proposal* for director Adrian Lyne, and scripting a television show pilot which has been picked up for six episodes.

Jones's choices make sense for various reasons. As a writer, she has more control over how and when she works than she would have as a director, something which, as a mother, she values; she is able to work on bigger films and she earns more doing it. However, she still wants to direct and believes that success as a writer will give her 'some clout' as a director in the future. As money for independent production has started to dry up, she has felt it necessary to establish herself in the world of studio features, even though she would be happy making independent pictures. Jim McBride, similarly, sees the present atmosphere, in which most independent companies have been pushed out of business, as not very favourable for individual work, and he, too, has been obliged to make some kind of accommodation with the studios. As Jones concedes, if she were purely a director, she would probably have ended up working in television, which has seemed the logical, even if not desirable, option for many.

Directors' relationships with producers and studios depend on circumstances, though the expectation is always that directors will be to some degree at odds with those in control of production. In low-budget, independent film-making the directors are likely to have more control and freedom; as budgets increase, more people are involved in creative decisions. Mick Garris had enjoyed exceptional creative freedom working on *Amazing Stories* and then made the low-budget independent *Critters 2* and *Psycho 4* for cable, but making his first studio picture for Columbia, *Sleepwalkers,* 'I found that I've been allowed a lot more creative choices, with nobody interfering, than on anything I've done. I was quite surprised by that.' Garris puts it down to the power that successful directors have gained spreading out to other directors.

It is certainly true that the enhanced status of directors in general (rather than of just a few exceptional figures) over the last twenty years or so has given more potential power to directors, but it is also much more common for directors to report struggle and tension over creative choices. This is not a situation peculiar to the new Hollywood – it was how the studio system functioned, too – but there is a widespread feeling that the nature of studios' control has changed. Interviewed at the time of *The Player* (1992), a movie precisely about power in the movie industry, Robert Altman expressed the feelings of many. Altman, like others, has a strong feeling of nostalgia for the old style of movie studio bosses, 'because the old moguls had control, and they had passion, and they had hate . . . It wasn't computerised. And now it is . . . The power has been taken away from more people, and the bottom line has become more strongly the power . . . It's all based on money . . . I don't know anybody who runs any of the studios who could make a decision about what to put their money into that will follow their instincts . . . Nobody follows hunches any more – it's all marketing, it's market research.'

Such sentiments help explain the affection in which Roger Corman is held by so many of those who began with him: Corman seems to them to exemplify the way Hollywood ought to be, but no longer is. Of course, the directors with such feelings never actually experienced the old-style moguls in action. And, until the 1950s, anyway, the

Still: left to right, Mädchen Amick, Alice Krige and Brian Krause in Sleepwalkers.

movie industry had a virtually guaranteed audience, which perhaps allowed the system to operate somewhat differently, without the market-research techniques that are characteristic of the new Hollywood. When Coca-Cola acquired Columbia, for example, it brought its research techniques with it: it was reported that Columbia was to seek out 'heavy users of entertainment' and 'concept test' possible film plots by sampling this audience, a technique long used by the networks for made-for-television movies. Market research was undertaken with a sample of some 19,000 consumers on the demand for feature films and the most profitable pricing and release schedule for theatrical exhibition, cable transmission and home video release. It was no surprise that Coca-Cola brought its methods to bear on selling Columbia's products, but research and marketing cannot guarantee success for movies, and Coca-Cola soon got out of the movie business. The succeeding regime at Columbia under David Puttnam presented itself in a very different, more 'artistic' guise; it, too, was soon replaced by another with more 'commercial' instincts.

As Joe Dante puts it, 'The studio people have their own agenda of what they need, and I'm firmly convinced that if these people could make movies without directors and writers and actors, they would do it. If they could make computer movies, they'd just do that, because they really don't understand the creative process, and most of them are afraid of it. They get easily intimidated sometimes. I know of directors who rant and rave and scream and kind of get what they want, though try as I might, the best I can do is work up some withering sarcasm. It's not that they're bad people. It's simply that their interests are not the same as yours. Yeah, they'd like to have a good picture, but it's much more important to have a successful picture, and whatever they think will make the picture successful is what they want to do, and they don't care if it makes sense or not. Thank God, they don't know what works, because if they did, they'd make you make that. The only freedom you get is in the areas where they're not sure.'

Still: Dee Wallace in Cujo.

Pressure and compromise come in many different forms. Jonathan Demme's first studio picture with big stars, *The Last Embrace* (1979), was an ambitious and fascinating, though not wholly successful, stab, at a big-budget Hitchcock-style thriller. He had problems both with casting – having to find a female star whom Roy Scheider would agree to work with – and with needing to start shooting, because Scheider was available, and United Artists thought the script was viable, when he felt another month's work was needed. On *Swing Shift* (1984), everything went well, with Demme and star Goldie Hawn sharing much the same vision of a film about working women during World War II. This was a film that Warner were making only because Hawn wanted to do it – she commanded considerable power after the massive success of *Private Benjamin* (1980). Then, partly as a result of the personal relationship between Hawn and co-star Kurt Russell that developed during the making of the film, Hawn's and the studio's requirements changed: 'I liked the movie we had already, with the theme of solidarity among women during the war; it was an ensemble piece. Goldie felt the emphasis should be on the love affair which would help the film reach a wider audience and that's what it turned into.' Demme was told he had to reshoot scenes, especially close-ups of Hawn and 'Tracy-and-Hepburn' scenes with Hawn and Russell. Demme was advised by friends not to quit, to stay in the job and fight for his own version of the movie in the hope that they would get exhausted. Instead, Warner quickly organised the requisite two previews of Demme's version and took back control.

Lewis Teague's route to the film industry was rather circuitous. He started at the top, as he puts it, going to a director's apprenticeship at Universal in the mid 1960s after film school at New York University, but he did not want to direct for television and left. In retrospect he feels he was probably too young and unprepared for the opportunity. After running a cinema, doing odd jobs on documentaries and working for public television, Teague gravitated towards New World, where he edited Monte Hellman's *Cockfighter* (1974) and was second-unit director on a number of Corman

Still: Michael Douglas and Kathleen Turner in The Jewel of the Nile.

films, finally directing *The Lady in Red* (1979) and *Alligator* (1980), two vigorous exploitation films with strong political implications, both from scripts by John Sayles.

Fighting Back (a.k.a. *Death Vengeance,* 1982) was a significant step upwards in budget, at about $6 million. It was made for Dino De Laurentiis, and turned into a political struggle between Teague's conception and De Laurentiis's. Teague, who stepped in to replace another director just two weeks before the start of principal photography, was attracted to the story (based on the real case of Anthony Imperiale, a former city councilman in Newark, New Jersey, who organised a vigilante group) for its portrait of growing fascistic tendencies in the United States as people became more frightened by the violence of inner-city life. Teague wanted to make a film about a 'flawed hero: I'd always imagined a *Raging Bull* type of story, with this fascinating villain as the main character.' But De Laurentiis wanted to do another *Death Wish* and insisted that Teague put in a couple of scenes in an attempt to make the character more heroic. Teague bent to De Laurentiis's will, 'so the picture's a little schizophrenic in its point of view – you don't know whether to like the guy or detest the guy.'

Teague's next two films were medium-budget, independent pictures which nevertheless had major release. They are both interesting horror movies from the work of Stephen King, *Cujo* (1983, with Teague again stepping in to replace another director, this time with only three days of preparation) and *Cat's Eye* (1984). Now established as a safe pair of hands, Teague was offered *The Jewel of the Nile* (1985), the sequel to *Romancing the Stone* (1984), produced by Michael Douglas's The Stone Group for Twentieth Century-Fox. Teague commented at the time that 'the scary thing about *Jewel of the Nile* is that it's a sequel to a film that grossed $75 million, so everybody's expectations are very high. It's one thing if a Roger Corman picture doesn't do very well – nobody notices, and you move on to the next one – but here, a lot of people are going to be watching to see how well you did. You have to constantly discipline yourself to ignore that.' In retrospect, he realises that he was rather intimidated by the scale of the

Still (left): deadly comic – Ray Liotta in Something Wild. *Photograph (right): Lewis Teague on the set of* Navy Seals.

production – $17 million – and the stars (Douglas, Kathleen Turner, Danny De Vito) and so was rather more conservative than he had been on earlier movies.

After *The Jewel of the Nile*, Teague spent a year and a half on a movie for Orion, and directed *Collision Course* (1990) as a favour to De Laurentiis when the Orion film fell through. Then Orion interested him in *Navy Seals* (1990), a big-budget action picture about Navy commandoes pursuing Arab terrorists in the Middle East (which was not very favourably received in the United States on its release in 1991, and very unfavourably received when it was released in Britain some months after the Gulf War). This was a film of significant compromises. Teague had grown up with war movies – Samuel Fuller's *Fixed Bayonets* and *Steel Helmet* had made a great impression on him – and he had later shot second unit on Fuller's *The Big Red One* (1980). The *Navy Seals* project, then, had some interest for him, but Orion already had a script, which included a love triangle. The problem became how to keep the elements Orion wanted and still incorporate what interested him from the research he had done on terrorist scenarios. Teague agrees that the result was somewhat unwieldy.

Directors' experience of the system inevitably leads them to reflect upon their relationship to it. Demme confesses that he was so disoriented by the debacle of *Swing Shift* that he more or less used *Stop Making Sense* (1984), a vivid documentary record of David Byrne and Talking Heads in concert, as a way of reorienting himself with something completely different. It picked up on Demme's long-standing interest in music and was made outside the normal channels of movie production: 'It was such a great thing to be able to go out there with David Byrne and those guys and, in a very free atmosphere, make *Stop Making Sense,* where nobody had any concerns other than making the best possible film. That was really invigorating and brought me back in touch with a lot of things that had come to be the joy of work for me, which more than any-thing is collaboration, working with gifted people and seeing the exciting results you get.'

After *Stop Making Sense,* Demme dabbled in some quite experimental television: David Byrne and Rosanna Arquette in *Trying Times – A Family Tree.* His other experience of television had been in 1978, when, desperate for work, he had directed a *Columbo* episode. His next film was another record of a performance, *Swimming to Cambodia* (1987), with Spalding Gray. Demme came back to features with the offbeat, darkly comic *Something Wild* (1986), which he talks about as being almost like a first film, starting again after the experience of *Swing Shift*. From there, he took a different route, this time less marred by loss of creative control, back to mainstream features, with *Married to the Mob* (1988) – 'a blatant attempt at a full-tilt, crassly commercial entertainment, let's make no bones about that' – and *The Silence of the Lambs* (1990), which was hugely successful, commercially and critically.

Demme is one of a growing number of film-makers who have succeeded in steering a course between the major studios – he is currently, in 1992-93, developing projects at TriStar – and independent production. But despite the often distinctly (and deliberately) blurred line between the two, there is a strong and widespread sense of the diffence in possibilities available to film-makers through the studios and through independent (especially very low-budget) production. As John Sayles said at the time of *Matewan* (1987), 'many of the movies we've made independently could never have been made through the studio system.'

Even someone apparently as closely associated with studio film-making as Lawrence Kasdan (*Body Heat*, 1981, *The Big Chill*, 1983, *Silverado*, 1985, *The Accidental Tourist*, 1988, and *I Love You to Death*, 1990) sees very clearly the dangers of the studio approach and the attractions of independent film-making: 'The easiest moral threat to avoid in Hollywood is something you know is dishonest. But even doing what you consider to be good and honourable work, you can become part of a system that is inflated in every way.' Kasdan certainly does not believe that he has worked with the studios by systematic choice: 'I feel that it's only chance or coincidence each time that I've done something within the system. And while I probably will continue to make this kind of movie, I hope to also do things where the price is much lower and you can do whatever you want and still have it be feasible economically . . . It's so limiting otherwise. The commitment of time and energy is enormous, and [the life of a completed movie] can be over in a weekend.'

Teague says of *Navy Seals*, 'I'm happy because I did a "yeoman's" job on it. It works, it cuts together, the action sequences are exciting, but it has nothing personal in it.' Big movies also take a long time to make – not so much for the actual production, but to

Still: Charlie Sheen and Michael Biehn in Navy Seals.

get projects greenlighted – and that means much less time practising the skills of directing. Teague had not enjoyed the episodic television (including *Vegas*) that he did between *The Lady in Red* and *Alligator*. Before *Navy Seals*, he joined up again with John Sayles to direct the pilot for *Shannon's Deal*, a critically well-received show about an unconventional lawyer, written and produced by Sayles. He found the experience refreshing, more like the Corman days. Teague therefore decided to take some time off to contemplate his next move, wanting to be more involved in the offers made to him and to work on projects more 'from my own experience and my own instincts, themes and points of view which are personal . . . I don't always want to be a "gun for hire".' Since then, Teague has directed a cable movie, *Wedlock* (1991, with Rutger Hauer and Mimi Rogers).

After the bad experience making *Explorers*, Joe Dante wanted to make something quickly and was offered a segment of *Amazon Women on the Moon* (1987), a comedy compendium of sketches vaguely parodying late-night television – in Dante's segment, *Critics' Corner*, a discussion between two television reviewers goes from movies to real life. A low-budget, non-union film, made as a pick-up for Universal, it was shot very much off the cuff – 'a lot of fun' after a difficult studio picture. Dante thought it could have been a much better movie, but it was not his project: 'I had a lot of ideas about how to make it better, but I was just a hired director, so I didn't have anything to say.'

Michael Mann reckons that 'any film is going to be personalised,' and, certainly, being a director-for-hire does not in any sense preclude a very deep engagement with a project. Jim McBride spent two years after *Breathless* writing and trying to start up projects with no success, until new agents gave him a script he could probably direct. It became *The Big Easy* (1986), 'my first job as a director-for-hire'; the film was about police corruption and its investigation by a woman prosecutor. McBride did not like the script much. It was set in Chicago, which he thought was too obvious, and it had interesting ideas that were not explored very far, but he felt that the core, the corrupt cop and the woman prosecutor, was there. McBride thought a New Orleans setting could give greater ambiguity to the corruption theme. He was hired as director to work with the

Still: Winona Ryder and Dennis Quaid in Great Balls of Fire.

Still: Ellen Barkin and Dennis Quaid in The Big Easy.

author of the script, which had been written some time before. The writer, Daniel Petrie Jr, had become successful as the rewriter of *Beverly Hills Cop,* and so had all kinds of deal going. According to McBride, he was not really interested in reworking this old script. During pre-production, when the shooting date was being set, McBride and colleague Jack Baran were secretly rewriting, and, as production began, there was hardly an agreed script.

McBride thinks that the lack of script enabled the actors – the main stars were Dennis Quaid and Ellen Barkin – to be more collaborative and to bring him ideas, and to improvise on the day. This was fine for McBride, for whom it was a 'great experience', recalling the beginnings of his career in the 1960s with films like *David Holzman's Diary,* but it did not suit the producer. Conflict continued after shooting; McBride had decided he would fight for what he believed in, arguing over almost every cut, right up to the moment when he would be fired, and then he would back off. Despite his satisfaction with the final product, it was agony for McBride when they could not find a distributor for six months, during which time the producer insisted they shoot a new ending. As it is so expensive to release a film theatrically, and with sales to cable and video depending on theatrical release, what was planned for *The Big Easy* was what happens to a lot of films: a theatrical release in three southern cities for one week, then release to video. But, two weeks before this was to happen, David Puttnam, who had just become head of Columbia, saw the film and bought it (so that what spelled the end for Rockne O'Bannon's horror script at least turned out well for McBride). Now McBride was able to write to Puttnam, who agreed to replace the new ending with the original one (but because the film had been sold abroad before this, the version released abroad had the new ending).

The Big Easy was a critical success and did reasonably well at the box office, which enabled McBride to make development deals and earn good money, but he still spent the next two years writing and working on projects that proved not mainstream enough or too ambitious. *Great Balls of Fire* (1989) came out of the blue when Orion sent him two scripts, one of which was the Jerry Lee Lewis story (probably because Dennis Quaid, whom McBride had directed in *The Big Easy,* was attached to the project). McBride, a longtime fan of Lewis, wanted to start the script from scratch and got the go-ahead, but the more they found out about Lewis, the less he appeared like someone

Still: Candy Clark and Paul Le Mat in Citizens Band.

you would want to make a movie about. Everybody, however, was happy about the script they were coming up with and, though interrupted by the writers' strike, they went into production without hitches. The smoothest of McBride's experiences, however, was also his biggest box office flop. It throws a little light on market research in the industry: the film had enjoyed a lot of publicity while in production, and market research had shown a very strong awareness of the picture, but it failed to register a low level of desire actually to see it.

After *Storyville*, an independently made picture but a relatively high-budget one, Mark Frost was planning his next project, a romantic comedy in the spirit of the 1930s or 1940s by, say, Mervyn Leroy, as a more expensive studio picture. He sees room in the system for the kinds of movie he wants to make, even if he does not want to spend two years of his life working on the sort of action blockbuster he sees as typical of hard-core Hollywood. Recalling his 'apprenticeship' with John Schlesinger, Frost recalls that 'Schlesinger said his rhythm was always to do one for them, and then do one for himself.' He points to John Huston, who began as a screenwriter at roughly the same age as Frost, as someone who managed to achieve that kind of balance in his work and 'that may be the way to do it. That doesn't mean that the one you do for them has to be a piece of garbage, it just means it's somewhat different.' As a more contemporary example, Frost offers Clint Eastwood, 'arguably the most successful personal modern film-maker over the last twenty years,' as also having achieved that kind of balance between 'personal' work and more frankly 'commercial' work. We might also think of the career of someone like Barry Levinson as alternating between more and less personal pictures.

Big studio pictures do have much to offer directors in the way of technical expertise and experience, as well as first-rate actors. As Mark Frost comments, 'what I particularly enjoyed was working with actors of that calibre [*Storyville* stars James Spader, Jason Robards, Joanne Whalley-Kilmer and Piper Laurie] and having the time to really build performances.' In theory, bigger budgets should offer more time, at pre-production, shooting and post-production stages, and less necessity to cut corners. In practice, these advantages are not always so clear. Mick Garris comments that, despite the apparently big leap to $15.5 million on *Sleepwalkers*, 'it didn't feel like it – what made the difference was that it was a studio picture, but it felt every bit as strapped, every bit as tight as the $4 million *Critters 2*, which was non-union and made on location.' Garris calculates that the $250,000 it took to build a whole town set for *Critters 2* would probably have built only one tiny set on *Sleepwalkers*.

Lewis Teague recalls that differences in size of budget are sometimes less important than differences in priorities about where money can be spent; the big budget of *The Jewel of the Nile* did not allow as large a crew to be taken to some locations as he would have liked, while *Navy Seals* was organised to make that possible. Size of budget may mask other factors. At $22 million, *Explorers* was Joe Dante's most expensive film to date, costing twice as much as *Gremlins,* but it would not have been so costly had the film not been rushed to be finished by a certain date; millions of dollars were spent, for example, on building sets on Sundays – 'a tremendous waste of money, just so that the picture could open on the day of the Live Aid concert, the weekend nobody went to the movies.'

Release date pressures affect any film, and Lewis Teague notes an increasing tendency for films to be brought out quickly because of high interest charges. Michael Mann describes as a 'Faustian bargain' (which he lost) the deal he made with Paramount's Frank Mancuso to finance his 1983 picture, *The Keep* (which Mann describes as 'a fairy tale for adults which shows something of the psychopathology of fascism'), for $20 million providing he could deliver it in a year.

Dante took on *Explorers* (1985) as a nice little film about three kids and as something different after all the complicated effects on *Gremlins,* but in negotiations in August-September 1984, Paramount said they wanted the film for release the following summer. As Dante tells it, he said that was too soon; work was needed on the script, spaceships needed to be built, and so on. The studio agreed, but wanted him to agree to *try* to get it done. Dante agreed: he thought it meant yes, he would do the film and try to complete it by their date. He did not realise that in effect he had committed to it being ready for the following June-July. Dante plunged in, but during the course of production he discovered that all the studio people who hired him were leaving and moving to another studio, except the person who had originally got Dante into it and who now told him not to worry. A week later, this executive also left. This is not an unusual phenomenon in an industry where executive personnel move around with some frequency: Demme recalls that he got his 1977 picture *Citizens Band* ready to the satisfaction of the Paramount

Photograph: 'Faustian bargain' – Michael Mann on the set of The Keep.

hierarchy and went into production, but by the time shooting was finished, there was a new studio regime which did not like the project, could not understand why it had been made and, as a result, failed to market it with any commitment.

In the case of *Explorers,* it was the former head of distribution who took over at the studio. As his main interest was inevitably distribution, he wanted to know when Dante's picture would be ready. Dante had already realised that he could not make the original date and said he needed another two weeks, but was shown a graph to explain why Paramount needed the picture at a particular date. Dante protested that his contract specified a date two weeks later. 'Basically, they said "We don't care, sue us." ' Dante therefore went back to work knowing that the picture would be screwed up. He also knew that if he left they would put someone else in to finish it. In retrospect, he thinks he should have left, but he was aware that Peter Bogdanovich had just been in a squabble with Universal and was looking bad: 'Dante vs. Paramount Pictures – this I didn't need. I just couldn't leave. I felt like I'd be walking out on everybody who had trusted me and worked so intensely with me. OK, I'll bite the bullet, I'll stay and try to make the picture as good as I can in the amount of time I've got.' After a disastrous preview (though Dante likes the film: 'for me personally, it was the most expressive and personal movie I had made'), he tried to make cuts, although he could cut only from the end of the film because the time pressures had meant that the first reels had already been printed. With more time, he feels he could have made it into something more palatable about which he could have said he failed on his own terms; with the pressure, he can now say 'they made me do it.'

Amy Jones remarks how difficult it is to find people in the studios and the Hollywood system in general who really understand how movies are made and what makes a movie good. This is why such respect is earned by film directors who also function as producers – Corman obviously, but also, say, Ron Howard with Imagine Films, or Rob Reiner at Castle Rock, or Joe Roth, a founder of Morgan Creek and director of *Coupe De Ville* (1990), who was chairman of Fox for two years, up to late 1992, when he left to run his own production company at Disney. Jones argues that most people at the studios do not even pretend to know what makes movies work and go only on who is 'hot'. In other words, they pick film-makers who everybody else wants to work with (a similar principle lies behind 'bidding wars' for scripts: if everyone wants it, it must be good). Comparing his experience of studios and the low-budget independents, Joe Dante comments: 'When you go to a studio and the dailies are perused by hordes of people, many of whom have no idea not only of what you're doing, but also of how a movie is made, you start to realise that it's a lot more difficult to do something off-beat on a studio picture than in what looks like the very regimented formula of the cheap exploitation picture. When you make a studio film, there's a feeling that everyone has to like this movie to justify the expense. You say you want to do this or that, and they say, well, we don't know, people might not like that, and before you know it, you've got these bland, homogenised movies that nobody likes, because they're just dull.'

Dante's experience of the studio system with *Gremlins* (1984) is instructive, not least because of the 'Spielberg factor.' Before *Gremlins,* on the strength of the success of the independently-made *The Howling* (1980), Richard Zanuck and David Brown offered Dante *Jaws 3 People 0,* for Universal. The storyboards were already done, and all from eye level, just like MCA television. Even so, he could change it a little; Dante had in mind a dream cast which included Orson Welles, and remembers being told 'Orson Welles? You must be kidding – we'd have to put his name on the poster.' 'I had never encountered studio reality before,' and it was disillusioning; he suddenly understood why Welles and Samuel Fuller had not been able to find work. A friend of Dante's at the studio had said he would be his liaison there, and when agreement could not be reached on what kind of movie was wanted, and Dante was being offered another picture (which, in fact, he accepted), he tried to find out from his friend whether this movie

Still: Joe Dante directing River Phoenix and space creature Wak in Explorers.

was really going to happen (in fact, it collapsed). He never got an answer, and the friend later said he was not allowed to answer Dante's calls. 'I thought, OK, I've learned my first big studio lesson: don't trust anybody. It's stood me in very good stead. And the only time I've ever gotten screwed was when I made the mistake of trusting somebody. You could trust Roger [Corman]. He might screw you out of every dime, but he's an honest guy, he did what he said. It seemed like that was the way the business should run.'

After some time developing various projects – *The Joy of Sex* at Paramount, which he dropped out of, and *The Philadelphia Experiment,* which was shelved when the new owner of Avco Embassy did not want to make more slick action pictures – as well as directing some *Police Squad!* episodes for television (which got him a DGA card), Dante was sent the script for *Gremlins* by Spielberg. 'I assumed it had gone to the wrong address,' but it turned out that Spielberg had liked *The Howling,* and they met to discuss *Gremlins.* Originally, it was intended that it would be a cheap, non-union picture shot in Utah, but it soon became clear it could not be cheap. While he was preparing it, Dante directed his first studio picture, an episode of *Twilight Zone: The Movie. Gremlins* was the first production of Spielberg's Amblin company, and all concerned were feeling their way forward.

Even for Spielberg, as producer anyway, it was not easy to get a movie set up. Warner Brothers needed to be convinced that they should be making it, and gave it only rather grudging approval. Dante had heard the stories that Spielberg had been very interventionist on *Poltergeist* (1982), finally replacing Tobe Hooper as director. However, Spielberg went off to direct *Indiana Jones* (1984) and left Dante largely to his own devices: he did not want to see it until it was finished, but he did not want it cut at under two hours, to leave him room to make changes. Dante felt that it was very like working with Corman, because 'you're working for people who know what they're talking about.' The Warner Brothers executives, who had not really understood the dailies on *Twilight Zone* and had not seen how it would cut together, were vociferous about the *Gremlins* dailies,

Still: Zach Galligan and Phoebe Cates in Gremlins.

particularly because, as the movie progressed, the gremlins themselves got wilder and funnier than had been implied in the script. But Spielberg thought it the best work Dante had done ('did that mean it was any good?'). Even so, during the screening, he remembers seeing Spielberg frequently putting his hand to his forehead, but not knowing what the gesture meant.

Spielberg thought the first half a little slow and wanted it speeded up. Dante did not make all the radical changes Spielberg wanted, but they agreed to show it to the studio. Dante talks about 'the empty room syndrome': 'studio executives like to see films by themselves in an empty room. Very few films – certainly very few films of mine – are made for studio executives. You don't think about them while you're cutting it and you don't plan things while you're shooting so that executives will like it, but somehow this movie has to stand its first test in an empty room, with people whose ages range from maybe 25 to 60, sitting there, staring, wondering where their money has gone. And they hated the movie, except one guy, and he left the company right after.' They disliked the movie for the opposite reasons to Spielberg: they thought the first half was very sweet, but did not like all those gremlins running around all over the place. To get the studio off their backs, Spielberg told them, 'OK, we'll cut all of the gremlins out and we'll call the movie *People* – would you like that?' and they backed off. Meanwhile, Dante was trying to stop Spielberg cutting some major exposition at the start of the film. Spielberg's Amblin colleagues Kathleen Murphy and Frank Marshall persuaded Spielberg to have a preview in San Diego. 'It was astounding. I'd never seen anything like it. The audience were berserk. It was the greatest thing they'd ever seen. Warner Brothers were thrilled. This movie that was so terrible a week ago is now a wonderful movie. They wonder what Steven did to it. What magic did he work to make this picture so great?'

Gremlins has a wonderful – because so unexpected – scene in which Phoebe Cates's character explains why she hates Christmas: her father died by getting stuck in the chimney. While they shot it, the crew told Dante he was crazy and the scene would never end up in the movie, and later the editor thought the same. After the preview, Warner said it was great, except one thing: 'as soon as we take out that scene where she talks about her father getting stuck in the chimney, it'll be perfect.' Dante loved this scene. For him, it 'encapsulates the entire tone of the movie – it's a funny story if it doesn't happen to you, but if it does happen to you, it would be a horrible story, just like the whole movie.' Warner started to work on Dante; the president called him and said they wanted to help him, victory was in sight, and so on. Dante felt they did not understand the movie anyway. Although he knew Spielberg did not like the scene much either, he explained to him that the scene was important to him, and was only fifty seconds long, 'and I'll be disappointed if you don't stand up for me, because after all, you hired me to do this.' Spielberg agreed and told Warner that the scene was to stay, which was the end of the matter – except that Spielberg told Dante later that for months afterwards they kept trying to get him to persuade Dante to take the scene out.

Much to Dante's surprise, *Gremlins,* which cost only $11 million, was a gigantic hit, one of Warner's biggest grossing movies ever (and the only movie Dante has made any significant money on). 'Everybody's happy. Now they want *Gremlins 2*' – and this was only a week after *Gremlins* opened. It had been the most difficult film Dante had made; he felt nobody had been sure they were doing the right thing and that consequently there had been little support. He felt burned out on gremlins; the last thing he wanted was to do it again. He worked half-heartedly on some treatments and then bowed out, only to be offered *Batman* which he worked on it for a while before turning that down too, finally taking Paramount's offer, the 'nice little picture about three kids', *Explorers.*

Not all Dante's previews were as successful as the one for *Gremlins.* Dante's idea with *Explorers* was that the aliens would not be god-like; when the kids meet the aliens they expect to get the secrets of the universe but just get bits of television reruns, because that is all the aliens know about Earth. Although Dante feels that he could have made the picture better with more time, he believes in retrospect that it could never be successful because 'as soon as the audience realises that the aliens are not all-powerful, all-knowing, all-Spielbergian, they're disappointed.' Dante remembers the preview as disastrous, with three- and five-year-olds carrying enormous preview cards. 'They've identified with the kids in the movie, and when the kids in the movie are disappointed, they're disappointed. When the alien says he doesn't have the secret of the universe and instead says "What's up, doc?" there's dead silence in the theatre. They don't get it, and there's no way they're going to get it.' The film did no business, and *Hollywood Reporter* called it 'a monstrosity'. It is no consolation to Dante that he himself loves it and that people in strange places come up to him and say they loved it too.

Jim McBride had never experienced previews before *Breathless,* and the process of accepting other people's ideas was new to him. Everyone had particularly struggled to find the right ending, and the studio thought the one they came up with was a mistake. They shot three or four alternative endings and came up finally with two – McBride's and the studio's. McBride felt they were lucky to be making the film for Orion, whose reputation was that it was relatively director-oriented. The Orion executives said they thought the ending should be their way, but told him it was his movie. Two preview screenings were held, one with each ending, and McBride's was marginally better received and so was used.

Dante says of *Gremlins* that 'my success was tainted by it being a Spielberg picture. [The studios] do hire the director and they know that I do something, but I think they felt that whatever my excesses and idiosyncrasies, which would make my movies less popular, they will be filtered through Steven, who seemingly has a pipeline to the national psyche. With any Amblin picture, the studios feel that Steven will exert a popular influence and that your movie will become more commercial because he's involved. And it's true.' Dante remembers that the original idea was that the gremlin Gizmo would become the leading gremlin, but just before shooting, Spielberg suggested it would be better if Gizmo remained the same for the whole film, an idea which Dante thinks works to the movie's advantage.

The experience of working with Spielberg was good enough for Dante to work with him again on *Innerspace*. Once again, he was generally left alone by Spielberg, although, near the start of shooting, Spielberg offered advice on some casting problems raised by the studio. Dante was enjoying making the movie until he was called to a lunchtime meeting with the studio people, at which he recalls them saying, 'We don't know what to say to you, it's just not funny, it just isn't any good. We don't know what to tell you, we don't know how to make it better, we just wanted to let you know. Goodbye.' Dante went back to his 'comedy', which he still thought was funny, but maybe wasn't. 'This [turned] out to be one of the most destructive meetings I've ever had in Hollywood. To me, this is the opposite of the way to make a movie. If you have a constructive opinion about why something isn't funny, or how to make it funnier, that's one thing, but to call a guy up to a meeting to tell him that you don't like it and don't know what to say, it's just no good – and not fire the guy – is a big mistake.'

Dante finished the film, and Spielberg wanted only a few additional special effects. The studio loved it, but Dante's troubles were not yet over: 'They think it's so great that they don't even have to advertise it, and in service of that vision, they decide to have the worst ad in the history of motion pictures, with a giant thumb, with a tiny little spaceship in it, and the title, *Innerspace,* with no indication that it's a comedy, or what it's about.' Even though the reviews were good and people liked it when they saw it, it was a disaster, and an expensive one at $25 million – Dante's second expensive disaster. 'It's better to have a well-reviewed disaster than a badly-reviewed disaster, but a disaster is a disaster, and really the bottom line is what they look at: does this guy make movies people want to see, or doesn't he?' It was from this very difficult career point that Dante tried unsuccessfully to set up something more like an art movie, with *Little Man Tate,* in order to do something different, where box office success would not be so crucial. Then he agreed to do *Gremlins 2,* but took on *The 'burbs* first. After *Gremlins 2,* Dante's arrangement with Warner which had run, on and off, for ten years came to an end. He decided to make a similar deal with Universal, from which base, and with some European funding, he has been trying to set up *Matinee,* with John Goodman and Cathy Moriarty, as well as doing some work for television.

Still: 'now they want Gremlins 2 *– John Glover and gremlin in* Gremlins 2: The New

THE LITTLE PICTURE

Both economically and industrially, the film industry and the television industry are so indissolubly linked that it makes little sense now to think of them as separate entities. Since the 1950s, production for television has soaked up a lot of the technical and creative personnel who had lost their jobs in the movies with the break-up of the studio system and the decline in the number of theatrical features being made. Television also gained the regularly-attending mass family audience once enjoyed by the cinema, and it took over many of the forms of routine production once carried out by the movie industry – B features, cartoons, general interest shorts, newsreels, and so on.

Although many writers and directors (and others) are employed in television as well as film at some point in their careers, their television work often remains, if not hidden, at least not much spoken about. There are a number of fairly obvious reasons for this. The financial constraints on television production are often much tighter than on theatrical features, particularly in the amount of time available for production – a typical shooting schedule for a made-for-television movie is about three weeks. Even so, television budgets do not look too bad in comparison with much low-budget independent production, if only because a great deal of television uses union personnel. Many directors who started out in low-budget outfits like New World gained their director's or editor's union cards by working for television.

In some ways, the most important constraints are on freedom and control over both style and content: the family audience for television and the power of the advertisers often result in blandness. A much discussed example of this process was the loss of $1.5 million in cancelled commercials when conservative pressure groups and advertisers reacted to *thirtysomething*, which included a scene of two gay male characters in bed together. Television's fear of giving offence was also clear in a report by *TV Guide* about NBC toning down the recent television movie *Roe vs. Wade* (1989), which was about the Supreme Court's ruling that legalised abortion; changes were apparently made in the script to make it less 'pro-choice'. Alex Ben Block, editor of *Show Biz News*, was quoted as saying that 'movies tend to have a very hard edge. They can do things that are negative and have characters who aren't likable; TV needs likable characters as a central focus.' One of Mark Goldblatt's reasons for *not* working for television is that 'network television is all about "maybe we can soften it . . ." ' Such pressures have detracted from the status of working for television. However, both the nature of television and its relationship to film have been constantly in flux. Until the 1970s, television was essentially restricted to the three main national television networks, ABC, CBS and NBC. From the 1970s, the advent of cable television, and particularly pay cable, meant that different kinds of entertainment began to be made for delivery through television sets in the home.

In the 1950s, television drama enjoyed high status, and indeed the period is now commonly referred to as a 'golden age' of television. Certainly, it provided the launching pad for several future movie directors. For some, live television drama was a staging post between a training in legitimate theatre – a frequent source of film directors since the start of talkies – and movies: Sidney Lumet, Delbert Mann and Arthur Penn, for

99

example, all took this route, directing their first feature in the mid to late 1950s, Lumet with *Twelve Angry Men* (1957), Mann with *Marty* (1955), Penn with *The Left-Handed Gun* (1958), though Penn continued for some years as primarily a theatre director before making more movies. Others, like John Frankenheimer, Irvin Kershner and Franklin Schaffner also moved out of television to make their first features during the same period (respectively *The Young Stranger*, 1956, *Stakeout on Dope Street* – made for Corman – 1958, and *The Stripper*, 1963). The status of television drama shows like *Playhouse 90* and the *Kaiser Aluminum Hour* is amply demonstrated by the fact that both *Twelve Angry Men* and *Marty* began life as television dramas before being remade as theatrical features.

Such drama was very far from the norm for television. Very early on, television established its own episodic form (taken more from radio than from film or theatre) in massively popular shows like *Father Knows Best* and *Bachelor Father* in the 1950s or *My Three Sons* and *Marcus Welby M.D.* in the 1960s. The episodic format, filmed rather than live, produced in Hollywood rather than New York, and drawing on Hollywood for many of its ideas and performers, became the stuff of prime-time television. It lacked the status that had accrued to television drama, and its Hollywood origin was evident in the use – and enormous popularity – of ageing movie stars, such as Robert Young *(Father Knows Best, Marcus Welby)* and Fred MacMurray *(My Three Sons)* or Donna Reed and Barbara Stanwyck, in their own shows (a film/television relationship still with us, for example with Burt Reynolds in *Evening Shade)*. Another Hollywood legacy was the prevalence of the western, with series like *Rawhide, Wagon Train* and *Bonanza.* Episodic television was another starting place for future-film-makers. Robert Altman had made a low-budget feature debut in 1957 with *The Delinquents,* but, until his re-entry into the movie business in 1970 with *M*A*S*H,* he worked extensively in television on shows like *Alfred Hitchcock Presents* and *Bonanza,* while Sam Peckinpah wrote and directed for television on shows including *The Rifleman* and *The Westerner* before making his first theatrical feature, *The Deadly Companions,* in 1961.

The episodic format has continued to be standard for prime-time television. From the vantage point of the present, with costs being drastically pruned as the audience share has dropped, many have begun to talk of the 1970s and 1980s as another 'golden age' of television – a golden age purely of episodic television, with high-status (and/or very profitable) shows like *M*A*S*H, Hill Street Blues* and *Miami Vice.*

The advent in the mid 1960s of the made-for-television movie, followed from the 1970s by the mini-series format, was mainly economic in motivation, stemming from a shortage of material. From the 1960s onwards, though, television began to show more recent Hollywood features, and by the early 1970s the three networks were broadcasting ten movies at prime time each week; again there was a shortage of the right kind of product. Made-for-television films were produced in greater quantity to fill the gap and soon established themselves as popular prime-time fare; their production more than doubled between 1970-71 and 1971-72.

The form itself had first been established in 1965, when NBC contracted with MCA for a series of movies to be premiered on network television, the first of which was *Fame Is the Name of the Game* (Universal, 1966). Initially, made-for-television movies were not a regular feature of programming and were considered somewhat risky. The made-for-television movie is something of a hybrid: it is a movie, made on film and within the industrial framework of the film industry (though it has tended to be made by independents rather than the majors, despite Universal/MCA's prominence in the field), running at feature length (where quality live television drama in the 1950s would usually have been one hour in length), but it is television, which implies that it is subject to content – and perhaps formal – constraints, despite its frequent exploitation of highly controversial subject matter (not just abortion in *Roe vs. Wade*, but also domestic violence in NBC's *The Burning Bed*, 1984, incest in *Something About Amelia* and nuclear war in *The Day After*, both part of ABC's 1983-84 season). Made-for-television movies are made less expensively than major theatrical releases, using known performers rather than stars. In the late 1960s, television movies typically cost $450,000 to $700,000, rising to about $1 million by the early 1970s and to twice that in the late 1980s, though some cost much more; a mini-series like the western *Lonesome Dove* (1989), for example, was budgeted at around $20 million. It is their comparatively low cost that has made them economical propositions compared to the expense of broadcasting popular Hollywood theatrical features.

Nevertheless, the made-for-television movie did not displace episodic television as the dominant prime-time filmed product. The general pattern for episodic shows is of 22 or 23 episodes for the autumn-to-spring season on network television, with reruns in the summer. Successful shows can continue for four or five years, or even longer, but most shows are cancelled after only part of a season or, in many cases, after the feature-length pilot show which is traditionally used to test audience response. The standard forms are half-hour shows (in fact, more like 25 minutes to allow time for commercial breaks), generally sit-coms like the current *The Cosby Show, Golden Girls, Cheers, Roseanne* and *My Two Dads*, or older shows like *I Love Lucy, Happy Days* and *M*A*S*H*, and hour shows, generally episodic dramas like *Starsky and Hutch, Columbo, Kojak, Cagney and Lacey, Police Story, Charlie's Angels, The Rockford Files, Magnum, Hill Street Blues, Miami Vice, LA Law, Dallas, Dynasty, Quantum Leap* and *Twin Peaks*. There are also anthology shows, among them *Twilight Zone, Amazing Stories, American Chronicles* and *Lifestories*, where each episode is a separate, half-hour or hour long story. The economics of television production are very different from those of theatrical film production. Until the rise of cable, made-for-television movies had very limited possibilities for making significant profits, since their sole outlets were the networks for which they were made. They were produced for a flat fee from the network, which would have the right to two broadcasts, and any profits for the producers had to come from any difference between the flat fee and the actual cost of production or from foreign sales. Television films and shows have been widely sold abroad and some, though relatively few, have had the possibility of theatrical release abroad (Steven Spielberg's 1971 Universal television movie *Duel* is a well-known example).

Although major studios, in particular Universal/MCA, have made television movies, the small profits available are more attractive to independent production companies, many of which have been non-union and therefore have had a budgetary edge over the majors. More recently, in a highly competitive market, majors, such as Paramount, have been setting up their own non-union offshoots to produce television shows. The majors have tended to be more interested in episodic television, which is 'negative' or 'deficit' financed on a formula by which the networks pay about 20 per cent less than the overall costs of production – a level generally thought to cover the costs of production but not overheads. The networks, in fact, get the shows for less than their actual cost, and also tie producers into long-term contracts in advance with a set price for a series season by season (so that the producers of hit shows cannot seek higher bids from other networks).

The pay-off for the production companies was that they retained their rights to the shows after the network broadcasts. The relatively few shows that were successful and ran for several seasons were well positioned for widespread and long-term syndication sale to local television stations and, of course, for export. The domestic and foreign market for televison show reruns is estimated at about $5·5 billion a year. Predictably, the networks have fought for a share in this lucrative market, but the long-running 'fin-syn' dispute about syndication rights was decided in favour of the producers and against the networks in the 1991 ruling of the Federal Communications Commission (FCC). With the international television market in almost constant growth, major producers expect sales to foreign markets to account for some 40 per cent of total revenues from telefilms. The production

Photograph: an hour show – Cagney and Lacey *with Tyne Daly and Sharon Gless.*

costs of a television series are said not to be fully recouped until about 88 episodes, or four full seasons, have been made; this ensures off-network syndication, allowing local stations to transmit continuing episodes of old shows for five days a week ('strip syndication'); very few shows achieve this. In the mid 1980s, it was estimated that the cost of an episode of *Dallas, Magnum* and similar shows was between $1 million and $1.2 million. Half-hour sit-coms, often studio-made, with lower production values and smaller casts, are much cheaper to produce – one reason why, in the cost-conscious present, they are preferred (they are also favoured by local television stations as they can be more flexibly scheduled).

Given the level of cost, it is not surprising that the major studios – for which episodic television provides virtually continuous work and use of studio space – are central to its production. Among them are Paramount with *Cheers* and MGM/Pathé with *thirtysomething;* the shows are often made jointly with their original creators. Some independents have also been signally successful with series: The Carsey Werner Company with *The Cosby Show* and *Roseanne,* Spelling Entertainment with *Beverly Hills 90210,* Lorimar with *Dallas* and *Knots Landing,* and MTM with *Hill Street Blues* and *St Elsewhere* in the past and with *WKRP in Cincinnati* and *Evening Shade* more recently. Although the chances of really big success are slim, the rewards, when they come, are great. When $M*A*S*H$ was originally syndicated in 1979, the series was sold for $250,000 per episode; this rose to $900,000 per episode when it was resold in 1984. In 1986, *Magnum* sold for $900,000 per episode. In 1988, *The Cosby Show* was selling to syndication at $3-4 million per episode – the most profitable show ever, grossing over $500 million in syndication by the end of 1991. However, on a more usual scale, even a hit show like *The Golden Girls* has as yet grossed only about $100 million.

Given the general crisis in the networks, some new forms of production have begun, or have been revived, with sponsors helping to finance shows in return for reduced advertising costs (and a share in any profits) and with cable companies producing shows (more cheaply than elsewhere) for their supposed enemies or rivals, the networks. The decline in the networks' power has also meant that, following the example of *Star Trek*, some shows like MTM's *WKRP in Cincinnati* and Berk-Schwartz's *Baywatch*, which have been cancelled by the networks, have survived on first-run syndication and foreign sales, if only by cutting costs to do so: *Baywatch* was rebudgeted at about $800,000 per episode as compared to the $1.2 million per episode when it was being made for NBC.

Indeed, in the new climate of television broadcasting and the decline in power of the networks, the *Baywatch* example begins to look increasingly typical. *Variety* reported the producer of *Quantum Leap*, Don Bellasario, who produced *Magnum* in the 1980s, as observing, 'it used to be our primary concerns were creative ones. Not anymore. Now the first question is, "Can we make it for the budget?" ' Austerity has meant a squeeze on production costs, with hour dramas now getting six- or seven-day shoots as opposed to eight days, and special effects being reduced in number. It is reckoned that budgets are on average 20 per cent lower than in the 1980s. Increasingly, shows that would have once been produced for the networks – like the current Paramount projects *Star Trek*, *Deep Space Nine* and *The Untouchables* – are being made for the syndication market (where costs are covered in advance of production) and for foreign sales. Paramount's *The Young Indiana Jones Chronicles*, costing some $2 million per episode, looks exceptional in these austere times, but then ABC is in partnership with the studio on the project, and the show's name guarantees strong international sales (reportedly $800,000 an episode). *Twin Peaks*, on the other hand, did not make enough episodes before it was cancelled to earn much money in syndication sales to American stations, but it has sold extremely well abroad and has led to a theatrical feature, *Twin Peaks: Fire Walk With Me*, for which there is a dedicated core audience. As producer Mark Frost puts it, the real pay-off from the series would be if the theatrical feature was a big success, and he envisages that in this case there could be more *Twin Peaks* features in the future, along the lines of the *Star Trek* features.

Gradually, the already symbiotic relationship between theatrical film and television film has changed and intensified. Although Burt Reynolds in *Evening Shade* continues the tradition of ageing movie stars moving to television, movement in the other direction increased significantly in the 1980s. Bruce Willis, for example, moved very quickly from co-star in *Moonlighting* to major stardom in theatrical features; actors established in television have become much more likely to move up to features while still being able to work in television as well. Ted Danson and Kirstie Ally from *Cheers*, Roseanne Barr and John Goodman from *Roseanne* and Jimmy Smits from *LA Law* have all made a significant impact in theatrical features while continuing to play their television roles.

Although television shows have generated theatrical features, as with the *Star Trek* films, *Twilight Zone* and, most recently (though a rather special case), *Twin Peaks*, the 1980s boom in cinema admissions encouraged television production companies to exploit on television the success of theatrical features. In many cases the television producers, often the major studios, were exploiting their own properties. It makes economic sense to extend the exploitation of a property in which large sums of money have already been invested. At the end of the decade, the hit movies being turned into series included *The*

Little Mermaid, Steel Magnolias, Uncle Buck, Parenthood, Bill & Ted's Excellent Adventure, Bagdad Café, True Believer (as *Eddie Dodd*), *Alien Nation, Beetlejuice* and *The Outsiders*. There are also rip-off series, which borrow the concept rather than the exact title of the feature, like *The Young Riders* (ripping off *Young Guns*), *Baby Talk (Look Who's Talking), Parker Lewis Can't Lose! (Ferris Bueller's Day Off,* a 1986 movie that also has a series named exactly after it). Many other series based on features have been tried, some successfully, such as *In the Heat of the Night,* based on the 1967 movie, most unsuccessfully, such as *Dirty Dancing, Baby Boom, Down and Out in Beverly Hills* and *Fast Times at Ridgemont High.* As with television shows of any kind or origin, many more fail than succeed, but there may be special reasons why there are so many series based on movies and why so many of the shows tend to fail. With a hit movie it is not, in many cases, necessary to make a pilot for the show, and this saves an estimated cost, currently, of about $2.2 million per hour, as the title, the concept and the projected series have already been massively promoted. On the other hand, the danger is that what audiences liked about a theatrical feature will have to be absent from a series based on it, as television will not usually be able to afford the high-profile stars of the original and may need to tone down language and content. There is also the question of whether the original movie provides a workable enough basis for the continuing episodic form.

What constituted television underwent further redefinition from the late 1970s onwards as pay cable began to become a major force. The repercussions of the rapid growth of cable have had vital effects on the movie industry, but even more vital effects on the television industry. Since the main attractions on offer from pay cable are not only feature movies, but also sports coverage and music, and, of late, news too, much of the bedrock provision of the networks is available elsewhere. But it is the opportunity to see feature movies without the insistent commercial breaks of network television that has been one of the major attractions of cable and has undoubtedly been an important reason for cable's rapid growth at the expense of the networks' audience share. Home video is another force that has undermined the dominance of network television: although it also offers music, sports and general interest material, it has essentially been a means of delivering feature films to the home.

For its filmed entertainment, cable – predominantly Home Box Office – was oriented primarily to the feature film industry. As early as 1977, finding a scarcity of product there to buy for cable screening, it instituted the 'pre-buy', putting up a percentage of the production costs of features in return for cable rights (and a share of the profits) and began to produce its own features, rapidly becoming the largest financier of motion pictures in the world. Since pay cable was not dependent on advertisers ('movies sell themselves, but television has to sell soap,' as Mark Goldblatt puts it) and did not have the same image of national public exposure and responsibility, it was not inhibited by the same constraints on subject matter and language. Indeed, pay cable actively sought the strong and adult material that network television found difficult to handle. As pay cable prospered, the budgets for its own feature-film production were generally higher than those for made-for-television features, often around $5 million. As well as providing its own programming, features produced by cable entered the world media market for sale to cable and network television abroad and, quite often, to foreign theatrical distributors.

As all these developments in small-screen home entertainment begin to imply, the point of comparison for filmed dramatic entertainment on television is always theatrical film production: this is what television films of various kinds are measured against, whether by the audiences watching them or by the creative personnel who work on them. Accordingly, for creative workers like directors and writers, the status of working for television of any kind is almost without exception lower than that of working on theatrical features. Despite all the evident industrial overlap between film and television, everyone acknowledges a divide between the two. Within television itself, a fairly well-defined hierarchy of status attaches to working on different kinds of television production (just as there are hierarchies in theatrical film production). As Rockne O'Bannon put it: 'Every episodic television director aspires to do pilots; pilot directors aspire to do television movies; television movie directors aspire to do features.'

Cable movies, particularly those for HBO and Showtime, now occupy a status very close to that of theatrical features. Although the budgets are rarely above $5-6 million, and schedules accordingly rather short, directors, writers and actors can all have considerable input and creative control. The cable companies themselves have been anxious to attract top-line talent and to give the chance for it to become involved in projects that would probably not be viable as theatrical features. Many directors and actors have responded to this. Distinctions need to be made between cable movies for pay cable premium services channels like HBO and Showtime, and normal cable movies for a channel like USA Network, which depends primarily on advertising for its revenues. HBO movies (some twenty a year) certainly enjoy the highest status, with budgets up to around $8 million, while Showtime movies (about twelve a year) have budgets up to $5-6 million. Movies for a company like USA Network are made more cheaply and will be broken by commercials while being transmitted, but the constraints imposed on network made-for-television movies do not apply to the same degree.

Pilots for episodic television are in a different category from one-off features, but as pilots are also intended to stand on their own, they are in effect made-for-television movies. A pilot has higher status than a one-off made-for-television movie, because much more rides on its success; with some of the investment in a pilot also being investment in the series it is supposed to inaugurate, the budget is likely to be higher than for a made-for-television movie. Directors hired for pilots are very often recruited from the ranks of those identified primarily as theatrical feature directors; they are hired because their input is sought in establishing the look and feel of a show.

Some time may elapse between the pilot and the creation of the initial episodes of the series, and responses to a pilot may encourage the network and/or the production company to make changes in the original concept, look or feel. Thus, when the first episodes of a series come to be made, much may remain to be established or re-established and directors may still have considerable space for invention. Directing the initial episodes of a new television show therefore has considerably higher status than directing later episodes, when the format is well established, and a director's job becomes something very different, with conspicuously less space for creative intervention. Once a successful show has established itself, the actors have a tendency to refuse direction – quite rightly, in some respects, as they will know the characters they are playing better than someone hired to direct a single episode.

The lowest status of all probably attaches to television daytime shows such as soaps, the most derided form of dramatic television. But here, too, movie directors have long learned their craft – most recently, black film maker Mario Van Peebles, whose first feature, *New Jack City* was a considerable hit in 1991. There is a whole series of variations on the broad hierarchy of status attaching to shows. Very often, one-hour dramas enjoy higher status than half-hour sitcoms, but powerful producer-directors like James Brooks (who went on to make *Terms of Endearment*, 1983) came from a background in sitcoms. Anthology shows, like the revived *Twilight Zone* and *Amazing Stories,* have a rough format but not one as standardised as episodic shows, and directors thus have more freedom on them. These shows are often seen as privileging the writers, but they are also likely to mark their status by hiring directors who are firmly identified with features. Both the new *Twilight Zone* and *Amazing Stories* almost set themselves up as 'cult' shows, which has again changed the status of working on them. Cult status and/or very high prestige also attaches itself to successful episodic shows, prime examples in the 1980s being *Hill Street Blues, Miami Vice* and *Twin Peaks,* all of which had an extraordinarily high profile, critically, with the viewing public and the industry itself. They contrast with shows like *Quantum Leap* or *LA Law,* which are popular and successful but do not enjoy any

Photograph: Aaron Lipstadt (right) with Willie Nelson during the shooting of El Viejo, *an episode of* Miami Vice.

particular prestige. On a different scale, 'quality' shows like John Sayles's *Shannon's Deal*, though not big hits, enjoy a critical and industry reputation and may actively seek out theatrical feature directors. On shows like these, directors with reputations in features can work without acquiring the usually negative associations that working for television would normally bring. *Shannon's Deal* also encouraged top theatrical feature writers, like Tom Rickman (*Coal Miner's Daughter*, 1980) and Joel Oliansky (*Bird*, 1988), to write for television by offering them the chance to direct.

There is no doubt either, as Jim McBride says, that feature-film people look down on television, or that people in television feel feature people don't understand television. Theatrical feature people will usually work for television when it is the only employment they can find, and the experience generally confirms their antipathy to the medium. After *Over the Edge* was made and then shelved, Jonathan Kaplan could not get theatrical feature work he wanted – he was offered only truck movies similar to *White Line Fever*. Television movies offered the opportunity to work with other kinds of material, and the chance to work: 'I'm a director, I want to direct movies. I don't want to sit around and have fantasies, or let a project go down the tubes when we can't get some star to read the script.' So he finally decided to direct a made-for-television movie, *11th Victim*, for CBS in 1979, and subsequently made three more, *The Hustler of Muscle Beach* (1980), *The Gentlemen Bandit* (1981) and *Girls of the White Orchid* (1983). When Jonathan Demme directed an episode of *Columbo* (*Murder Under Glass*, 1978), it was after the box-office failure of *Citizens Band*: despite the film's critical success, no projects were being offered, and Demme was broke, about to lose his apartment and desperate to work. 'It was absolutely a life-saver: it saved the apartment, it gave me a little bit of confidence back.' Joe Dante made some episodes of *Police Squad!* (a short-lived comic police series produced by the Zuckers – 'it overestimated the hipness of the American audience') in 1982, after he had been involved with several projects – *Jaws 3 People 0*, *Joy of Sex* – which had come to nothing or from which he had removed himself; he had been developing *The Philadelphia Experiment* for Avco Embassy and was not paid for it, so he, too, was broke. Aaron Lipstadt was feeling that the failure of *City Limits* had buried his career, and then he was hired to direct for *Miami Vice,* when it was in its second season and very hot, which gave him much-needed work as well as restoring some (also much-needed) status, partly because *Miami Vice* was self-consciously hiring directors whose names were associated with theatrical features rather than with television. Although he himself does not quite put it that way, even Michael Mann was at a difficult career point when he became involved in what became *Miami Vice:* of his two theatrical features to that point, *Thief* had not been a box-office success, though it was a critical success, while *The Keep* had been a box-office disaster and had received a critical mauling.

Others have, as far as possible, avoided television altogether: Mark Goldblatt would rather edit top-quality theatrical features than direct episodic television ('if I wouldn't actually invest forty minutes of my time to watch it, I don't want to work on it' is his bottom line) or make made-for-television movies (though he would be happy to make a film for pay cable and would have loved to direct an episode for *Twin Peaks*). Amy Jones would prefer to write quality feature material than direct for television (though she had planned a pay-cable feature and has originated a series as a writer). Lewis Teague backed out of a directing apprenticeship at Universal because he did not want to direct episodic television, though he did later work on, for example, *Vegas,* and, much later, directed the pilot for John Sayles's *Shannon's Deal* and shot a cable movie, *Wedlock,* in 1991. George Armitage began his career in the 1960s producing made-for-television movies, and the experience encouraged him to stay well away during the long gap in his career in the 1980s – he preferred to develop scripts, even though they did not get made, rather than direct for television.

Mann also belongs to another – large – group of film-makers, who were in television before they worked in film, but almost always with a very precise sense that this was a way of getting into the business and graduating to theatrical features. Having established himself as a hot television writer with four scripts for *Starsky and Hutch* episodes (1975-77)

Still: Peter Strauss in Michael Mann's made-for-television feature The Jericho Mile.

107

and four for *Police Story* (1976-78), directed an episode of *Police Woman* (1977) and scripted the pilot for *Vegas*, Mann was able to set up a made-for-television movie, *The Jericho Mile* (1979). According to Mann, the script for *Thief* was already written and the conscious plan was that a successful ABC movie-of-the week would make it possible for him to make it as a theatrical feature. He recalls that *The Jericho Mile* 'aired on Sunday – by noon Monday I was offered twelve or thirteen movies to direct, so it was immediate.'

After meeting Steven Bochco, Mark Frost went straight from college to writing for the children's television show, *The Six Million Dollar Man,* but left after a year to work as a PBS (Public Broadcasting System) documentary producer and as a playwright attached to the Guthrie Theater in Minneapolis. He returned to Hollywood to work as a writer on over fifty episodes of *Hill Street Blues*, 'apprenticed' to Bochco and contributing stories and scripts, particularly during the third and fourth seasons, 1982-83 and 1984-85. Even at that time, says Frost, he knew he wanted to have the kind of creative control over his material that could come only from being a director and he wanted to work in film (so his next move was his association with John Schlesinger on *The Believers,* which he scripted). In television, the way to control was to become a producer as well as a writer, since producing was where power lay in television, and it was as a producer that he worked on *Twin Peaks* (on which he also scripted and directed some episodes).

Though, by their own accounts, they had less definite senses of a career path that would lead to directing features, both Rockne O'Bannon and Mick Garris, got their film education in television. Both were writers and story editors, respectively on *Twilight Zone* and *Amazing Stories,* shows on which writers' work was valued and the writers, unusually, were closely involved in the whole production process (casting, choice of director, production design, and so on). These shows hired feature directors: Garris's scripts were directed by the likes of Martin Scorsese, Robert Zemickis and Joe Dante, and O'Bannon's by Wes Craven, Dante and Martha Coolidge (and, in fact, Garris). It was observation of the creative process that helped O'Bannon and Garris to a large degree to become directors (though O'Bannon feels he may have learned more from the lousy directors: 'Gee, I know I can do as well as this person – at least I can articulate partially what I want and have some imagination. . .').

Photograph: working on The Equalizer – *left to right, composer Stewart Copeland, director Aaron Lipstadt, camera operator Alec Hirschfield and director of photography Jeffrey Erb.*

It is indicative of the low esteem in which television is held and of the creative working conditions within it that it is very often seen as an environment where film-makers can learn their craft before moving on to 'better' things – it is, after all, where such powerful figures as Steven Spielberg, Richard Donner and John Badham began. 'Definitely a place you can learn a lot' is how Jim McBride describes television, and Rob Cohen, who got into directing features somewhat by chance and then had a disastrous experience with a second feature, wonders in retrospect if he would have done better to have worked first in television and have learned the craft elements of directing on a daily basis. Given television's reputation for tight budgets and the new mood of austerity in the feature industry itself, television might seem a very appropriate place for recruiting new film-makers used to cutting corners. Certainly, this is the position which *Variety* reported as being taken by Brandon Tartikoff when he moved from NBC Television to become chairman of Paramount in the summer of 1991 (a position he held until late 1992) and resolved to bring costs down: 'The simple reality is that people who have worked in television are more accustomed to low-budget productions.' While earlier directors from television have made a considerable impact in the cinema, many film-makers are not convinced by Tartikoff's argument, insisting that television directors often lack the vision and patience needed to make good features. Mark Goldblatt notes that many producers think it is difficult for television directors to make the jump; the habits that directors learn in television are not necessarily the best ones for feature production. As Mark Frost puts it, television is a place to learn, but it can also be a trap. Rockne O'Bannon considers that it is partly a question of attitude, but also a matter of learning bad habits; when directors 'learn to shoot very quickly as their primary goal, to get the coverage but don't care much what it looks like, then unfortunately their features look like that, too. The important thing is to know how to do it when you need to – that's what saved Spielberg's neck a few times.'

Directors who move from features to television are most aware of the constraints of working for television. Jim McBride feels that despite great (usually union) crews, the time pressures always make things difficult and prevent directors feeling satisfied with what they do. 'It just happens too fast', Bobby Roth comments. Even if the writing is good, which it normally is not in television as compared with features, 'I don't think you can direct terribly interestingly [on a one-hour episodic television-show schedule of] seven days.' In particular, thinks McBride, you do not have the chance to correct your mistakes, or, as Joe Dante puts it, you cannot fine-tune things as you would on a feature – everything has a certain roughness – 'you go for what's *acceptable*, you compromise.' Directors do often feel there are compensations, some of them down to the general lack of consequence associated with television. For Dante, 'The appeal, for somebody's who's been spending two years on every picture, is that you go in and within two months you've got a product,' in his case, *Eerie, Indiana* (1991, a children's show, though it is also calculated to appeal to adults; Dante is 'creative consultant' and is directing four segments). Here, thirty-minute shows were produced from six days of shooting on the pilot episode, five days for subsequent segments: 'It happens, it's instant gratification; you're not doing something you planned six months before.' Rob Cohen also likes directing television because it is fast and 'if it's good, it feels good and if not, at least it's over quickly.'

The constraints of network censorship are usually slight but nonetheless real. *Eerie, Indiana* was scheduled for 7.30 p.m. on Sundays – considered children's programme time – and the networks were worried about it being too scary. The rules specify that nothing can be shown that children would imitate, which caused problems for an episode in which a kid drives a car. The producers of the show had *Tom Sawyer* in mind as a source for the show, but Dante feels it is more like *Twilight Zone*; although it is kids' programming, it needs a certain adult edge, a difficult formula to arrive at under the rules. Mick Garris's work on *Amazing Stories* as a writer and story editor got him his first chance to direct (as well as produce and write) a one-hour Disney Sunday Night Movie for television (with

John Landis as executive producer). *Fuzzbucket* is about a twelve-year-old boy with an imaginary friend who turns out not to be imaginary. Though there was a side to it that had a Spielberg sweetness, Garris's original story gave the boy a troubled childhood; when Disney took that out, the overall tone of the film inevitably changed.

Jim McBride recalls that directing a *Twilight Zone* episode *(The Once and Future King*, 1986, 'a marvellous story about an Elvis imitator who goes back in time to 1954 and meets Elvis'), though difficult to do and be satisfied with, was like making a 'mini feature'. This was very different from his experience in 1990 of directing some episodes of *The Wonder Years*, a series on which the characters, style and format were already established: 'You really don't have any creative participation beyond actually directing the actors and the camera . . . it's just not satisfying, because you're not in there at the beginning, and you're not in there at the end.' Although the Directors' Guild has built into contracts that directors have three or four days with the show's editor after the first cut is made (air dates permitting), McBride's experience is that the producers go and recut anyway.

It is ironic, but typical of television, that Peter Falk hired Jonathan Demme to direct an episode of *Columbo* on the strength of having seen *Citizens Band*, but that the range of choices available to Demme once he was directing on the show was strictly limited. Directors often refer to what they do on episodic television as like being a traffic cop, which is clearly one step down even from being a 'gun for hire' on features. The more successful and straight the show, like, say, *LA Law*, the less freedom for directors. Once any show has been renewed by the network, producers feel justified in saying 'this is what we do.' Aaron Lipstadt, who has worked on many episodic shows, including *Miami Vice*, *Crime Story*, *The Equalizer*, *Hard Copy*, *Tour of Duty*, *Private Eye*, *Houston Knights*, *Quantum Leap*, *Nasty Boys*, *Law and Order*, *Shannon's Deal*, *The Young Riders* and *The Untouchables* says it is very rare to be told, say, to 'shoot this close-up,' but it has happened. Rob Cohen, who has directed episodes of shows such as *thirtysomething*, *Miami Vice*, *Private Eye*, *Nasty Boys* and *Hooperman*, reflects that if the show's producers are going to say things like 'kill the fluorescents' or 'we don't do that', 'why not direct it by numbers?' Inevitably, directors look upon episodic television as, in Lipstadt's phrase 'a journeyman's job' in which, everyone agrees, invention is not really welcomed.

Paradoxically, at least for directors coming to television from low-budget independent film-making, union crews and often relatively good budgets offer opportunities within the constraints. *Miami Vice* had studio resources at its disposal and was budgeted at $1.5 million for a seven-day shoot to produce 48 minutes of screen time (more than most shows, and *Miami Vice* spoiled directors like Lipstadt for episodic television in general); the total budget for Lipstadt's feature-length *Android* had been one third of that. A lot of the money in a show like *Miami Vice* goes on overheads rather than directly into what appears on the screen, but a budget that allows for cranes and expensive set items can nevertheless be liberating. Abel Ferrara, coming from even lower-budgeted movies like *Driller Killer* (1979) and *Ms. 45 (Angel of Vengeance*, 1980) to *Miami Vice* (two episodes, *The Home Invaders*, 1984, *The Dutch Oven*, 1985), was also very conscious that there were a lot more things at his disposal in television than in B movies. 'It has to do with the budgets, how fancy a shot you can pull off. When you have the crew and you have a hundred people, then you say, All right, let's lay a few thousand feet of track – why not, the money's there anyway.'

Having got into episodic television by default, after one feature that flopped, Lipstadt thought that if he did the greatest ever episode of *Miami Vice*, he would be able to get back to making features. His first episode for *Miami Vice*, *Yankee Dollar* (1986), was very good, but, as he says, 'people don't see the director in television episodes.' What does an episodic television director do? 'You have minimal input on the script, and the style, tone and pace are there, but you've got to make the choices in telling the story.' The details of scenes are not usually in the script, and Lipstadt admits that early on in his

Still: Stewart Copeland (left) and Edward Woodward in an episode of The Equalizer.

work for television, he would consciously ignore any camera direction in the script. In the script, the writer indicates how he or she sees the script being played, but for a lot of reasons – not just disagreement, but also, say, because the set does not work as the writer envisaged – the director will have a different interpretation. 'What I try to do is ask myself "What's it about?" and try to express that.' But isn't that what any television director will do? 'No, I think most directors say, here are the words . . . I think what directing is about, at its most rudimentary, which is what television is, is the blocking, which I think is really underrated in terms of understanding what a director does: where are people physically in relation to each other, when do they move and how, and how is the camera expressing those relationships? When are you in a close-up, and when are you in a close-up on a 20mm lens, and when with a 75mm lens, when are you in a two-shot, who's looking at who, when, and what are you seeing?' Lipstadt likes doing things which are 'stylish but which speak to what the show is about and in an interesting way, in order to avoid the conventional; so much television is conventional that you value what's new and different.' The television norm is to do master shots and then lots of coverage for each scene, so that, to a large extent, scenes can be assembled in the cutting room. Directors like Lipstadt prefer to decide how a scene would play and shoot only what is needed, without providing much coverage, but 'some shows don't like the directors to be too stylish because it gives them less freedom in the cutting after the directors have gone.'

According to Lipstadt, 'The best shows hire directors who they have confidence in and say, go ahead and do what you do, because we like it and that is the kind of show we want to do.' Inevitably, this is most likely to happen with the pilot for a new show, or in its first episodes. Tim Hunter has directed episodes of *Falcon Crest* and *Twin Peaks*, but he also directed the pilot for *Beverly Hills 90210*, which he described, before its massive success was clear, as 'a very middle-of-the-road high-school show, but one where I thought the characters had some appeal.' Directing episodes for an established show and directing a pilot were for him very different – he does not look upon a pilot as much different from a feature, apart from the special pressure on the director: 'There's enormous pressure on you from the network and the producers because there's so much at stake; if it sells it could mean millions of dollars in weekly instalments to

Photograph: shooting the Miami Vice *episode* Payback, *with Aaron Lipstadt (centre) directing Don Johnson (left) and Frank Zappa (right).*

these people. Really there's no pressure on a television episode beyond sticking to the schedule.' The pilot itself is a special kind of category: 'It's a strange kind of hybrid: it has to stand up on its own and yet it's the template for a whole series. They hire you to establish a style and a look and a tone for the thing, and yet at the same time they put enormous pressure on you. There's a lot of confusion over what people want and what they think will sell. Television is not a director's medium, yet they count on a director – in a pilot especially – to put the thing over and make them all rich for the rest of their lives.'

To avoid the traffic-cop situation, many directors prefer to make pilots or the early episodes of a new show, as Rob Cohen has done. Cohen directed the pilot for Dan Pyne's criminal law show, *The Antagonists* (1991), and Lipstadt produced the series which followed. It can often be some time between the making of the pilot and the ordering of the series – six months in the case of *The Antagonists* – and first episodes can differ sharply from the pilot, sometimes because the network may dislike the pilot but want the show and will thus expect to change things. In such a case, the first episode will need to do some of the same things as a pilot. As Lipstadt puts it from the director's point of view, 'A producer may have no clue about what look is being sought, or may have particular ideas, but yet be willing to concede that the director's ideas are right.' In addition, since pilots are shot entirely separately from the series, there is very often a new crew and even actors.

Though first episodes are more prestigious and offer greater latitude for creative intervention, there are also more potential problems: Cohen talks about 'centering the crew and style' at this point. Lipstadt respected Cohen's work on the pilot of *The Antagonists* but intuited that some of the ambivalence of the network related to the choices of stylisation. As producer, Lipstadt needed to shift the style for the series, making it a little more 'in with the characters' and trying to get a lot of movement on long lenses. As Lipstadt knows from his experience as a television director, 'the bad shows are the ones that don't care what it looks like and just want to do what's easy. They always give you convincing arguments, like "hey, you want to move to this location, but the time you spend moving is time you could be shooting," and to some extent you've got to weigh up, is it better to have the time on the set, or have the better set?' As he concedes, he has made the mistake of opting for the better set, but then shooting in such a way that it has not made much difference.

By common consent, television, and particularly episodic television, is a producers' medium, and perhaps to some extent a writers' medium, rather than a directors' medium. When Mark Frost wanted to know the film business he apprenticed himself to John Schlesinger, a director; when he had earlier wanted to know about the television business, he apprenticed himself to *Hill Street Blues* producer Steven Bochco. Lipstadt believes that 'a show won't succeed on the basis of one or two well-directed episodes, but on the basis of the concept and the casting, which is what the producer does.' According to Mann, 'It's a producer's medium: the producer calls all the shots, deciding the look of the show, casting the show, etc., normally the functions of a director on a movie, because it has to stay consistent.'

Mann's vital contributions as executive producer on *Miami Vice* are not in doubt, but there has been some disagreement about the conceptual origins of the show. It was by chance that Mann became involved in a television pilot, then called *Gold Coast*, written by former *Hill Street Blues* writer and supervising producer Anthony Yerkovich, who claims that much of the central idea of the series – location, characters, use of music – was already in the script that had been put to NBC and Universal, well before Mann was involved. There is no doubt at all about Mann's impact on the first season of the show (1984-85), or indeed about his continuing influence over the next four seasons.

It is typical that once the format of a show is established the producer can move back from such close involvement: during the second year of *Miami Vice*, Mann was directing his feature *Manhunter* (released 1987); during the third year, he was producing his new television series, *Crime Story*, devoting about eighty per cent of his time to it and only some twenty per cent to *Miami Vice*. Mann reflects that as a television series producer he gets some of the same kinds of satisfaction that he gains from directing and producing a feature, but certainly not all, because the producer is not working on the episodes in detail: 'You don't get that deep involvement in a given story . . . and one year of successful *Miami Vice* episodes doesn't mean as much to me as one day's good writing.' On the other hand, 'You're impacting on a culture every week in a very dynamic way. It's very quick – a terrific work-out in terms of the fluidity in coming up with story ideas. That part of it is great – you're very directly designing every aspect of the way it's impacting on audiences.' The bad part is that 'there's too much other crap on your mind, there are a lot of business headaches, which to me is like being a janitor: everything is going fine, and then someone reports that the plumbing on the fourteenth floor is out and needs fixing.' Mann recalls as 'enervating' the various battles, for example, to try to figure out how to do episodes of *Crime Story*, material which he really loved and was committed to, for $100,000 less per episode (which he says he was finally unable to do). After the success of *Miami Vice*, produced for Universal, and *Crime Story*, produced for New World Television, Mann was in a strong position in television. 'After that I did not want to do any more work in television in which I was working for a studio – I wanted to own the negatives myself and be my own boss,' and this is how his subsequent work for television *(Drug Wars* in particular) has been produced.

Rob Cohen sees clashes or tensions between directors, who are used to being the leading and decisive voice in features, and episodic television producer-writers, who feel they are in charge, as almost inevitable (which is why he prefers to do pilots or early episodes). Bobby Roth was one of a number of feature directors engaged by Michael Mann for *Miami Vice* and directed one of the early episodes (he says he would never work on a show in its later stages). Roth had been a friend of Mann's, and he became involved because Mann would come by and look at Roth working on *Heartbreakers* and talk about his new series. Roth remembers that *Miami Vice* never had a finished script – because Mann liked to change things at the last moment – and that he had freedom to shoot as he wished, but then what he had done was cut beyond recognition. Roth, however, feels that this was only right, because Mann knew what he wanted, and Roth had not shot with the same vision as Mann's. Roth, for example, had made an episode quite humorous and he remembers that, although Mann laughed, the comic elements did not survive in the cutting room.

Acknowledging that in episodic television the producer rules, Roth remembers that his later experience directing for Mann's *Crime Story* (the seventh and eighth episodes), was very different: he feels that on *Miami Vice* he somehow resisted what he was being asked for, and it did not work out, while on *Crime Story* he 'went with the flow and got in touch with Mann's vision,' and it worked out well. He cites other reasons, too – having an unambitious cameraman on *Miami Vice* but a very fast one, who allowed him to 'really direct again', on *Crime Story*, for example, or the fact that *Miami Vice* was centred on big stars, while *Crime Story* was very much an ensemble show. When Aaron Lipstadt directed his two episodes of *Miami Vice* (he was hired because Mann had seen *Android* in London, when he was working on *The Keep*), the show had already been on for a year and was hugely popular and publicised. He remembers that what an associate producer told new directors about the use of colour and the overall look of the show was therefore largely redundant: Lipstadt already knew the show and shared its thinking about its look. He also remembers being told that it was a producer's show – 'the kind of stuff you say to intimidate people.'

It is not at all surprising that film-makers like Roth and Lipstadt, who think of themselves as directors, should want to become series producer-directors in television, for the possibility of creating the style of the show, rather than having to fit into an established style. Roth's experience as executive producer and director on his own show, *The Insiders*, was not very good; he did not even enjoy directing it, mainly because his (Universal) crew was so slow, the slowest he had ever worked with. It is clear that the organisation of shows varies considerably, and that good organisation makes it more possible for all involved to do good work: Tim Hunter recalls that *Twin Peaks* was very well organised.

When Lipstadt came on to *The Antagonists* as producer, the pilot had already been made, the principal roles had been cast and the look of setting and costumes established, but for the episodes there was a new crew and new sets and some changes were made to the look of the pilot. Lipstadt was involved in choosing directors for episodes, directing some himself, and in getting scripts into shape, which was much more than he had ever undertaken in his television work before and meant that he was directing material on which he had had a real input. 'Most directors,' says Lipstadt, 'acknowledge they're working for a producer and trying to do their job, recognising that it's not their creation, and if someone can tell you what they want in a precise way, then you can respond in a precise way . . . the biggest flaw in television is that there are competent directors who can tell a story but who have no attitude about what they are doing – it's very conventional and you feel anybody could have done it.' The problem is how to find directors with personality and attitude who can nevertheless fit in with and be comfortable with the overall look and approach of a show.

The Antagonists was a good experience for Lipstadt, 'primarily because I had a good working relationship with Dan Pyne, the show's creator,' though the show did not survive beyond one season (1990-91). Lipstadt, too, agrees that television is a producer's medium, but mainly because producers are very often also writers, as Pyne is: 'writing is valued more than directing – scripts are valued more than anything a director can bring to the scripts.' Joe Dante agrees on the importance of the producer-writer emphasis: on *Eerie, Indiana,* he was 'creative consultant', but this did not mean much more than general involvement and seeing episodes other than those he directed – 'It's not my show, the final decisions are theirs.'

Mark Frost remembers that on *Hill Street Blues*, Steven Bochco enjoyed relative freedom from the network's demands, because of his reputation, and shielded the show, especially

Still: left to right, Joe Spano, Michael Warren and Charles Haid in Hill Street Blues.

from the third season (the first full one, 1982-83), during which Frost also directed an episode. It is, however, well documented that the network did succeed in making the series more conventional in both look and narrative patterning than was implied by the pilot. Frost nevertheless recalls a 'liberating atmosphere': the formula and the characters were there but there was some freedom in the kinds of story that could be told, and the increasing number of characters also expanded the range of stories possible. The typical experience, though, of people in episodic television – producers and writers rather than directors because directors would generally not be so lengthily involved – is that after three or four seasons, they begin to feel restricted and worn down by what Frost calls 'the long haul of the daily grind of a series'. This is also why a producer like Michael Mann will step back from day-by-day supervision once the format has been established; even so, although he thinks the network and the studio would have gone on for another year of *Miami Vice*, Mann and, he says, star Don Johnson, felt that five years was enough. As Mann himself says, he was in many ways the 'wonder boy' of television in the 1980s, and his success gave him considerable power in Hollywood to pursue his own plans, for both features and television (even though, for example, he did a pilot for a series that did not get taken up – *LA Takedown*, 1989, a police story set in a rarely seen contemporary Los Angeles: 'there's a whole city out there that nobody seems to shoot').

Twin Peaks did not run so long, being cancelled after two seasons, although it did lead instead to the spin-off 'prequel' feature. Mark Frost and David Lynch had been brought together some years before by their agents as a writer-director pair that might work well, and several ideas had been pursued by them but came to nothing. As a television project, *Twin Peaks* combined Lynch's cultural cachet and Frost's knowledge and experience of the television business (where Lynch had none). While Frost and Lynch 'noodled the idea around', they kept expecting the studio to stop the project, given its nature, and they were surprised to be allowed to go on with it. 'All of a sudden,' Frost recalls, 'the network, ABC, was saying, we'll let you do basically whatever you want. That was what I'd insisted upon if I was going to go back and do television – the process is too debilitating otherwise.' As many commentators and ordinary viewers have observed, *Twin Peaks*, so consciously pushing at the boundaries of the medium, is a

Still: Dennis Farina in Crime Story.

surprising series to have come out of network television. Frost and Lynch were surprised too. In retrospect, Frost understands that it was 'the product of a particular moment in time that a network was willing to be that open, and that moment may not come again.' At the time, the networks' audience share was free-falling as cable gained ground rapidly, and one response was that maybe television should be more experimental and take more chances. So *Twin Peaks* became something of a test case; would the networks open up and welcome innovation? Sadly, Frost thinks, they turned their backs on this possibility. Frost's partnership with Lynch in Lynch/Frost Productions came to an amicable end in 1992, with Frost likely to be more television-oriented in the future and Lynch likely to be concerned more with theatrical features.

Twin Peaks was another show that adopted a conscious strategy of attracting quality directors, a lot of whom would probably not have worked on other television shows – people like Tim Hunter, Caleb Deschanel, Diane Keaton and Steve Gyllenhall – and encouraging experiment. But *Twin Peaks* was still a network television series, and some of the paradoxes remained. The vision of the show was that of the producers, yet they invited strong personalities to become involved and wanted them to do good work. Frost says that 'for the most part, they were left alone' and the idea was to give directors 'complete freedom'. Nevertheless, as producer and writer, Frost had the dominant creative input, even if he and Lynch wanted the show to be shared: during the first season (seven episodes), 'I was working very hands-on with all the directors, about the look of the show, and so on. The second year I wanted to step back and let it breathe a little bit,' but by then the show's shape and look had been well established; and whatever its aspirations, it was still tied to the same tight schedules as other shows. Tim Hunter, who enjoyed working on it and whose direction on it has been much admired, did not feel it was particularly different than being on, say, *Falcon Crest,* simply because of the schedule: 'it's the same experience when you shoot eight or nine pages a day.'

In spite of the constraints felt by directors and producers, working for television has its attractions. Michael Mann obviously enjoyed 'impacting on a culture every week' in a way that he could not through individual feature films, and claims that since the youth audience was traditionally not at home on Friday nights, when *Miami Vice* was broadcast, the show had to change the nation's habits. More precisely, though, Mann was positively interested in the possibilities which television offered. Although he got into television by accident, he then wanted to do what he could within the medium. Moving from directing his theatrical feature, *Manhunter,* to producing the television crime series *Crime Story,* he found 'the experience was of going from one piece of material that I loved doing as a director, to another piece of material that I really wanted to do as a story-teller.' The story, of the evolution of organised crime in the 1960s and 1970s, from Chicago to Las Vegas, 'that whole story was a big story to tell and I really wanted to tell it. And if you want to tell a story that long, perforce, it has to be a television series. And if you're doing series television and you want to be the story-teller, you're the executive producer – you're not the director, even of episodes.'

Mann continued his interest in this 'long-form' drama with *Drug Wars: Camarena* (1990) and *Drug Wars: The Cocaine Cartel* (1991), two television 'docu-drama' mini-series about the DEA (Drug Enforcement Agency) which, at six hours and four hours, are, in Mann's view, 'exactly as long as they should be' and not something that would have been possible in the feature film industry. Others, such as Robert Altman, have also been interested in long-form drama which only television can really contain: his series *Tanner 88,* about a presidential hopeful and political in-fighting, shot in a very improvised way over six months during actual party nomination campaigns, was an example of this interest. He has also wanted to make five two-hour films from *Tales of the South Pacific* and would love to do a 'never-ending story, a continual story', which he recognises is necessarily a television rather than a film project. John Sayles cultivates the image of a film-maker, and a fiercely independent one at that, avoiding television (though he did script the made-for-television movie, *Unnatural Causes,* about the Agent Orange controversy), yet he too has been attracted by the series form in his show for NBC, *Shannon's Deal,* which is intelligent and socially aware, as one would expect; it is about the travails of a Philadelphia lawyer coping with debt and a failed marriage. Robert DiMatteo has commented in *Film Comment* that 'the one-hour dramatic series requires broad strokes, maybe even favors them. And it's a good form for Sayles, whose ideas have sometimes seemed a little thin when stretched out on the canvas of the big screen.'

The danger for a director of being identified as a television director has diminished somewhat in recent years, with high-profile shows going out of their way to hire people associated with features rather than television. Although top-flight feature directors would not usually have been involved with such shows, those who did would not have suffered any serious loss of prestige. When Rob Cohen began working in episodic television he was, as he says, in most people's eyes a failed feature director, and he considered it better to be a working television director than a failed and unemployed feature director. Cohen appears not to be too worried about his status, preferring to generate all kinds of work, for both television and film, whether as director, producer or writer. Among others who share this view is Abel Ferrara, with his background in low-budget exploitation. He is reported as saying 'I'm not afraid to shoot anything – I'll do an episodic TV show, I'll do a soap opera. We're ready, we're just rocking, we just want to keep the show on the road. Whatever it takes, we're not hung up on our quote-unquote cult reputation.'

Joe Dante's forays into television, some episodes for the short-lived *Police Squad!*, *Amazing Stories, Twilight Zone* and, most recently, *Eerie, Indiana,* have also not hurt him as a feature director, though for slightly different reasons. Dante's feature reputation rests largely on his off-beat comic imagination and his quirky approach to popular culture; all his television work is in very much the same vein, with a slightly cultish appeal, and such work does nothing at all to hurt his feature status, any more than it hurts Spielberg's to be involved in television in such a substantial way. It would be somewhat different if Dante were making episodes of, say, *Murder, She Wrote* or *LA Law.*

Rockne O'Bannon, who struggled for a long time to get out of television writing and into feature writing and directing, considers that Mann ran considerable risks and perhaps hurt his feature reputation by going into television in such a big way and by returning to it again after *Manhunter,* so that it was some years since he had been involved with a feature. After *Drug Wars,* Mann certainly came to the conclusion that he did not want to be another Steven Bochco, that he had directed far too few features and that he must direct more. He had four scripts he wanted to do, the first being *Last of the Mohicans* (1992, for Twentieth Century-Fox), which, at $35 million, is by far his most expensive feature yet, and moves away from the contemporary, urban concerns of most of his previous film and television work. The industry will be waiting to see if Mann as feature director can find the same popular audience as Mann the television producer.

The situation for someone like Aaron Lipstadt, without Mann's prestige and without a theatrical feature since *City Limits* in 1984, is very different. Lipstadt positively did not want to become a television director, but force of circumstance has made him one in the eyes of the industry. He has consciously tried to make all the television work he has done interesting and exciting, despite scripts that were often not very good and were difficult to become committed to. He has succeeded to the degree that much of his television work has been highly regarded but, well thought of or not, television work tends not to be much noticed. A cable movie or a television movie-of-the-week would enable him to show what he could do outside the confines of episodic television. However, television movies are very often topical and issue-oriented, not the kind of material that immediately attracts him: 'The five words which give me greatest pause are "based on a true story", and that's the kind of thing they like in television movies.'

When Jonathan Kaplan was contemplating whether to make his first television movie, he 'was told not to do it. I was told I would never work again in features. But I had to make a living.' Kaplan, of course, got back into theatrical features. He sees the low prestige of making television movies as being largely because 'in television you are an employee, much more than you are executing your vision. You get there when the script is done and maybe even when several parts are cast, and you get maybe two weeks to cut – so you can't expect to have the [same] personal influence over what's going on.'

With the growth in power and prestige of pay cable during the 1980s, industry attitudes have changed. Indeed, *Variety* reports a strong feeling that the increasing willingness of producers, directors and actors associated with theatrical features to be involved with cable television projects is helping to break down the traditionally deep divide between film and television, or the big screen and the little screen. Demi Moore, for example, was reported to be planning a pet project on abortion as a cable movie, and Arnold Schwarzenegger was reported in late 1991 to be working towards his debut as a feature director with a remake of the 1946 film *Christmas in Connecticut,* with Kris Kristofferson and Dyan Cannon, for the cable network TNT, which was also planning an Alec Baldwin remake of Fritz Lang's *Fury* (1936), a remake of George Cukor's *The Women* (1939) to be directed by Diane Keaton, and a Jeff Bridges project on hunger in the United States. Stars of the stature of Cybill Shepherd, William Petersen and Kelly McGillis have also starred in recent TNT cable movies. HBO projects have included actors and directors like Robert Duvall, Laura Dern, James Garner, Barry Levinson and Richard Dreyfuss (in a movie about the Dreyfuss Affair and anti-semitism in late nineteenth-century France, *Prisoner of Honor,* 1992, which he had tried for many years to set up as a theatrical feature). While it offers directors, actors and others only a fraction of the fees they might expect to get on a theatrical feature (Schwarzenegger's fee for directing was said to be $150,000), work for cable can offer other advantages. Projects considered too uncommercial and, in some cases, too controversial, for features can often get accepted as cable projects, as the companies are anxious to attract well-known names. As cable movies are often more modest than theatrical ones, with lower budgets and shorter shooting schedules, people can become involved in more projects than if they were engaged solely in theatrical features. Finally, since cable movies are not subjected to the scrutiny of weekly box-office returns, they run little risk of being branded as failures, while a well-regarded success can help rejuvenate a sagging career.

Directors have therefore begun to look favourably towards pay cable features as not much different from theatrical movies in terms of status and as an opportunity to work on more offbeat material. Examples are two cable features that HBO has made from classic American short stories, *Women and Men* (1990) and *Women and Men 2* (1991). Both were produced by David Brown, the producer of *Jaws* and *Cocoon*. The first featured Mary McCarthy's *The Man in the Brooks Brothers Shirt*, adapted and directed by Frederic Raphael and starring Elizabeth McGovern and Beau Bridges, Dorothy Parker's *Dusk Before Fireworks*, directed by Ken Russell and starring Molly Ringwald and Peter Weller, and Ernest Hemingway's *Hills Like White Elephants*, adapted by Joan Didion and John Gregory Dunne, directed by Tony Richardson (among the last work he did before his death in 1992) and starring James Woods and Melanie Griffith. The second was culturally only slightly less prestigious, with Irwin Shaw's *Return to Kansas City*, directed by Walter Bernstein and starring Matt Dillon, Carson McCullers's *A Domestic Dilemma*, produced by Jonathan Demme, directed by Kristi Zea and starring Ray Liotta and Andie McDowell, and Henry Miller's *Mara*, directed by Mike Figgis and starring Scott Glenn and Juliette Binoche.

Such material, adult and challenging, and not readily adaptable into feature-length stories is almost as unlikely to be made into theatrical movies as to be made for network television. There is now general agreement among directors that HBO and Showtime are undertaking some adventurous projects, and that HBO is almost the only place to go now with something that is intelligent but risky. As Mick Garris points out, most studio projects are now budgeted at $25-30 million and very few take risks, whereas HBO actually wants to take risks, since its product differentiation is precisely to be different from studio projects. Rob Cohen agrees that HBO's openness to unusual and substantial ideas, often polemical or political, which would be anathema to the studios, has opened up new possibilities. He puts this down in large measure to the fact that HBO's policy is decided by one man, its president Bob Cooper, reflecting his own, and what he calculates to be his audience's taste – in much the same way as the majors were run in the era of the studio system, which Cohen contrasts with the 'pack mentality' of committee-run studios today. Since it is financed by subscriptions and accepts no advertising, HBO is free from the pressures that can be brought to bear by advertisers on content. This can give film-makers a lot of leeway in dealing with sex and violence; TNT, which is financed roughly 60 per cent by subscriber fees and 40 per cent by advertising revenue, would tend to steer clear of material with too hard an edge. Rob Cohen has been wanting to set up a project that would tell the notorious Nussbaum-Steinberg story as an 's-and-m love story', featuring frank drug use and sexuality, with the child as the innocent victim; as he says, such a project could be done only for HBO.

After *Critters 2* and scripting *Fly 2*, Mick Garris had decided 'no more movies with numbers in the title', but he found himself making *Psycho 4* as a cable movie, for Showtime. 'I probably had the same reaction to the idea of *Psycho 4* as everyone else who hasn't seen the film, "Oh, great, another one",' but Garris loved the script – it did not try to be a Hitchcock movie, but went back to Joseph Stefano as writer. Because it was a prequel as well as sequel (and because 'a little of the pressure was off' because of *Psycho 2* and *Psycho 3)*, it was a freer project, less tied to the original: 'I wouldn't have made a movie which was one I didn't want to see – that would be a horrible way to spend six months of your life.' Part of the aim was to make the film as unlike *Psycho* as possible, while remaining in some way true to its spirit. Since it was in colour, 'let's really use colour', instead of making a black-and-white film in colour. *Psycho 4* had been turned down as a theatrical project, but cable snapped it up as something with in-built publicity; as it would have no theatrical life – it would feature on Showtime cable and then go to home video – the budget, at $4 million, was lower than for a theatrical feature, but 'you don't need a hook to sell it, and since expectations are lower, the opportunity to do something unusual is higher on cable than in theatrical.' Garris says he made the film because he liked it rather than as a career move, but he recognises that the lack of any feeling of a paying audience aside, a cable movie is 'a no-lose situation: if it succeeds, good, if not, no-one worries.' As it turned out, one of the reasons that the studio picture *Stephen King's Sleepwalkers* became Garris's next project was that Stephen King had liked *Psycho 4*: 'with the incest and all, you're our guy.'

After his low-budget independent feature *Heartbreakers* in 1984, Bobby Roth fell into the cable feature world and has now made four cable movies. *Baja Oklahoma* (1988), with Lesley Anne Warren and Peter Coyote, about a small town Texas barmaid aspiring to be a songwriter, and *Dead Solid Perfect* (1988), with Randy Quaid, about the world of professional golf, were both for HBO. The other two were for Viacom's Showtime, *Rainbow Drive* (1990), a police thriller with Peter Weller, and *Keeper of the City* (1991), with Lou Gossett Jr, Peter Coyote and Anthony LaPaglia, about a cop's mission to track down a killer who is murdering Chicago's mob leaders. Viacom movies are budgeted at around $5 million, about half of which is accounted for by the transmission on Showtime cable, leaving half to be earned from foreign television and sometimes theatrical sales, and from home video. They generally have 25-day schedules, closer to those for television movies, rather than the 33 days that are usual for HBO movies. 'That difference of eight days,' says Roth, 'makes a huge difference in what you are able to do as a director.' But in preparation and post-production time, cable movies are comparable with theatrical features: directors make a larger and longer commitment – nine months each on Roth's cable movies – than they would on a television movie.

In some ways, Roth is resigned to, even embraces, the 'nice little niche' he has in cable movies, but part of him would rather be making theatrical features, mainly because of 'the fantasy of the bigger audience, but the truth is that most features don't get seen – they play for two weeks, no-one sees them and then they go to cassette.' He recognises that 95% of those who have seen *Heartbreakers* will have seen it on television or video, and that *Baja Oklahoma,* basically a cable movie though it also had a brief theatrical release, will have been seen by many more people. In industry terms, Roth's work for cable is not as visible as theatrical features would be, 'but industry perception can be a pretty overrated thing. For many years I thought that [working in theatrical features] was what I wanted, but last year I hit forty and I was at a film festival in Italy, walking with my wife, and I said, "You know, maybe I'm never going to get to make big movies." And she said, "You hate big movies, why do you care?" And it occurred to me for the first time that I'm not really that far from doing what I want. I've made nine pictures and I like five of them – that's pretty good.' While planning further cable movies for Showtime ('what they want is romantic, erotic and action'), Roth still recognises the need to get the energy up to do movies for himself and plans to do another independent movie from a script of his own. He knows that he will probably not be able to raise more than about $2 million for it, and that it is likely, in common with his other features, to be seen by more people on the little screen than on the big screen.

Cable also functions as an outlet for theatrical features that have not been released in the United States – just two examples are Dennis Hopper's *Catchfire* and Mike Hodges's *Black Rainbow* (both 1989). Showtime was reported as paying as much as $500,000 for 18 months exclusive cable rights for unreleased features with some name recognition, part of the deal being that they would not go to home video release until three months after the first Showtime cablecast. Cable (and home video) have also made it possible to show versions of films different from those released theatrically. Michael Mann has made particular use of this new freedom to re-edit his features. 'A little bit of time goes by, and with 20/20 hindsight you fix this, fix that.' Mann took 30 minutes out of the released version of *Manhunter* and put back a different 35 minutes, so that it was quite a different movie on cable; for both network and cable showings of *The Keep* he took the ending off, realised that was a mistake and has now put it back on.

The future remains unclear for dramatic filmed entertainment on television, particularly for episodic drama. This is still largely the preserve of the networks, but has also been taken up by cable, often involving prestigious figures from theatrical film: *Dream On*, for Universal, has John Landis as its executive producer, and the executive producers of *Tales from the Crypt* are Joel Silver, Robert Zemickis, Richard Donner and Walter Hill, who have all directed episodes (and the show has provided Arnold Schwarzenegger, Tom Hanks and Michael J. Fox with their first chances to direct). Episodic television remains a problematic, though still central, element for the networks.

As producer of *Twin Peaks*, Mark Frost saw the show as giving 'complete freedom' to directors: 'give them a script that had something to it and say "go make a movie." ' This is a line that Aaron Lipstadt says he has heard many times in his work for television: 'producers are fond of saying, "We're making a little movie here" and, indeed, with a good budget, the chance to mix the film on a big screen with stereo sound, and so on, directors can feel that is what they are doing. 'But when you see it on a television screen, you're not "making a little movie"; you can fool yourself for years but it doesn't look like that on television, so acknowledge that: what interests me is finding out what does work on television, how do you compose for that frame – it's not just close-ups.'

The medium is clearly different from theatrical features in the questions that it poses about dramatic narrative construction, and it is uncertain how the nature and shape of series television narratives will develop over the next few years. Although the problems of composing for the television image may change as it becomes bigger, wider and in high definition (television image quality is at present notably worse in the United States than in Europe), Lipstadt's concerns seem important ones. And the importance of aesthetic and dramatic considerations is highlighted by economics, in the shape of the continuing decline in the networks' audience share and power. The climate of increasing austerity in television production has made the one-hour episodic drama a particularly endangered species and has led networks (in a trend shared with Europe) often to prefer cheap, so-called 'reality-based' material such as game shows.

In 1988, Lipstadt took a producing credit on ten episodes of *The Street*, another show originated by Dan Pyne, with John Mankiewicz, which was shot on video, very fast, without internal scene editing. It was very cheap to do – and looked it, too, in comparison with something like *Crime Story*, but it could also be seen as simply different. The cost was about $60,000 for a thirty-minute show, or about a tenth of the cost of a typical network episode, partly because it was non-union. Because it was cheap, it could afford to take risks and was a lot of fun to do. The experience made Lipstadt think about doing television which does not try to pretend it is 'a little movie' but on the contrary 'plays to the strengths of the physical medium' and is able to be innovative. Why not make 13-episode, short-run shows with union agreements on reduced crews budgeted at the network licence fee, which is to say not on the deficit financing basis of most network shows, but for what the network will actually pay, so that there is nothing to lose? Thinking ahead to an idea for a show being developed with Pyne about two characters on the road, going from one small Texas town to another, Lipstadt asks 'If you can shoot 22 pages [of script] a night in Newark in January [on *The Street*], why can't you do nine or ten pages a day in Albany, Texas in April? Why can't you do a television show in five days, in 16mm, with hand-held masters, day exteriors and less complicated lighting, not build sets, make the show on the road for thirteen weeks at a stretch?' It's a fascinating idea, which seems to respond to both the nature of the medium and the current economics of television production, and it will be interesting to see if the networks and production companies begin to adopt such approaches and, if they don't, how they will manage to respond to the current problems of dramatic shows for television.

UNEQUAL OPPORTUNITIES: WOMEN FILM-MAKERS

Hollywood's equal opportunities record is by general consent not very good. It is not necessarily worse than that of other major industries, but very few other industries are so constantly in the public eye, and the media have a crucial ideological role in the propagation of images of gender and race. For this reason, as well as for all the other reasons of natural justice which would apply in any other context, the movie industry has been a very visible fortress to be breached both for women and for black and other ethnic minority film-makers (black film-makers have been the most visible ethnic group to break through in the last twenty years, but it is clear that the demands of Hispanic film-makers will be being made with increasing urgency over the next decade).

For women, the 1970s and 1980s have seen significant – and now surely irreversible – changes in the numbers and status of women in the film industry. But, as elsewhere, their rise has been limited by the 'glass ceiling' syndrome: although women are present in significant numbers in middle management, 'natural' bias in male-dominated organisations and family responsibilities in which women still take the major role mean that very few make it through to the top echelons of power, and women directors are very aware of this.

Amy Heckerling, whose work (most prominently *Fast Times at Ridgemont High,* 1982, *Look Who's Talking,* 1989, and *Look Who's Talking Too,* 1990) has been entirely within the studios, observes that 'I've been finding that a lot of the women I really enjoy working with seem to get to a certain point and then men get promoted over them much more easily, and I find that discouraging.' Heckerling concedes that this is clearly not a problem exclusive to the movie industry, and adds that the worst person she ever had to deal with in show business was a woman.

Joan Micklin Silver began as a feature director with independent pictures like *Hester Street* (1975) and *Between the Lines* (1977), before working with or close to the studios on *Head over Heels* (a.k.a. *Chilly Scenes of Winter,* 1979), *Crossing Delancey* (1988), *Loverboy* (1989) and *Big Girls Don't Cry . . . They Get Even* (1992, retitled *Stepkids* in Britain). She points out that 'Women are in high places but very few women are in the places you have to be to greenlight a movie. There's always one person at the top who can say yes, and, in almost every case, it's a man.' One case where it was not a man was that of *Desperately Seeking Susan* (1985), produced by Midge Sanford and Sarah Pillsbury and directed by Susan Seidelman. Barbara Boyle, formerly Roger Corman's lawyer at New World, and by the mid 1980s a vice-president at Orion, had liked Seidelman's independently-made first feature, *Smithereens* (1982) and took to the screenplay for *Desperately Seeking Susan.* Seidelman remembers that it 'was the kind of project which a lot of women who were vice-presidents of development had responded to – women tended to like the script. And then they would show it to their male bosses who didn't like it enough to give it the go-ahead. For a brief period of time, there was a little window in which Barbara Boyle at Orion was given the opportunity to develop and give the go-ahead to movies which could be made for $5 million or under, and *Susan* was one of the projects which fell into that category. Luck and good timing play a huge part in so many people's lives. It was chance that at this one studio, this one woman was given the power.'

In fact, in the 1970s and 1980s, there have been one or two other instances of women in – mostly short-lived – positions of executive power at the major studios, most noticeably Sherry Lansing, who was briefly head of production at Fox in 1981-82 (and was later the producer on such projects as Jonathan Kaplan's *The Accused*, 1988) and more recently Dawn Steel, the only woman undisputedly in charge of a major studio: she was brought in to replace David Puttnam at Columbia, only to be ousted when Sony bought Columbia and brought in Peter Guber and Jon Peters to run it. Neither Lansing nor Steel showed much sign of encouraging women film-makers during their tenures, and it would have been amazing if they had. Steel is generally recognised as having brought Columbia back to its mainstream commercial senses after what was seen as the aberration of the Puttnam regime.

Women have been much more prominent as producers. After *Desperately Seeking Susan*, the Sanford-Pillsbury team went on to produce independent features like Tim Hunter's *River's Edge* (1987) and John Sayles's *Eight Men Out* (1988), as well as features for the majors like Jonathan Kaplan's *Immediate Family* (1989). Debra Hill, who was co-writer and producer on much of John Carpenter's late 1970s/early 1980s work, including *Halloween*, *The Fog* and *Escape from New York*, later produced such movies as David Cronenberg's *The Dead Zone* (1983). Like Hill, Gale Anne Hurd has been involved with action-oriented and genre pictures: after learning the production ropes at Corman's New World on, among other pictures, *Battle Beyond the Stars*, she went on to produce James Cameron's major pictures in the 1980s, *The Terminator* (1984), *Aliens* (1986) and *The Abyss* (1989), when Cameron was respectively her boyfriend, husband and ex-husband. She was also involved in the production of other movies, such as *Alien Nation* (1988).

Women have long played important creative roles as writers and editors and have done many more technical jobs in production, but until very recently, the rarity of women directors has been very striking, particularly in view of the pressure from the women's movement for equal opportunity in all fields. Although women have sometimes had a high profile in independent and avant-garde film (the most obvious example being Maya Deren's experimental work in the 1940s, right on Hollywood's doorstep), women film directors within the mainstream industry have been so rare as to be freakish. Before the studio system was firmly established, when film production was a little more loosely organised, it was perhaps marginally easier for women to work creatively in the industry. As in other fields, feminist critics and historians have worked to recover a suppressed

Stills. Left: John Travolta and Kirstie Alley in Look Who's Talking. *Right: Rosanna Arquette and Madonna in* Desperately Seeking Susan.

history, pointing to the work of Alice Guy, active in France in the late 1890s and around the turn of the century and then in the United States from around 1910 to 1920, and of Lois Weber, who worked as a director from 1911 to 1934. During the period of the studio system, the only significant woman director was Dorothy Arzner, who worked at several major studios between the late 1920s and the early 1940s, often on reasonably prestigious projects with major stars like Katharine Hepburn, Joan Crawford, Merle Oberon, Rosalind Russell and Claudette Colbert. Although Ida Lupino began as a star in the studio system (at Warner Brothers), her work as a director was mainly on a series of films made between 1949 and 1953 (though she directed her last film in 1966), on subjects considered daring at the time, including rape (*Outrage*, 1950), unmarried mothers (*Not Wanted*, 1949) and bigamy (*The Bigamist*, 1953). These were relatively small-scale productions made for her own independent production companies at the time when the major studios' divorcements had begun and independent production was growing.

This minimal participation of women in movie-directing began to increase slightly in the 1970s. Elaine May, with a background of acting, writing and performing, and, in particular, a long comedy partnership with Mike Nichols, made three features in the 1970s – two very off-beat comedies, *A New Leaf* (1971, starring herself) and *The Heart-break Kid* (1972), then *Mikey and Nicky* (1976). But other women were working more independently in the 1970s: among them was Joan Micklin Silver who moved from directing educational films and writing to make her first features, *Hester Street* and *Between the Lines*. Barbara Loden, also from an acting background and the wife of Elia Kazan, made a remarkable, very low-budget feature in 16mm blown up to 35mm, *Wanda* (1970), starring herself as an alienated, semi-destitute woman cast adrift.

This was also a period in which Hollywood made a lot of 'women's pictures', movies that consciously tried to address some of the questions raised by the women's movement, such as women's independence in relation to family and career, women's sexuality, women's friendship and solidarity. These were pictures like *Alice Doesn't Live Here Anymore* (1974), *An Unmarried Woman* (1977), *Julia* (1977), *The Turning Point* (1977), *Girlfriends* (1978), *Norma Rae* (1979), *Looking for Mr Goodbar* (1977), *Old Boyfriends* (1978) and *Lipstick* (1976). There was another group of pictures that began to imagine women as active protagonists in generic, action situations, like *Coma* (1977), *Alien* (1979) and *Gloria* (1980). In only two cases were these films directed by women: Claudia Weill's *Girlfriends* began life as a documentary, was transmuted into a fictional short and became a low-budget feature only when it was picked up for distribution by Warner. Joan Tewkesbury, who directed *Old Boyfriends*, had been an associate of Robert Altman, scripting *Thieves Like Us* and *Nashville*. *Girlfriends* was successful enough to win Weill a big-budget film with Columbia, *It's My Turn* (1980).

Neither Weill nor Tewkesbury has subsequently been prominent in features, although Weill has worked in television. Joan Micklin Silver's first studio feature, *Chilly Scenes of Winter*, also made at this time, ran into problems with the studio, United Artists, which changed both the ending and the title (to *Head Over Heels*); the film was re-released in 1982 by UA Classics with its original title and ending. Then the sense that women were at last beginning to direct movies abruptly disappeared. Around this time, Amy Heckerling was just beginning to develop scripts with the studios: 'When I started in development, there were a number of women working and it looked like it was all starting. There were suddenly a lot more women than there had been before. When I was in film school [New York University in the mid 1970s, then as a fellow in the American Film Institute's directing programme], there was only Elaine May that I knew of. So it seemed like there would be this whole slew of women and it would start, and it kind of didn't.'

As the 1980s progressed, however, a growing number of women, from a wide range of backgrounds and working on a variety of projects, have become established in feature film production. Among them are performers like Penny Marshall, Jodie Foster, Sondra Locke and Barbra Streisand, film school graduates like Amy Heckerling, Susan Seidelman

Still: Keanu Reeves and Patrick Swayze in Point Break.

and Marisa Silver (one of Joan Micklin Silver's daughters) and women with backgrounds in exploitation movies like Amy Jones, Penelope Spheeris and Martha Coolidge (though even earlier, Coolidge had worked in radical documentary), as well as in theatre and television (Randa Haines), documentary (Joyce Chopra) and art (Kathryn Bigelow). In the early 1990s, there seems little doubt that attitudes to gender in the industry have changed, but it will be some time yet before the depth and permanence of the changes can be properly assessed.

Mary Lambert is one director who objects to the label of 'women director', as a 'sexist idea – I resent being called a woman director: you don't call a man a "man director". I do a job which should be genderless in its classification.' Kathryn Bigelow agrees: 'I don't think of film-making as a gender-related occupation or skill. I think a film-maker is a film-maker. Nobody talks about "man directors" as constituting a group.' While such objections are fundamentally valid, looking at women directors as a group is useful, for example, in pointing to institutionalised disadvantage and discrimination.

Both Bigelow and Lambert have worked in genres like action and horror that have often been characterised as masculine, and both are relative newcomers to big features; they have therefore worked in a climate in which prejudice may have diminished. But being labelled a 'woman director' can still severely restrict the kind of material a film-maker gets a chance to work with. Martha Coolidge admires directors like Bigelow who refuse to fit the mould and make what might be considered typical women's films: 'Look at *Point Break,* for instance. Kathryn Bigelow is proving that women can do action. What's hard is that women are not considered for most of the jobs, that people still think, I can't have a woman direct this, it's too macho, too big budget, too much action, too much this or too much that.'

In the normal way that Hollywood works, it was perhaps inevitable that after the big success of *Fast Times at Ridgemont High* (1982), an ensemble teen comedy set around school and shopping mall, Heckerling should have been offered lots more projects about preppies and girls losing their virginity, but other directors' accounts make it seem that this kind of material was considered by the studios as suitable for all women directors, even for someone like Randa Haines whose early work in television *(Hill Street Blues* and other shows) was in a very different area. This can have its bad effects, even if directors can afford to turn the offers down. Heckerling looked for something different and 'unfortunately, I was looking to be too different'. The result was *Johnny Dangerously*

(1984), a comic 1930s-style gangster movie: 'As a woman, I wasn't doing a movie about a girl losing her virginity, I was doing something with a lot of male stars running around with guns, with beautiful deco sets and a cast of people I loved [among them Michael Keaton, Jo Piscopo, Marilu Henner, Peter Boyle and Griffin Dunne]. If you grew up watching movies, it's the kind of stuff you want to do. I've since then formed a theory about what went wrong. If you remember the 'thirties and you're on drugs, it's the perfect movie to watch, but there aren't that many stoned people that remember the 'thirties, so it was doomed to failure.' Though not expensive to make (it was shot on the revamped sets of Mel Brooks's *To Be Or Not To Be)* and not a massive failure commercially, Heckerling thought 'Uh, uh, I'm in trouble, I've got to do something quick, so I went off to Europe [to make *National Lampoon's European Vacation,* 1985] without a script . . . It was living hell.'

Penelope Spheeris struggled hard and for many years on low-budget independent pictures before achieving huge box-office success with the studio picture *Wayne's World* (1992): 'Until you have a box-office hit, you are not a viable commodity. But now I am, and things have changed a great deal. The problem is, after working for twenty years on some pretty serious, hard-edged pictures, I do one comedy and now I am only being given offers to do comedies.'

Penny Marshall starred in the television show *Laverne and Shirley,* a spin-off from *Happy Days* and similarly produced by Marshall's brother Gary Marshall, who went on to direct *Pretty Woman* and *Frankie and Johnny.* She also directed some episodes – the offer to direct is a common ploy (though not perhaps where the star is the producer's brother) to encourage stars to renew commitments to long-running shows – and she directed a television pilot. She was brought in on *Jumpin' Jack Flash* (1986) some two weeks into production: 'I called my brother and I called Jim Brooks [also a successful television producer who had made the transition to theatrical features] and said whaddya think. And my brother said, "They pay you to learn, straaange business." And Jim said, "You have nothing to lose: if it doesn't do good it's not your fault, you didn't start it, and if

Still: Phillip Kimbrough and Tina L'Hotsky in The Loveless.

you complete it, you've done good." ' Having made a success of this first feature and then making a resounding success of *Big* (1988), Marshall was hot property and could have made almost anything she wanted, but took on the serious drama of *Awakenings* (1991) almost in order to prove to herself that she was really a comedy director.

Kathryn Bigelow's work, though so far extending to only four features, has been recognised as important by other women directors: *The Loveless* (1981, co-directed with Monty Montgomery) is a biker movie and *Near Dark* (1987) Bigelow calls a 'vampire western'; both have elements of pastiche but both are definitely action genre pictures, as were *Blue Steel* (1990), a vigilante cop picture with Jamie Lee Curtis as protagonist, and *Point Break* (1991), a male bonding, cop and heist movie set in the world of surfing, which Bigelow refers to as a kind of 'wet western'. Bigelow argues that 'fantasies of power are universal' and counts among her cinematic mentors Walter Hill, Samuel Fuller, Sam Peckinpah, Sergio Leone and Martin Scorsese (though also Kenneth Anger). Bigelow: 'Conventionally, hardware pictures, action-oriented, have been male-dominated, and more emotional kind of material has been women's domain. That's breaking down. This notion that there's a woman's aesthetic, a woman's eye, is really debilitating. It ghettoises women. The fact that so many women are working as directors now and not exhibiting specific types of material – they're working across the spectrum, from comedy to horror to action – I think in itself is incredibly positive . . . You're asking the [Hollywood] community to reprogramme their thinking, to re-wire their brains. [Women] should just be encouraged to work in an as uncompromised form as possible, be that tougher or softer.'

For there to be much progress in the range of subjects available to women, films made by women needed to achieve box-office success. The commercial successes of Marshall's *Big* and Heckerling's *Look Who's Talking*, both of which took over $100 million at the box office (*Look Who's Talking* was the most successful film ever made by a woman) are important not only for those particular directors but for all other women directors, just as the box-office disaster of Elaine May's *Ishtar* (1987), which had the biggest budget for any film undertaken by a woman, was potentially problematic for them. In a community where box-office success counts for almost everything, successful films by women are the surest way to removing any doubts attaching to women directors. As Susan Seidelman put it, 'Let's face it, Hollywood is an industry. It's about selling a product. And one of the fallacies was that they thought that a woman could maybe make a nice sensitive little movie, but they can't make anything that's going to sell. So to be able to compete on their terms is really important . . . One of the good things about *Desperately Seeking Susan* is that, regardless of whether it is a good or a bad movie, it made money, and in Hollywood that is the bottom line. The fact that a film produced, directed and written by women made money at the box-office makes it easier for that kind of arrangement to happen again.' Women directors are liable to feel that they carry a responsibility for more than their own work, and that this imposes an extra burden on them. As Randa Haines expresses it, 'Every woman working maybe even still today feels that she's carrying an added responsibility, that every time a woman succeeds at doing something, it opens the door a little bit further for everybody else, and if you fail, it closes the door just that little bit. So in addition to all your own terrible fears and nightmares of failure, you've got that, too, you're carrying this race of people.'

Most women film-makers feel to some degree that they are participating in an activity whose terms and conditions seem predominantly male, particularly in the all-important process of setting movies up. Producer Gale Anne Hurd talks of 'the boys-only club' and Susan Seidelman of the industry being 'a bit of a boys' club', while Amy Jones talks of the 'game' being 'very male'; all have experienced a kind of exclusion. As Martha Coolidge put it, 'If I were a man, I would have been directing major features long before this, but what's the point of dwelling on it?' Penelope Spheeris, with her background, since the mid 1970s, of making television, rock promos, documentaries and low-budget independent features, puts it a little differently: 'As a film director, I have to work

Still: Jamie Lee Curtis in Blue Steel.

harder because of being a woman, but that's OK: I'm lasting longer. The guys I went to UCLA with, their careers have peaked and are on the downward slope by now. My way was more frustrating in the beginning, more gratifying in the end . . . This is something of a redemption, you know, that I finally have a successful picture [*Wayne's World*]. It's beeen a rough ride. A person with less tenacity would have quit a long time ago but I won't be defeated. I have to keep going and prove I can do it.'

Some have argued that the industry has begun to recognise its forms of discrimination. Thus Paramount president Ned Tanen thought that when *Children of a Lesser God* won 1986 Oscar nominations for best movie and best actors but not for best director for Randa Haines, 'that pushed a lot of buttons in the community about women really being – it's an unspoken law, but – second class citizens.' When Kathryn Bigelow talks about the heroine of *Blue Steel*, she could very easily be describing the experiences of women film-makers in the industry and in some ways what she says makes more sense in relation to film-making than to what happens in the movie itself: 'The thinking was that you had a woman in an otherwise male-dominated world fighting for a voice and during the course of the picture she has to fight two hundred or five hundred per cent of herself just to be taken seriously at all. So it really is a woman in a role that you had previously seen a man in and in an environment having to fight very much. The result is you see this woman who is incredibly capable, incredibly strong. Yet in order to succeed she does not have to become a man. She can be incredibly capable, incredibly strong, incredibly tough, and still be vulnerable and be a woman. Her strength of will carries her through.' Maggie Greenwald, director of an adaptation of Jim Thompson's tough crime novel *The Kill-Off* (1989) adds, 'Women can't go on making generous films . . . Audiences have found it refreshing to see a strong film by a woman.'

Sondra Locke's route to directing was in some ways very particular: she had a lot of experience as an actor, most notably in movies like *The Gauntlet* (1977), *The Outlaw Josey Wales* (1976) and *Every Which Way But Loose* (1978) with Clint Eastwood, whose partner in private life she also was, before she started directing, but in other ways her experience echoes that of many other women. 'There's no doubt that being a woman makes it much more difficult. It's hard enough for anybody, because it's just an impossible industry, so frustrating, so arbitrary, such a roll of the dice. I used to think that what makes it so difficult as a woman was the large amounts of money involved and some idea that women are irresponsible with money, but in most households it's the women who do the book-keeping. So much of what makes it more difficult for women is that – probably like a lot of businesses, but maybe it's more so with the movies – it is a 'club'. People do business with the people they're hanging out with, and it's a tit-for-tat kind of thing, so much about contacts and connections and who do you know who can get you this and who owes you a favour, and so on. That's the way a lot of deals get made, on the tennis court. And they're mostly men, and women don't really hang out with them. Women are just not in the running in that way of doing business, because we just don't have those kinds of relationships with the men. Either there just aren't enough of us or we just don't have the same kind of buddy system. So you're going in at a disadvantage. And unfortunately the relationships that women do have with men can so often actually hurt as much as they can help. I'm a prime example. My relationship with Clint certainly helped a lot in my having the opportunity to be around a fully operating production company [Eastwood's Malpaso Company] for many years, so that was a good learning ground. But as "Clint's woman", or whatever, I wasn't really taken seriously, so it helped on the one hand and took away on the other hand, in establishing myself as a serious separate identity . . . *Impulse* [1990] has helped in that people say, "Well, I guess she's determined to do this after all," so maybe I'm wearing them down a little bit. They say, "It got some good reviews, and she did an OK job as director," so I'm getting a little more attention paid to me, but nobody's rushing to hire me for their next movie.'

Part of the problem for women may be that the dominant image of the director and what the director does is a very conservative one, an old-fashioned idea of the director as, in Seidelman's words, drill sergeant (though as Locke says, 'I firmly believe that most executives in this town don't have the vaguest idea of what a director does or what his or her contribution is.') Maggie Greenwald has felt that many have seen the process of direction as a military operation that only a man could lead. The favoured language of male directors and executives, who talk in western or sporting metaphors of directors as being 'guns for hire', big hit movies as 'home runs' and moderate successes as 'base hits', tend to sustain such images. Certainly some women, Mary Lambert for one, have found that, as in society at large, men can find it hard to accept women as authority figures: 'A lot of men . . . don't like to take orders from a woman.'

Both Lambert and Greenwald felt that this was a particular problem on the set, where the director needed to give direct orders, but that it was probably easier for producers, more off the set. This was certainly not the experience of Gale Anne Hurd who reported that when she went to Britain to produce *Aliens* in 1985-86, 'A couple of top crew members said: "I cannot take orders from a woman." I was told that no woman had ever produced a film at Pinewood in its fifty-year history. I don't know if they were having me on, but it was quite a shock.' Not that there is anything peculiarly British about this – Hurd has reported that when she started her career at New World, 'Roger [Corman] gave me this naive idealism that this was an industry with no barriers to sex or age. Initially, when I went to the studios after Roger, I got a lot of "How can a little girl like you expect to do a big movie like this?" '

When Joan Micklin Silver talked about 'flagrant sexism' in the movie industry in the 1970s, the implication was that the situation had changed, but this is far from clear. A Columbia-TriStar spokesman, commented, officially, on anticipated problems between Debra Winger and Madonna on Penny Marshall's *A League of Their Own* (1992), on which Winger was later replaced by Geena Davis: 'Penny Marshall is sweet, but she's a lightweight. She never has her picture figured out when she directs. She just figures it all out in post-production. Would you want to put her together with Debra Winger and Madonna? That's how the guys at Columbia saw it – women are frail and have to be treated with kid gloves, except the bitches. Penny Marshall might survive with one shark in the tank, but with two?' Even allowing for the fact that Marshall herself concedes that she spends little time in detailed preparation of shooting and sees her strength as working with actors, it is difficult to imagine such comments being made so unashamedly about a commercially successful male director working on a prestige picture for the spokesman's own studio. Sexism is not confined to the industry itself; Penelope Spheeris remarked that being referred to as middle-aged by a critic was probably not something a male director would expect (even if the context was the youth movie *Wayne's World*).

Many women film-makers make a distinction between attitudes to them in the industry as a whole and attitudes to them when they are actually working on the set of a film. Recalling the shooting of *Desperately Seeking Susan*, Susan Seidelman recalls that 'there wasn't any prejudice, but there were odd looks. When I first came on the set I'm sure they thought it was kind of weird that a) I was a woman, b) at that time I was only about thirty and c) I was five feet tall. I know for a fact that they didn't think I was the director until a few days in.' She remembers that some technicians would take her for an assistant and ask her for cups of coffee, 'but after a while, if they feel you know what you're doing, they do respect you; it takes a little longer because you have to prove yourself. But I love crews – that's the fun stuff. To be honest, the hardest part of making the movie was working with one actress – and it wasn't Madonna' (Seidelman had some problems with the other woman lead, Rosanna Arquette).

Randa Haines's experience is very similar: 'I think that I made some kind of an unconscious decision early to not think about sexism and in fact to put blinders on, because it must have been around me and must have been present in some of those crews. When I did *Hill Street Blues*, it was very rare for a woman to work on what was a very male show, but I can't say I remember a single instance where any negative thing happened that I would attribute to that. Either I'm simply naive and stupid or I really did shut it out, or it didn't happen – but that's a little hard to believe when I hear the stories that everyone else tells. I think it helped a lot that I came from a crew background [as a script supervisor in theatre]. I know what the crew needs from a director: I know they need to feel safe, that you've done your homework, you're not going to abuse their time. I know the jokes – they're like family to me, so I was never intimidated.' And as Amy Heckerling, who also derives the most fun in movie-making from working with crews, points out, 'People often talk as if there's a bunch of gorillas out there with mechanical stuff, but if you've hung out on a film set, it's not really like that.' Actors are of both sexes, the script people are usually women, the art department and the beauty people are integrated – 'you've got a lot of men and women running around.'

Several women film-makers have thought of themselves as 'feminists', but there is a strong sense that feminism has become much less an overt issue for both film-makers and the companies producing their films than it was in the late 1970s and early 1980s. Martha Coolidge, after training as an actor, working in Canadian television and going to New York University film school, made a series of independent, generally very personal, documentaries in the 1970s, of which *Not A Pretty Picture* (1975), a semi-autobiographical film about rape, became very well known and admired in the women's movement. It was perhaps not surprising, then, that the producer of her hugely successful teen comedy, *Valley Girl* (1982), Atlantic Releasing, 'was worried I was a feminist . . . Although my point of view is feminist-influenced, my films aren't political pictures – and certainly Hollywood is not interested in making political pictures. Nor are the studios interested in dealing with an obnoxiously political person. Or anybody who would be abrasive in any way.' Discussing her 1983 picture *Love Letters*, Amy Jones observed, 'I'm a feminist, but I don't think it's a feminist film in the sense that the heroine gets a gun and kills the guy who has done her wrong. It's feminist in that it's rare to have a film that's entirely about a woman, and an experience that's very female, and which treats her and her

Photograph (left): Susan Seidelman during the shooting of Desperately Seeking Susan. *Still (right): Roseanne Barr in* She-Devil.

female friends as worthy of sustaining an entire movie, focusing on her relationship with her mother as opposed to some guy's relationship with his father or friends for the hundredth time.'

If feminism as a burning issue has faded somewhat, the more general question of whether particular kinds of subject matter are favoured by women, or whether there is a distinctive woman's point of view, is still very much debated. As Susan Seidelman puts it, 'The films I'm interested in making come out of the fact that I'm a woman. [Although] there are more women directing movies . . . I do feel a little bit out on an island by myself, because not only am I a woman who wants to direct movies, but I'm a woman who directs movies with very strong female subject matter. All my films have a strong female protagonist, and I've always tried to show the women from an insider's point of view as opposed to an outsider's point of view. There are other women who are directing more genre stuff or stories where there are male and female protagonists.' Seidelman feels that, for her, finding the right subject matter is perhaps the hardest part: 'If I wanted to direct teen comedies or horror movies, I think it would be a lot easier . . . I could be directing neutral movies, movies where you can't tell whether the director is a man or woman – but without wanting to be moralistic about it, I'd rather make movies from a feminine point of view.'

When women film-makers talk about their films, there is often a strong sense of obligation to wider issues about the representation of women. Thus, Martha Coolidge on *Rambling Rose* (1991), set in the South during the Depression and dealing with the sexual frictions that are stirred up when a poor young girl, played by Laura Dern, comes to live with a family: 'A man might really have simplified the women in this movie and cast Rose as a bimbo. I felt that I was sympathetic to the male point of view but I was also the guardian of those women.' One of the reasons that Seidelman adapted Fay Wheldon's novel *The Life and Loves of a She-Devil* into her 1989 movie *She-Devil* was that she was 'intrigued by the whole idea of female revenge – especially a dumpy housewife's revenge not just on her husband but on a whole world which presents beauty as the ideal we are supposed to aspire to.' Seidelman's sympathies were such that she even changed the ending: 'I liked the idea of a dumpy heroine who says, "Fuck this, I'm going to get even" and I didn't want to kill her off.'

Working with genre material like the crime story of *Impulse*, Sondra Locke found a different kind of problem: 'What really challenged me was the love story and the woman,'

Still: Phoebe Cates and Jennifer Jason Leigh in Fast Times at Ridgemont High.

but this was a commercial crime picture with a lot of plot about gangs and drugs and arresting people and getting them to court on time which 'didn't really interest me, and it was difficult to keep that alive and simple enough so you don't have to spend time on it.' Locke feels that if there are differences between men and women directors, it could well be in their choice of material; her own favoured material would have 'a bitter-sweet quality and an edge. I don't like things too lyrical, and you have to be very careful of those as a woman.' She also feels that her love of layering things and of detail may also be a gender difference: 'Gender has to make a difference. I'd say the majority of male directors have a sparser attack on things. I don't know if it comes out of being Sondra or being a woman, but I'm interested in a tremendous amount of detail and I love to load and layer things.'

Randa Haines is also very uncertain: 'People always say to me, is there a woman's point of view, or a woman's style, and I honestly don't know. People say that they can see something in my work that they would say has to do with my being a woman as opposed to being a man. I don't know. I don't think consciously about that . . . I think it's only when we've seen a whole body of work by women that we will really be able to say. But as a woman you do perhaps identify with certain characters and you say, "I'm not going to make every woman in this film a mindless bimbo" and, "Yes, you do have a responsibility to all your characters." ' Haines's two theatrical features, *Children of a Lesser God* (1988) and *The Doctor* (1991), centre on male characters, both played by William Hurt, although the deaf female protagonist of *Children of a Lesser God* was one with whom Haines strongly identified; she sees the common thread in the three characters as 'the isolation, the difficulty of communicating, the person who looks on the surface to be someone who really gets along and is very verbal, but is really not speaking, not connecting, is afraid of intimacy.' Both films feature central characters whose attitudes and assumptions, very male in many ways, are challenged by female characters (Marlee Matlin's deaf woman in *Children of a Lesser God,* Elizabeth Perkins's character, dying of cancer, in *The Doctor)* reconciled to adversity and disadvantage. As directors always emphasise, the problem is to find material that they have a commitment to, rather than to find material with particular 'women's themes'.

One area where women directors' sensibility almost inevitably finds itself challenged is in the representation of sex and female nudity. Given the kinds of film Hollywood makes, and in particular the kinds of film young directors, women included, find themselves making, this is an issue that cannot be avoided. Thus, on Coolidge's *Valley Girl,* 'They said there had to be skin in four scenes . . . I said fine, as long as I can do it in my own way.' Similarly, Amy Jones had to do a women's changing room shower scene in *Slumber Party Massacre* and just 'did it as straight as possible'. *Love Letters,* also made for Roger Corman, who, as before, imposed nudity requirements, posed different problems because this was much less an exploitation picture and much more personal a project for Jones: 'In the modern age, when two people meet, they go to bed . . . People learn about each other in bed rather than before. In my film, Anna and Oliver's relationship is based on sexual passion, which is ephemeral. They haven't got that much to talk about, so their relationship only takes place in bed . . . I like the sex scenes because I think they're at least different and interesting and very brief. I did not like the nudity where Anna and Oliver are just standing around the house, or she's in the tub – I find that a little gratuitous. There are only two scenes like that, but those were required by Roger, and we did them as discreetly as possible.'

Amy Heckerling says that she has never felt she should do anything because it might be expected of her as a woman, but 'just one thing. In *Fast Times* as a woman I felt that I'd always been seeing movies where there are love and sex scenes and men take off their shirts and reveal basically nothing and women are buck naked and you could say exploited. Not that I want to say we should all look at naked men, but I wanted to show a sex scene with these two teenagers and make it very awkward and uncomfortable, to say that this first time it was not this romantic, beautiful thing, it was scary. And, to me, scary for a teenage girl would be the jarring sight of the naked boy. So I had the girl take off her bathing suit and you saw her breasts, but you didn't see anything else. I wasn't going to show her stark naked, but I was going to show him stark naked. The rating board wanted to give us an X because of that one scene. There was no way the studio could allow it to be an X, so we had to take the shot and blow it up, so I wound up having to do exactly what I had always seen in movies – a man's shoulders and a woman's breasts. I felt bad about that and, in fact, there were reviews that asked how

Stills. Left: William Hurt and Marlee Matlin in Children of a Lesser God. *Right: William Hurt and Elizabeth Perkins in* The Doctor.

could I, as a woman, do that. And my mother said, "I'm going to write to them and tell them," so I said, "No, Ma, forget about it . . ." That was the one example where as a woman I would like to have done something differently.'

Whatever the differences between women directors' perceptions and experiences of the industry and men's, in many fundamental ways, those experiences and perceptions are very similar and shaped by the same forces. Gender does not greatly affect the experience of yourself making a studio movie with a union crew for the first time. Amy Heckerling: 'I remember the first shot very vividly, because it was first thing Monday morning, and we were going to shoot a drive-by of a car before the actresses were ready. All the amazing possibilities of what a drive-by can be suddenly presented themselves. This was just a girl standing on a corner, she looks and sees a car go by, but how big should the car be, how long should we follow the car before it's out of sight, should the car leave frame or should we move with it? There just seemed too many choices and they all meant [such] different things. Somehow, the shot was over and then, you know, you just keep going. But that was the one which was, like aaah . . . It's like that first jump into the water, and then you swim.' Although being an actor had helped to prepare her for what happened on set, Sondra Locke's first experience of directing was complicated by the fact that she was starring in *Ratboy* as well. 'It was terrifying. The only thing that made it easier – the one sensible thing I did – was that I used the camera crew I had worked with as an actress many times, so I had a relationship with them already and that took some of the edge off the terror, but it was still a very scary thing. One of the good things about being an actress, as a director, is that you can go on the set and act like you know what you're doing, even though you don't.'

Women's and men's career routes to directing have naturally followed rather similar courses, quite often through exploitation pictures. With its appeal to the fantasies of a predominantly male audience, exploitation does not seem like an arena in which women could feel comfortable working. Roger Corman's New World, at least, did offer a reasonably congenial environment for women film-makers, much of which appears to have been due to Corman's attitude to them. Gale Anne Hurd's view was that Corman 'is and always has been, without question, a great champion of women in film . . . When I left Roger, I thought all of Hollywood was going to be like that, that women would be given opportunities and even considered better candidates for the job than most men. I think Roger prefers to work with women. I never even realised sexism existed in Hollywood until I got outside of New World.' Certainly, Corman's willingness as an employer to treat men and women equally meant that several women started out in exploitation and were able to use its requirements and conventions to their advantage.

Although Stephanie Rothman, with producer, co-writer and husband Charles Swartz, had made exploitation material before *(It's a Bikini World,* 1966), her work with Corman combined a feminist sensibility with the requirements of exploitation genres: *Student Nurses* (1970) incorporated issues of abortion, drugs and politics, while *The Velvet Vampire* (1971) was a female vampire movie which reversed the usual plot of woman as victim. Role reversal was also crucial to Rothman's later *Terminal Island* (1973, known in Britain as *Knucklemen),* a violent action picture (not made for Corman but dealing in the same generic material) in which imprisoned women revolt against a cruel system and set up an alternative society. Despite some other interesting films *(Group Marriage,* 1972, and *The Working Girls,* 1974) and an attempt to set up her own production company, Rothman did not continue to make movies. This also appears to be true of writer-director Barbara Peters, who made three films for Corman: *Bury Me An Angel* (1971) was a biker movie with a revenge-obsessed female protagonist; the title of *Summer School Teachers* (1975) is more or less self-explanatory; *Humanoids from the Deep* (1980, UK title: *Monster)* was one of a long line of Corman 'monster from the deep' pictures, which despite – according to *Variety* – 'more nudity and gore than carried by any exploitation film in recent memory' also attempted to play at times with gender identification and

Still: S.L. Baird and Sondra Locke in Ratboy.

camera point-of-view. What Amy Jones liked in *Slumber Party Massacre* was the 'subtext of a slasher movie from the point of view of the women.' Whether such films can actually meet the requirements of exploitation and yet at the same time work against them and turn them back on their typical audience is hard to judge, though the attempts can certainly be of great interest.

Most women did not work in such areas by choice. As Amy Jones succinctly put it: 'If women only made films with no sex and no violence in them, women wouldn't be making films.' Jones saw *Slumber Party Massacre* simply as a way of making a first feature, and *Love Letters,* despite some lingering exploitation elements, showed very clearly that her real interest lay elsewhere. Women's work in exploitation nevertheless raised questions about what kinds of subject matter might be appropriate to women long before they were raised by the work of someone like Kathryn Bigelow. So, for example, Joan Freeman, who made *Streetwalkin'* (1984), a tough urban thriller about prostitution and violence, for Corman, asked, 'Why is there this myth that women are incapable of making strong movies? A women's perspective on an exploitation movie can actually inform the audience in a different way – give them the format they know, then say different things. And why should women only make films about home baking? In some ways, being a woman, it's more dangerous to make a soft, sexy film because it typecasts you from the start.'

Penelope Spheeris's early fiction features, chilling explorations of alienated youth, *Surburbia* (1983) and *The Boys Next Door* (1985), made for New World after Corman had sold the company, also join in this debate, although Spheeris rejects the 'exploitation' label: 'Just because they're about roughneck teenagers doesn't mean that my films are exploitation. So were *The Outsiders* and *Rumblefish.* Exploitation films have nothing to say about the human condition and I always take responsibility for my films' moral statements.' Spheeris thinks that the uncompromising subject matter of her films contributed to her difficulties, as a woman, in getting her films financed: 'I believe one reason I have been held at arm's length in the business is that my films have always expressed a certain amount of brutality and anger, and that scares men. They don't want to see women dealing with such emotions.'

Television has figured in the learning experiences of many women directors. Randa Haines went from a long period as a script supervisor in theatre into the Directing

Workshop for Women at the American Film Institute – not a course, but a conscious attempt by the AFI to encourage women who were already professionals in the industry, like Anne Bancroft and Dyan Cannon (among whom Haines figured she was 'the token unknown'), by providing a little money and equipment so that they could show what they could do. She then made two films for public television, one of which, in the 'American Short Story' series, she used as her calling card to get into features. 'I would go to all these meetings and people would see the short story film and say "We think you're wonderful, we love you, we can't wait to work with you," and then nothing would happen. So I began to understand that the process was not about each meeting, it was about the totality of all the meetings and all the people you meet, and all the putting out of who you are, that will some day come back in some form. I tried to understand that I was never going to leave a meeting with something having happened. It would never be a tangible thing like that. That was a hard thing to grasp.'

She realised that she needed more to show and more experience before she could expect people to come to her with their projects. She did four episodes of *Hill Street Blues* during its second, third and fourth seasons (1981-82, 1982-83 and 1983-84), and later directed some other shows. The challenge of fitting into a format 'can be really good if it's something of quality, and even if it isn't. There's a good learning challenge in looking at something that has its own particular style and asking, "How is that style achieved, and how can I adapt myself into that style and yet bring my own strengths to it, yet not try to take it over and turn it into something else?" Especially if you're working with good material like that.' However, as well as the risk of being typed in the industry as an episodic director, television can be a trap in other ways: 'First of all, you can fall in love with making a lot of money. Second, you can get into some bad habits. The good aspect of it is that you have to think on your feet, make decisions very quickly. You may often walk on to a set and have to shoot something when you've never seen the location before. It's a great learning experience. Within seven or eight days of shooting, you may have a love scene, a car crash, a rainstorm, all crammed into one little hour. You learn to trust your instincts because you have to work so fast that's all you've really got.'

It was then a very different kind of experience to direct the television movie *Something About Amelia* (1983), about incest (Haines thought it had needed 'a real leap of faith to decide to tackle the issue at all'), which came to her from one of those people who had said, years before, 'We love you, we can't wait to work with you.' Here there was a much more important role for the director than in episodic television, not least because of the importance of the performances. Although, as Haines says, more people saw it than saw *Terminator 2*, television success hardly counts in film terms because it does not count in money at the box-office; there's 'still a brick wall between those two worlds', even if less now than in the early 1980s. Though offered lots of other television movies, as well as some routine theatrical movies, Haines chose – and was able financially – to gamble, turn down projects and wait, until *Children of a Lesser God* came up, though she 'thought at the time that this will probably be one of those prestigious development deals that never gets made.'

Amy Heckerling's experience of television came after she had made three theatrical features, before which, she, too, had experienced the vagaries of the system. 'Right after film school, I showed a short film I had made, went in, pitched an idea, had a deal [with Warner]. So I thought, that's easy. So I struggled with the script, and was very confused over who to try to please, the studio or the producer. I didn't know what that was all about – different executives and everybody having different opinions, and thinking that you did something because it's what you want, but it's also to please the people that you think will make the decisions, and finding out that other people make the decisions. Then it went into turnaround and was picked up by Universal, where there was a very similar situation of writing it for some executives and those not being the ones who say yes or no actually. It went into turnaround again, got picked up by MGM and

I wrote another draft, by which time I was pretty tired of writing this same thing, and yet I was very attached to it. Each draft takes a long time – handing it in, waiting for notes, waiting for someone to say what they think. Ultimately it was a go picture at MGM. We built all the sets, got all the locations, the casting was found, the costumes were being made, and the actors' strike happened. It's another situation where I don't know really what happened, why my movie was chopped as opposed to any other. I heard they had a similar project, *Rich and Famous,* that they picked up after my movie and because bigger stars were attached to that they decided to let mine go. I'll never know what really happened. All I know is that I had to call up over a hundred people and tell them they were out of a job. Then it was picked up by Columbia. During the time I was writing at Columbia, the executive, who I thought was our executive there, became no longer our executive there without even telling me, so I was little confused by this time. Years seem to have gone by . . .'

This is a not untypical tale of 'development hell', and *Fast Times at Ridgemont High* came from elsewhere, from contacts made at Universal. Heckerling's experience of television came after the disappointment of *Johnny Dangerously* and the bad experience of *National Lampoon's European Vacation:* after Europe, she got pregnant and had a baby and meanwhile, without her involvement, Universal had got network commitment to a television show spin-off from *Fast Times at Ridgemont High.* Heckerling came in, rewrote the pilot script, cast it and shot it: 'I enjoyed working on it so much, especially compared to how miserable I was on *European Vacation,* that I thought, I love this, I just want to do this. You get up in the morning, you know who your actors are, you run around the school, you shoot a show, you meanwhile rush over and mix the other week's show and you've got to come up with the idea for the last week's show. You're doing everything at once. It's not like our careers are dependent on the box office. A great experience, a lot of fun.' Heckerling was not, like Haines on *Hill Street Blues,* just a director for hire, and she would have been similarly in control of a series spun off from *Look Who's Talking* had the movie not been such a surprise success – it had in fact been on the shelf for some months for lack of studio faith in it. While she was editing it, Heckerling had told the studio they should make it into a television show, but there was no enthusiasm. When it became a hit, they wanted the show, but then decided they wanted the sequel instead, and since everyone by now was pitching baby shows to the networks, the sequel had to be made very fast ('I wanted to do the sequel – I liked the people I'd

Photographs. Left: Randa Haines on the set of Children of a Lesser God. *Right: Amy Heckerling directing* Judge Reinhold *in* Fast Times at Ridgemont High.

worked with, and I was into babies, but I didn't want to do it that quickly. It was "beat the clock", and that stinks'). As a result, Heckerling was not involved in the television show – except in trying to sue the producers.

Regardless of the director's gender, the process of setting up big-budget studio pictures and getting them made can be very debilitating. Against this, working for television or returning to one's origins in low, or lower, budget film-making can be revitalising. Like such other graduates from New York University film school as Jim Jarmusch, Spike Lee and the Coen brothers, Susan Seidelman set out to work independently rather than knocking on Hollywood doors and rising through the ranks, or working in episodic television. She pulled together a crew of fourteen or fifteen people from those she had worked with on her student films (on which crews were more likely to be seven or eight) and found a budget, in dribs and drabs, of about $80,000, to shoot, much in the style of a student film, *Smithereens* (1982), about a working-class, punk young woman who comes to the squalor of the Lower East Side to try to make her fortune. 'We had to do everything, but I enjoyed the communal aspects of that kind of "guerrilla" film-making.'

Knowing nothing about film distribution or film festivals, and more out of ignorance and naivety than design, she managed to get the Cannes film festival organisers interested in it, and success at Cannes brought recognition and distribution both in the United States and abroad. Good reviews meant that she got an agent and scripts started to come to her and, as 'that month's new flavour', she had lots of meetings with independent producers and development people at the studios: 'I had tons of lunches.' Some money from the distribution of *Smithereens* and some development money meant that she could take her time and be cautious. Having in mind the career of someone like Claudia Weill, who moved from the low-budget New York independent film *Girlfriends* to the big-budget studio picture *It's My Turn* and then nothing (in theatrical features, at least), Seidelman commented at the time, 'Of course, to start with, I was scared to death of Hollywood. A lot of independent film-makers get caught up in the studio system and then lose everything that was interesting about them as independents. Or else they flop, and then they never work again. So I had a hell of a lot riding on this movie.'

Desperately Seeking Susan, a script which had been around for some time, was one of the things she was sent. She liked it and felt it connected well with her earlier work, so it would be 'a comfortable leap to make.' In her first real experience of the film business, Seidelman discovered that you needed a sense of humour: 'I found the process bizarre, going from studio to studio, pitching the same idea over and over again, trying to find the terms in which to tell the story that people could relate to – "Well, sort of *Diner* mixed with *Saturday Night Fever*", or whatever. On that level it was kind of absurd. I do find it a humiliating process. You walk in and there are vice-presidents who are playing with wind-up toys as they listen to your story. I think if you take it all too seriously, you can go crazy.' Now, four big films later, Seidelman reflects that she still has not learned how to do it, but as her last few projects have been with Orion – by common consent the most director-friendly of the studios – she has not really had to. At the time of *Desperately Seeking Susan,* Seidelman commented that, 'At first I really had a problem with the notion of working for a studio. I thought about studio execs hanging around the set, telling me what to do. But they've been wonderful. We sent them the dailies, and they didn't interfere. If you want to do something offbeat, I think Orion are the best people to work for.'

Desperately Seeking Susan was budgeted at about $5 million, but the great difference from the budget of *Smithereens* was not too intimidating, partly because 'in some ways, it was more of a New York independent movie than a Hollywood film.' Seidelman chose a director of photography, Ed Lachman, who 'wasn't a slick Hollywood guy – he'd worked on a lot of European movies [like Wim Wenders's] and had also come out of the independent film world.' 'If I feel like I'm working on material I understand, I'm not afraid. Making a low-budget movie in a world I'm not comfortable with, that would be intimidating. I felt I knew the world and these characters, and I had made

Still: Laurie Metcalf and John Malkovich in Making Mr Right.

one more movie than the producers, so I didn't feel I was working with an overbearing producer. If I'd been working with Joel Silver, I would have been scared to death, but working with Midge and Sarah, we were all inexperienced. Maybe the fact that they were also women made it easier for me.'

Seidelman's next three pictures rose dramatically in budget, with *Making Mr Right* (1987), a science-fiction/screwball comedy mix following the complications which ensue when a 'male' robot falls in love, shot with a stylised 1950s look, costing $10 million, *Cookie* (1989), a screwball satire on Mafia movies, $15 million, and *She-Devil* (1990), from Fay Wheldon's novel, $17 million. *Making Mr Right* and *She-Devil* were part of a deal with Orion which gave them first look at projects developed by Seidelman herself; *Cookie*, made by Lorimar, was a project brought to her. One of the results of the increasingly large scale of the pictures was increasing pressure: 'The thing about your

Still: Susan Berman in Smithereens.

first studio movie is that there are no expectations, no-one's looking at you. No-one expects anything from you, and then if it's good, people embrace it. *Desperately Seeking Susan* was a sleeper. When you're doing a movie with much higher visibility, like *She-Devil*, the expectations are higher and the criticism is higher. With *Desperately Seeking Susan*, you're begging people to talk about your movie. On *She-Devil*, you're turning down covers, but when you're on the cover of *Premiere* magazine, people expect a certain thing. It's always much nicer to be a surprise than be a disappointment.' During the actual making of a picture, the pressure of expectations must often necessarily be pushed into the background: 'You're aware that you're working on a high-profile movie, but on the other hand, the day-to-day stuff – it's raining, or the sun's about to go down and how are you going to get the shot in the can – takes over. Once the ball starts rolling, it's such an all-consuming process that you're really worried about very concrete things – how to get the actors on the set, what time to do the lunch break, is there going to be a meal penalty? You're just worried about getting the next shot done.'

There are things in her last two pictures which Seidelman likes and thinks work well, but she has doubts about them and the context in which they were produced. (They were in fact done virtually at the same time: the pre-production on *She-Devil* was done before *Cookie*, and they used the same production office and virtually the same crew – 'you kind of felt you were on a roll . . . We just sort of slid from *Cookie* to *She-Devil*,' though she would have preferred a break). She likes the father-daughter stuff in *Cookie* but (like Sondra Locke's feelings about *Impulse)* likes the second half less, 'when the plot takes over,' and 'it wasn't the most personal of my movies.' Had she known about the BBC Television mini-series adaptation of *The Life and Loves of a She-Devil*, she would probably not have attempted to film it: 'To me, that was the biggest thing that hurt the movie. The mini-series was wonderful, but it was also eight hours long and did a lot of things you can do with the BBC that you can't do in America. I thought I was taking this unknown little novel that no-one had ever heard of and that I could borrow ideas from and turn into something else. I think had it been based on an original script, it would have been judged very differently.'

The relatively indifferent performance of both movies, both critically and commercially, has caused Seidelman to reflect more profoundly on the process of film-making than she has since *Smithereens*. She has never been a 'director for hire' and has mostly generated her own material. 'What I've learned after *Cookie* and *She-Devil* is that I am questioning the kinds of thing that interest me, and have become interested in doing things on a scale that I feel more comfortable with. As you go along, you begin to see where your strengths are. And I'm not a slick director who can take anything and do something with it. What I realise is that I'm not a great studio director, nor do I particularly aspire to be one. The weird thing is that when I was making *She-Devil*, I thought it was going to be a bizarre feminist film, not mainstream at all. But somehow it became mainstream and I think that was the problem. I don't blame that on the studio, I blame it on me, really. As much as I'd like not to think it, I do think that the more people you have involved, things weigh down a little bit.'

Seidelman feels that independent film-making has more energy and that her own films have had less energy as they have got bigger. 'When you're doing something like *Smithereens*, if you want to do a shot in the subway, you take three people, stick a camera in a suitcase, run out to the subway and do it. With *Cookie*, you have to rent the special filming subway, you spend two days putting up the lights, you spend another day putting up artificial graffiti that can be washed off, you spend an awful lot of money getting the right kinds of extras to look like subway people, whereas you go into the real subway and they're there. There is something energising about guerrilla-style film-making, and I do feel that *Cookie* and *She-Devil* were big productions. I actually think as a film-maker I am more of a street person.' Earlier, echoing the feelings of a number of other film-makers, including Jonathan Demme and Spike Lee, she was quoted as saying 'I've rejected the idea of working in Hollywood. It's like being on Valium. You can float away for a while, but I don't feel real there, whereas New York keeps you down to earth. Simply by living there, it ends up in your movies somehow.'

Seidelman does not argue that all movies should be low-budget, and she points to directors like Woody Allen and Martin Scorsese as being able to work creatively with the risks involved in bigger budgets, 'What I'd like to do is get back in touch a little with the more personal side of what I think made my stuff interesting in the *Smithereen* days and the things that excited me as a film-maker.' Accordingly, Seidelman opted for trying to make a low-budget (though at a hoped-for $6 or 8 million, not that low) independent movie, 'something set in New Jersey and New York, with younger characters.' So far, this project has not been realised. Seidelman feels she has not been helped in her endeavour by what she perceives as a polarisation in film production and the lack of middle-ground movies: 'Right now there are big blockbusters or there are quirky little art movies like David Lynch's.' More recently, Seidelman has divided her energies between two very different projects. *Confessions of a Suburban Girl* (1992) is a fifty-minute documentary – commissioned by BBC Scotland – in which she goes back to meet the girlfriends she grew up with in suburban Philadelphia, and she is trying to set up – with largely European finance – a $12-15 million feature project with Diana Keaton, about a dying middle-aged woman returning to Paris to seek out her former lover.

This perceived lack of opportunity for middle-ground films is of concern to many film-makers, but may be felt particularly by women. Certainly, Sondra Locke recognises the same problem: 'What I hope more than anything is that the business will turn away from such enormous budgets and give all kinds of directors opportunities to make smaller, more interesting films that will maybe never command the same kind of box-office, but then they won't cost that much either, so we can have a wider, more eclectic range of films.' The difficulty of setting up smaller, more personal films sometimes makes directors like Locke 'long for the good old days when you could maybe just go over to Republic Pictures and get a job as a director, and just make movies.'

For all the common ground between men and women directors, some differences of emphasis in their experience of the industry remain and perhaps in the way they talk

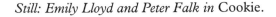

Still: Emily Lloyd and Peter Falk in Cookie.

about the process of directing itself. Susan Seidelman, for example, argues that she doesn't like directing enough to want to direct other people's material: 'I direct because there's a story or way I see the world that I want to try to get on screen, but the act of directing itself is not one I find particularly pleasurable in and of itself.' Randa Haines 'just began to feel this desire to use all the parts of myself. I remember the first job I had directing – the first three days I got back to my room at night and said, "Why am I doing this, why would anyone want to do this? It's horrible." And then, on the fourth day, it suddenly clicked and I realised why I wanted to do this: it was because I felt that everything I'd ever experienced or had even been interested in or good at was needed. As a child, I had a very strong imagination and suddenly I felt that all those things I'd ever cared about or knew about – drawing and making things and dance and movement – were being tapped. It wasn't about power or control. I think I had always felt as a person clogged up until then, as if I'd always been looking at the world and taking things in. Now all the stuff that I had taken in could come out of me in some form, in story-telling. And I felt the beginning of a kind of flow inside myself that I had never felt before.'

Having come to directing from acting, Sondra Locke feels that one of her strengths is with actors: 'We immediately feel a camaraderie and feel secure together, you can speak their language. As a director, one of the greatest things you can do for actors is for them to trust you, so that they're not constantly editing themselves. I really don't know how a lot of directors do it. A lot of directors think actors are aliens and they can't talk to them. They get them in and hope they do the right thing, and directing is all about the shots.' Though she is no longer actively looking for parts, she feels somehow that her career as an actor is somehow 'unfinished', and 'one of the things I like least about directing is that most of the people I really admire are other directors, so I won't get to work with them if I'm directing.' Despite feeling lost half the time on her first picture as a director and still thinking that 'you're always floundering to some degree,' Locke feels a strong affinity for directing, which she compares to her experience on her first picture as a performer: 'It was like the way I felt when I walked on to the set for the first time on *The Heart Is a Lonely Hunter* [directed by Robert Ellis Miller, 1968] as an actress. I came from a small town in Tennessee, I'd never been near Hollywood, I'd never been on a movie set, I could only imagine how it was done, and yet I felt instantly at home with all the equipment and the insane, fractured way it's shot. When I was directing for the first time, too, I felt that same sense of recognition of something that just feels right.'

Still: Sondra Locke on the set of Ratboy.

UNEQUAL OPPORTUNITIES: BLACK FILM-MAKERS

Because the 1980s and early 1990s saw a speedy and much-publicised growth in the number of black as well as of women film-makers in Hollywood, it is tempting to see the two phenomena as essentially parts of an opening out of the industry to previously under-represented groups. Certainly, black struggles in the 1960s and 1970s for greater equality, like the women's struggles which followed them, can be held partly responsible for a general change in social awareness that certainly filtered through to the movie industry as it did to other industries and social spheres. Certainly also, much of the struggle to gain access to the movie industry was motivated by the desire of black film-makers to have greater control over the images of black life propagated by the media. Images of blacks and black life, like images of women, were not lacking in Hollywood films; it was the generally limited and negative nature of those images that demanded change.

At the same time, there are some crucial differences between the histories of women and of blacks in their relationships to the movie industry (leaving aside the fact that taking blacks as a group appears to ignore any gender struggles within black culture itself). Although women had been very largely excluded from certain roles in the industry – whether as executives or as directors – they were, unlike blacks, employed in great numbers in the industry in other, generally more minor roles, but reached prominence only as actors and, perhaps, writers. Although women's struggles against discrimination and against limiting and negative representations have a long history, they were not widespread or widely formalised until the 1960s, whereas one of the early campaigns of the NAACP (National Association for the Advancement of Colored People) was in 1916, shortly after its formation, against the racist stereotypes of *The Birth of a Nation*. While the vast majority of women – publicly, at least – more or less willingly went along with, or at least did not openly challenge, their representation in Hollywood movies for most of the movie industry's history, the same cannot be said of black people. In the movie industry itself, women stars clearly did fight against some of the roles in which they were cast, but the struggles of Paul Robeson were clearly of a different, and much more public, order (he was pursued in the late 1940s for un-American activities and sympathies, and his passport was revoked by the State Department in 1950).

Given the relative powerlessness of the black population in American society as a whole, and their representation by stereotypes in Hollywood movies, it is perhaps not surprising that from an early date blacks made their own films. An early example was *The Birth of a Race* or *Lincoln's Dream* (1919), Emmett J. Scott's explicit riposte to *The Birth of a Nation*. During the 1920s and 1930s, there was a lively black movie business, with both its production and distribution centred in the industrial cities of the North, reflecting the rapid growth of black ghetto communities during the 1920s. Just as 'race' records were black music produced for black consumers, so 'race' films, fictions and newsreels, as Jim Pines has put it, 'were concerned primarily with depicting black life from "the black point of view",' making them very different from the all-black (at the time called 'All-Negro') productions made by Hollywood, from *Hearts in Dixie* and *Hallelujah!* (both early sound films dating from 1929) to *The Green Pastures* (1936) and *Cabin in the Sky* (1943). Some of the race film production companies were black-owned, like

George and Noble Johnson's Lincoln Motion Picture Company, formed in 1916, Colored Featured Photo Plays, Inc., formed in 1921, Million Dollar Productions, formed in the 1930s, and, perhaps the best-known and most distinguished, the Oscar Micheaux Company of New York, founded in 1918 and based in Harlem (Micheaux's *Body and Soul*, 1924, provided Paul Robeson's first film role). Others were white-owned, like The Colored Players Film Corporation of Philadelphia, formed in 1926, or the Goldberg Brothers, active in the late 1930s and 1940s. But whether they were owned by blacks or whites, they had very little chance of competing on equal terms with the products of the Hollywood studio system, which they generally tried to emulate in style. It was, however, mainly white-owned businesses that sustained the economic viability of race films, primarily through white ownership of theatres, and as the race film industry declined through the 1930s, there was no racial (as opposed to profit) motive to sustain it.

Part of the decline was due to changing representations of blacks in Hollywood films. The NAACP called its 1942 national convention in Hollywood to demand more and different roles for blacks, and World War II itself foregrounded the place of blacks in American society as a whole, bringing many whites into a degree of contact with blacks which they would not otherwise have had. The liberal postwar period, despite anti-communist scares, produced several Hollywood 'problem pictures' about racial prejudice and discrimination, some of which, like *Pinky, Intruder in the Dust* and *Home of the Brave* (all 1949) dealt directly with blacks. This was a theme continued into the 1950s and 1960s with actors like Ruby Dee, Dorothy Dandridge, Harry Belafonte, Ossie Davis and others. Pre-eminent among them was Sidney Poitier who came to represent the archetypally dignified and mainly stoical black figure in films like *No Way Out* (1950), *A Man Is Ten Feet Tall* (1957), *The Defiant Ones* (1958), *Guess Who's Coming to Dinner* and *In the Heat of the Night* (both 1967).

The memories of Hollywood and its commentators are notoriously short, and many accounts of the origins of the current wave of black Hollywood film-makers fail to go back further than 1986, the year of Spike Lee's independently made surprise hit *She's Gotta Have It* and Robert Townsend's (also independent) *Hollywood Shuffle*. Mario Van Peebles, whose 1991 movie *New Jack City* was one of the recent crop of hit films made by black directors, sees it differently: 'I think the film-makers look at our fathers in the 'seventies as starting it all off, not Spike Lee. Spike Lee is part of our generation, and maybe he was the first one of us, but we look to Gordon Parks, Ossie Davis and my dad Melvin Van Peebles in the 'seventies beginning all this.'

Socially and politically, the civil rights campaigns of the 1960s, and the Black is Beautiful and Black Power currents that came out of them, created a climate in which new representations seemed imperative. Culturally, some sectors of black culture, in particular popular music, were increasingly 'crossing over' to white audiences (Tamla Motown was the pre-eminent example), a phenomenon with important industrial implications. In the late 1960s, Hollywood was in deep economic crisis, primarily because the American audience had shrunk dramatically, and what was left was very different from the traditional clientele for Hollywood films. One element in the crisis was, therefore, who to make films for and what kinds of film to make, which allowed room for a degree of experimentation and left market sectors which independent producers could supply – this was the moment when Roger Corman began New World.

Indeed, the primary image of the films made mostly in the early 1970s by black directors and with black stars, though for white companies, whether major studios or independents was exploitation or, as it became known, 'blaxploitation'. The film that started the cycle was Ossie Davis's *Cotton Comes to Harlem* (1970), based on the novel by black crime writer Chester Himes, and starring Godfrey Cambridge and Raymond St Jacques. The film did well at the box-office, and *Variety* estimated that seventy per cent of its rentals came from black audiences, whereas only thirty per cent of the audiences for Sidney Poitier vehicles like *In the Heat of the Night* were black. *Variety* concluded

Stills. Left: Richard Roundtree in Shaft. *Right: Jim Brown in* The Slams.

that 'it is now possible to make pictures aimed specifically for black moviegoers – and expect to make a substantial profit – without worrying too much about what the rest of the public will think.' This was the commercial basis for the glut in the following years of violent blaxploitation films like *Shaft* (1971), with Richard Roundtree, *Shaft's Big Score* (1972), *Slaughter* and *Black Gunn* (both 1972, with Jim Brown, who was also in *The Slams*, 1973), *Cleopatra Jones, Cool Breeze, Blacula, Superfly* (all 1972), *Truck Turner* (1974, with Isaac Hayes), and many others. Only a very few of these pictures involved blacks as directors: Ossie Davis on *Cotton*, Gordon Parks on *Shaft* and *Shaft's Big Score*, Gordon Parks Jr on *Superfly*. Generally, they were white-made films aimed at mainly urban, male black audiences. Thus, Jonathan Kaplan, who had started off making exploitation pictures like *Night Call Nurses* and *Student Teachers* for Corman's New World, moved to MGM and AIP to make *The Slams* and *Truck Turner*. The opportunistic nature of such productions is made clear by Kaplan's account of *Truck Turner*: it 'was written for Lee Marvin or Robert Mitchum or Ernest Borgnine. Larry Gordon at AIP said, "Well, we can't get any of them, so it's a black picture." Isaac Hayes was cast, and that's how it came about.'

Many other black-oriented films in this same period were aimed at white as well as black audiences. Among them were Martin Ritt's *Sounder* (1972), a story about black sharecroppers in the Depression South and John Berry's *Claudine* (1974), a comedy about a black family on welfare. Berry Gordy Jr, chief of Motown, made a series of quite costly films designed to bring Motown music megastar Diana Ross to general cinema audiences: *Lady Sings the Blues* (1972), *Mahogany* (1975) and *The Wiz* (1978). The concentrated burst of black-oriented pictures in the early 1970s helped to establish the economic importance of the black sector of the audience, though movies aiming to 'cross over' rather than going purely for a black audience became most characteristic. A wider range of roles became available for black actors to play (even if some were new stereotypes, as in the case of *Shaft* and its successors), and it was possible for there to be black stars, such as Bill Cosby, Richard Pryor and, later, Eddie Murphy, with images very different from Sidney Poitier's. Outside the cinema, a parallel development was the astonishing success of the 1977 mini-series *Roots,* from Alex Haley's novel, which drew an all-time record television audience of 130 million.

The principal black directors of this period, Melvin Van Peebles, Gordon Parks and Ossie Davis, related only tangentially to early 1970s 'blaxploitation'. Even though Parks directed *Shaft* and *Shaft's Big Score*, he had already made a very different kind of black film, *The Learning Tree* (1969), which was elegiac and semi-autobiographical: he was in any case an exceptional figure, having been for some twenty years one of the leading still-photographer reporters for *Life* magazine. Ossie Davis, primarily an actor, had had

Photograph: Spike Lee directing Ossie Davis in Do The Right Thing.

a long career in theatre (where black actors had found it easier than in movies to work with some dignity) and then had some film roles in the 1960s. With his wife Ruby Dee, he had been very active in civil rights causes, and in the early 1970s he formed Third World Cinema Productions, to encourage black and Puerto Rican talent: he also made two US-Nigerian co-productions, *Kongi's Harvest* (1971) and *Countdown at Kusini* (1976).

Melvin Van Peebles had little to do with the blaxploitation phase, and his background, too, was very special: he had lived in Europe, become a novelist and then directed a film (*La Permission,* or *The Story of a Three Day Pass,* 1968) in France, before being hired by Columbia in 1970 to make *Watermelon Man,* a subversive comedy that explores a wide range of racist attitudes when a middle-class, married white character (Godfrey Cambridge in whiteface) wakes up one day to find he has turned black. Van Peebles insisted that blacks should form part of the production crew for the film, raising, like Davis in a different way, the crucial question of a trained black professional cadre in the mainstream movie industry.

Neither Davis nor Van Peebles particularly endeared himself to the movie establishment. Van Peebles used his earnings from *Watermelon Man* to help finance, quite independently of Hollywood, *Sweet Sweetback's Baaadasssss Song* (1971), an openly political film about the struggle of a persecuted black figure against white racist authority, produced, directed, scored, edited and starred in by Van Peebles himself. There were great problems in getting it shown, but it made a good profit from black audiences. As Van Peebles and subsequently others have recognised, it was important to show that this sort of film could succeed. As Reggie Hudlin, director of the hugely successful hip-hop movie *House Party* (1989), put it: '*Sweet Sweetback* was important not only because of its cathartic value – the main character kills a white cop and gets away with it – but because, as Van Peebles was quoted as saying, that movie made a million dollars before the first white person saw it. It was a business revolution as well as an aesthetic one.' The quotation from *Sweet Sweetback's Baaadasssss Song* in *New Jack City,* and the appearance of Melvin Van Peebles in a cameo role in his son's movie, like Spike Lee's casting of Ossie Davis (and Ruby Dee, too) in both *Do The Right Thing* (as Da Mayor) and *Jungle Fever* (as The Good Reverend Doctor Purify) express the debt that the current black film-makers feel to those of the 1970s. Another very successful black film of the 1980s, coming shortly after *She's Gotta Have It* and *Hollywood Shuffle*, Keenan Ivory Wayan's *I'm Gonna Git You Sucka* (1988) was emblematic of the time in being a splendid send-up of the violent early 1970s black films, with a clutch of the original 'superspade' performers, like Isaac Hayes and Jim Brown, brought back fifteen years on to parody themselves and definitively bury the earlier cycle.

One often gets the impression that a few black film-makers worked in the mainstream industry for a while in the early and mid 1970s and then there were none until Lee and Townsend had their surprise low-budget hits in 1986. Although the fashion, both for blaxploitation and, to a lesser degree, black directors, passed as saturation was reached and returns diminished, black film-makers continued to work and black subjects continued to be treated. Michael Schultz had a background as an actor and director in theatre, and then did some work for PBS and episodes for television shows like *Starsky and Hutch* and *The Rockford Files;* he made two commercially very successful, exuberant, music-based teen comedies, *Cooley High* (1975, for AIP, who did not know quite how to handle it, but it still grossed some $14 million from a budget of $3 million) and *Car Wash* (1976). Schultz continued to work within the industry, making generally more middle-of-the-road entertainment, usually with black subject matter: *Greased Lightning* (1977) – taken over from Melvin Van Peebles – and *Bustin' Loose* (1981) were Richard Pryor vehicles, and *Carbon Copy* (1981) was a race comedy in which Jewish George Segal copes with a black illegitimate son. Schultz's rap music movie *Krush Groove* (1985) was made in New York with a seventy-five per cent black crew: 'There was a lot of progress being made in Hollywood in terms of black involvement behind the camera, in the unions, on the crews, etc.; in New York, however, it was the same old story of not enough qualified people. I vowed to return to New York to make a film with all-black talent just to prove that these people existed.' Schultz's *Livin' Large* (1991) is about a black man from the ghetto getting caught up in the white world of television journalism. In television, Thomas Carter, who had begun as an actor, became during the 1980s one of the most prolific directors of episodes, mini-series and television movies and has directed for shows like *Fame* and *Hill Street Blues;* he was one of the most sought-after directors of pilots, with a very successful record of pilots that went on to become shows, including *Miami Vice* and *St Elsewhere*. Both his solid reputation and the current fashion for black film-makers have helped him set up his first theatrical feature, *Red Tails*, about a unit of black fighter pilots in World War II.

It is therefore not quite true to say that black film-makers went out of fashion in the mid 1970s and then came back with Spike Lee and Robert Townsend in the mid 1980s. Townsend goes even further: 'All of a sudden, here we are in the 1990s and people are suddenly talking about black film-makers, but we've been here since *Birth of a Nation.*' And yet there has been the feeling of a distinct phenomenon of new black film-makers and new black subjects, growing in pace from 1986 into the early 1990s. Initially, Spike Lee carried much of the weight, with *School Daze* (1988) and *Do The Right Thing* (1989), released by Columbia and Universal respectively after *She's Gotta Have It.* But 1989 also saw the successful release by New Line of Reginald and Warrington Hudlin's *House Party*, and the success of black subjects made by black film-makers (generally with a high proportion of black technicians in their crews) gathered pace so that in 1991 some twenty such films were being made and most of the major studios were involved in seeking and encouraging black talent. The phenomenon became known as 'the Singleton thing', after John Singleton, who was taken up by Columbia as a novice director at the age of 23 to direct his own screenplay, *Boyz N The Hood* (1991), becoming the youngest director ever to be nominated for Oscars for both best director and best film.

At base, naturally, the phenomenon is purely economic: *She's Gotta Have It* cost $175,000 and grossed $8 million; *School Daze* was the best grossing Columbia picture of 1988; *House Party* cost $2·5 million and grossed over $26 million; *Do The Right Thing* cost $6·5 million and grossed $28 million; *New Jack City* cost $8·5 million and will gross over $50 million; *Boyz N The Hood* cost $6 million and will also gross over $50 million. These are figures that Hollywood could not possibly ignore and, in its usual fashion, it eagerly wanted more of the same – exactly as it had in the early 1970s. As Spike Lee put it to *Playboy*, 'Every film studio, if you're black and even look like you're a director, they're signing you.' On the basis of the success of *House Party*, New Line rapidly invested in, of course, *House Party 2*, but also Joseph B. Vasquez's *Hangin' With The Homeboys* and Topper Carew's *Talkin' Dirty After Dark* (both 1991); the Hudlins signed a three-year deal with TriStar and Columbia offered Singleton a three-picture deal. As Warrington Hudlin said after the runaway success of *House Party*, 'Every studio in Hollywood has said they'd finance our next movie.'

Hollywood's current enthusiasm for black subjects and black film-makers was fuelled not only by spectacular successes. In the early 1990s, market research revealed that while blacks represented twelve per cent of the population of the United States, they accounted for some twenty-five per cent of the money spent in the country on entertainment, primarily movie-going and sports, and that sixty per cent of the black population attended a movie in a given month as opposed to 51·2% of the white population. This seemed to imply a solid base for films aimed at black audiences, but left open the question of how far films made by black film-makers could 'cross over' and appeal to the majority non-black audience. The revenues from *Boyz N The Hood* and *New Jack City* made it clear that they had managed to cross over. Bill Duke's *A Rage in Harlem* (1991) did much less well: with an audience reckoned to be 80-85% black, it failed to cross over, or failed to do so to a large enough extent.

The film-makers themselves are very aware that their chances to make movies and be successful have depended on the success of others. So the Hudlins recognise their debt to Lee's success with *She's Gotta Have It* and *Do The Right Thing*, and Singleton recognises that the successes of Lee and the Hudlins are what made *Boyz N The Hood* possible. There is general agreement that, as black film-makers, they have stories to tell that have not been told and that audiences, black and white, want to see (Reginald Hudlin said of *House Party* that he 'wanted to make a movie that I had not seen, but a movie that

Photograph: John Singleton directing Larry Fishburne in Boyz N The Hood.

Still: Spike Lee (far right) with Danny Aiello and Giancarlo Esposito during the shooting of Do The Right Thing.

I wanted to see'). However, there is quite a lot of resentment among the film-makers at being seen as a group apart, even if the media exposure this has generated has benefitted them. The story is told of two Columbia executives visiting the set of Singleton's new film, *Poetic Justice:* 'Executive 1: Did you see *Boyz N The Hood?* Executive 2: No, but I saw *New Jack City.*' Whether this is true or not, it is inevitable that Hollywood, always eager to exploit a trend, should be most conscious of similarities and see black film-makers as a group. As with women film-makers, there are some advantages attached to this – mainly that if one or two films by black directors do well commercially, other black film-makers are more likely to get their chance. The down side is that if one or two films by black directors fail, the opportunities for all other black directors are diminished; as Lee put it, 'If one black film-maker messes up, the rest of us will be made to feel it.' Inevitably, black film-makers feel a certain obligation to their race which is not be felt by white directors. As Singleton said of himself on his Filmic Writing course at the University of Southern California, 'I was one of the only black kids there, so I couldn't be caught slipping.'

The film-makers themselves certainly do not see themselves as a defined or definable group. Vasquez, the Hispanic director of *Hanging' With The Homeboys,* echoing Lee, complained that 'My problem with the Black Pack stuff is that if one of us fails, we all fail in a lump. If Coppola fails, it doesn't affect Scorsese at all, but with us, if Robert Townsend fails, it's "Uh-ah, black films never make any money." It's cool that it's happening, but it offends me that we're all looked at as the same, that we're not seen as individuals. In this country there's a lot of racism – they don't look at blacks or Hispanics as individuals, they just see us as a group of people stuck in poverty, or whatever the hell they look at us as. I think if the trend of black film-making goes on to succeed, eventually people will say, "They're films" not "They're *black* films," because when white films come out, we don't go, "They're white films," we just go, "They're *films*" . . .' Mario Van Peebles takes a similar line in observing that 'we're as different as Scorsese and David Lynch and Spielberg and Rob Reiner . . . and it's tragic that we're seen on the same basketball team, because our movies are *very* different . . . [studio executives] haven't a clue, but you can't blame 'em, they're just guys trying to make money, and they don't know how. To get offended is to take them too seriously. To get studio executives to make the intellectual jump and understand the difference between Spike's movies which are more art-house and mine which is action-oriented, and *To Sleep With Anger* which is again art-house and *Rage in Harlem* which is again different, is to ask too much of them.'

Whatever black film-makers have in common, there are certainly considerable tensions between some of them over what kinds of work should be done by black film-makers, and in particular how the black community should be represented. Thus, several film-makers have objected to Van Peebles's very obviously commercial and generic *New Jack City*. Among them is Ernest Dickerson, one of the newer directors with *Juice* (1992), about young blacks in Harlem becoming involved in a murder, but long a mainstay of black film-making as Spike Lee's (as well as other people's) cinematographer. He has commented that 'I thought *New Jack City* was socially irresponsible. It didn't go for any kind of balance; it glamorised the drug dealer played by Wesley Snipes and didn't deal with Ice T's character, the cop, and what drove him to take the direction he did.' John Singleton has been a little more outspoken: 'I didn't write some new-jack-shitty black exploitation film. I wrote a film about people from my neighbourhood who are strong and gritty . . . *New Jack City* was pure entertainment. It was not, quote, a serious film.'

The concern with 'authentic' black experience is taken up in a different way by Matty Rich, nineteen-year-old writer-director of *Straight Out Of Brooklyn* (1991), about black working-class life in Brooklyn's Red Hook housing projects: 'Don't compare me to Spike Lee. I'm more *real* than he is. He's a phoney. He's a middle-class, third-generation college boy. With me, what you see is what you get. I'm a street kid. I think and talk *street.*' Indeed in a sense, some of Lee's films can be seen as contemporary updates, certainly much more informed by a black point of view, of those liberal problem pictures that starred Sidney Poitier in the 1950s and 1960s. Lee himself has put on record his admiration for Poitier's work: 'His films might seem dated now, but if it wasn't for Sidney doing those films, I don't think that we would have made a lot of the strides we have. For me, his career . . . was closely connected to Dr King and the civil rights movement, and he had a great burden to bear: every time Sidney Poitier was in a film, he wasn't playing his character, he was playing the twenty million black people who were in the country at that time. He's a pioneer . . .'

Unlike some of the very young new black film directors, Charles Burnett and Bill Duke have been around, in the industry or on its edges, for some years. It is almost by historical accident that they have become associated with the new trend for black directors, but that trend has nevertheless had its effects on them. Neither Burnett nor Duke has had quite the press coverage of phenomena like Lee and Singleton, but both have useful perspectives to offer on the present and future of black film-makers. When Burnett became interested in film in the 1960s, there was no real chance to be involved

Stills. Left: Henry Gayle Sanders in Killer of Sheep. *Right: Everette Silas and Gaye Shannon-Burnett in* My Brother's Wedding.

Still: Ice T (far left) and Wesley Snipes (centre) in New Jack City.

in Hollywood, where the unions were still very strong and especially difficult for ethnic minorities to breach. So Burnett did not think of his own work in film as a way to make money, and this has not really changed. Before *To Sleep With Anger* (1990), Burnett made two independent features, *Killer of Sheep* (1977) and *My Brother's Wedding* (1983), both of which were largely dependent on foundation grants, although *My Brother's Wedding* also got money from German television channel ZDF (as a result of the international festival success of *Killer of Sheep*). *Killer of Sheep* cost about $10,000 and was shot in 16mm largely at weekends; Burnett produced, wrote, photographed, and edited the film as well as directing. *My Brother's Wedding* had a considerably higher budget, was shot in 35mm, with a lot more help – it had a co-producer and an editor – but Burnett was still responsible for writing and photography as well as directing. *To Sleep With Anger* was budgeted at $1.5 million and produced through Ed Pressman's organisation with money (raised only after several years of trying) from SVS Films, the feature film distribution arm of Sony before it acquired Columbia-TriStar. Burnett's functions on the film were therefore more like the industry's norm of writer-director; once made, the film was distributed by the prestigious independent Samuel Goldwyn Company and thus competed in the commercial arena in which the earlier films (which were pretty much distributed by Burnett himself) had no place. Almost certainly, the raising of finance for *To Sleep With Anger* benefitted from a late 1980s atmosphere that was welcoming to black directors.

Burnett found that making a commercial picture like *To Sleep With Anger* (though, by Hollywood standards, $1.5 million is a very low budget) was in some ways easier and in some ways harder than making his earlier independent features. Grant donors were often stricter and more rigorous in dealing with projects, often wanting changes, and decisions tended to be made by committees (he mentions a lot of argument with the Rockefeller Foundation about a current documentary project concerning the impact of immigrants on US society, *America Becoming*). On *To Sleep With Anger*, Burnett had an initial commitment from the Corporation for Public Broadcasting, but they pulled out over disagreements about the script. By contrast, once Pressman had agreed to the project, no changes were sought and the only issues to be resolved concerned budgeting and casting.

Still: Danny Glover in To Sleep With Anger.

Among the professional cast, the lead was played by Danny Glover, fresh from box-office success in *Lethal Weapon 2*; Glover's commitment to the project – doing it for a fraction of his normal fee – was crucial in securing funding. Having worked mostly with non-professional actors in his earlier films, Burnett found working with professionals in many ways easier, since they both wanted and knew how to work with the director. Burnett observes that when you are making independent films by yourself, there is always the feeling that you can come back and do something the next day. On a commercial production, with completion bonds hanging over you, 'you're locked into a time frame that's very rigid. Every moment is budgeted. It's a good thing because you have to make choices immediately, and then you're done with it,' though you have to be even better prepared than when working independently. Where in the earlier films Burnett was doing most jobs himself, on *To Sleep With Anger,* people were asking him what to do, and decisions were needed on things which had been done more or less intuitively before, such as where to place some prop in a set. Since this way of working was so much more compartmentalised, with specialists doing specialist jobs, 'you have to trust a lot of people,' where before he relied on himself.

The considerable strength of Burnett's earlier features lies less in their narratives than in their observation of everyday family life in South Central Los Angeles (the same area in which Singleton's *Boyz N The Hood* is set, and the scene of the 1992 urban disturbances). Burnett is very conscious that the images he is producing of black American life are not those that most Hollywood films offer. At the time of the release of *To Sleep With Anger,* Burnett was quoted as saying that 'The real problem is that blacks are still represented in a very conventional way in American films. If I wanted to get immediate funding for another film, all I'd have to do is write a story about a black making an ass of himself and I'd get four million dollars tomorrow. And if you argue with the makers of these films, they turn round and say, "But that's how blacks like to see themselves. Look at Eddie Murphy!". . . My view is that blacks are worse represented on the screen than they were twenty years ago, not better . . . Nobody is addressing the real differences between the races, except perhaps Spike Lee . . . Outside of Spike Lee, how many commercial movies are made that really talk about black people? There are a lot of black film-makers around. But they still have the greatest difficulty making movies in other than accepted forms. And there's still no dialogue being created about this representation of blacks on film.'

It was in this context that Burnett's films dealt with questions of community and earning a living and class. With *To Sleep With Anger,* Burnett 'wanted to show a normal African-American family placed in a crisis . . . a family that stayed together and worked things out. It's not the on-screen image that African-American people historically have, but it is reflective of the lifestyle that exists in a very large portion of our community.' The particular crisis in the film is provoked by the arrival of Danny Glover's devil-like character from the Deep South into the midst of three generations of an ordinary family, and the film looks at the way the family is upset by his influence. Burnett himself was born in the South but raised in Los Angeles where his family moved in 1944; he experienced a sense of community as he was growing up but feels that has got lost. He sees part of the reason as being a loss of roots and tradition: black people 'have their roots but they are being asked to forget them in favour of the aspirations of a predominantly white-led society . . . There's this terrible denial of our real culture going on. And the result of it is that young blacks know very little about it.' This is what *To Sleep With Anger* tried to be about.

One reason for doing a film on a bigger scale like *To Sleep With Anger,* with stars and a stronger narrative, was Burnett's frustration at his independently made films simply not reaching the audiences he was aiming them at. But Burnett feels – and other black film-makers have agreed – that *To Sleep With Anger,* too, did not find its larger audience. 'You spend all your time learning to be a film-maker. Then you feel you've got to learn about finding the financing. Hey, you better learn about marketing and distributing the film – that's where it's at.' Despite great hopes, Burnett feels that the marketing was handled wrongly and, as with his earlier films, *To Sleep With Anger* had more success at international festivals than with its intended audiences. Burnett learned that distributors and producers can have different agendas and that, surprisingly to him, power and ego can be as important as making money.

But it is a common complaint of black film-makers that promotion and marketing conventions work against them and that distributors are not familiar enough with the black press, black radio and black social life in general. Robert Townsend, commenting on the promotion of his *The Five Heartbeats* (1991), which also failed at the box-office, commented that 'Fox have a policy where they don't do billboards and benches or street advertising, which was what was needed for this film, that's where the minorities are, they walk and use the buses.' There is some evidence, too, that black film-going habits are not the same as white. Hollywood's general release strategy is to release a movie on many screens and decide from box-office grosses very soon, often after the first weekend of release, whether the film will be a hit. Black audiences, it is thought, often take longer to build. The industry image of the black film-makers as a group can also have its limiting effect: Warrington Hudlin has said that 'the conventional wisdom assumes films made by blacks have a ceiling on their potential gross. That becomes a self-fulfilling prophecy. They would talk about how Spike's movies would be in so many cinemas, and that was a ceiling for us. But *House Party* made more than twice that.' Perhaps some lessons are being learned: Warner and Columbia showed with *New Jack City* and *Boyz N The Hood* that committed promotion of black-made films can succeed. Films less easy to categorise generically may be those to suffer, but this is perhaps true of Hollywood in general.

Burnett argues that producers and distributors 'blame the victim. You're told that this just shows that blacks don't want to see movies like this because they don't support them. But, you say, that's not the issue because you haven't got to the point of making them aware of the film. And that helps them to continually make films they feel they know they can push successfully but which perpetuate this myth about people of colour, the same movies about violence and drugs.' It's because of these problems about promotion and marketing that Burnett admires the smartness of Spike Lee's relentless efforts (entrepreneurial – books, shop, etc – and in terms of media exposure) and his success in making his name such a recognised one, creating a market almost single-handedly for his own films. Burnett himself could not work like that. It may be that others apart from Lee are recognising the importance of promoting recognition of their names: Matty Rich appears to be following in Lee's footsteps in opening a clothing store, creating a comic-book series with black heroes and planning to direct commercials (Lee's commercials for Air Jordan/ Nike trainers are probably as well known as his features).

Burnett did not go on from *To Sleep With Anger* to another feature, that, for him, would be similarly large. He has gone 'back to the grindstone of independent films,' feeling that Europe may be a source of funding if he fails to find it in the United States, but he has also been working, without commitment, on a television pilot for Disney. He finds them nice people but always wanting to impose old formats, because, he thinks, those at the top relate to the world only through the scripts they read, which makes it hard trying to be original. Burnett says, for example, that he tries to develop a kind of narrative approach that might better evoke the way people experience life and is asked, 'Well, what's the first act?' – precisely the terms he wants to resist. More generally, he remains sad that young black directors may be going straight from film school to big-budget films, without having been 'out there' and accountable with small-scale projects: 'Film-making is like anything else; you have to know the direction by having gone through so many roads and roadblocks and then you find yourself on the right road by a process of elimination.'

Bill Duke's road to the feature industry has been as long as Burnett's, but very different. Like many other creative black people in the industry, his background was in theatre, producing, directing, writing and acting in plays in New York, never earning significant money, but feeling, in retrospect at least, that he was lucky to survive and not drift away from it as so many did. After coming to Los Angeles in 1972 as an assistant theatre director, he was unable to get jobs directing and went back to acting, appearing in, for example, *Car Wash* (1976), some television and *American Gigolo* (1980). He was then out of work for a couple of years; it was in any case often hard for black actors, and Duke was, as he puts it, 'not a traditional leading man' (for a start, he is about 6'5" tall). To get over his intimidation by the technical side of film – 'camera, lights, lenses, cables, dollies, all these people' – he spent two years at the AFI: ' "You want to be a film-maker? Here's a camera, here's a script, here's a crew." You come back with whatever you come back with and they critique it like you're Coppola. They tear it apart. You get very defensive, but it's a very good way to learn, because it's pragmatic, it's hands-on.' Back in Hollywood, the 40-minute film he made at the AFI and which won a couple of awards, *The Hero*, was sent around by his agent and Duke hoped for some kind of journeyman work as a director, but almost two years went by and nothing happened. Out of the blue, by a complicated accident – they thought he was someone else – Lorimar hired him to do two episodes, one for *Knots Landing* and one for *Flamingo Road*, both then in their infancy. They liked his work and engaged him for two more shows, then eight for the next season and twelve for the one after that.

Duke went on to direct an astonishing 130 or so television episodes, the titles of which read like a roll-call of 1980s episodic television, including *Miami Vice*, *Cagney and Lacy*, *Hill Street Blues*, *Crime Story*, *Matlock*, *Fame*, *Dallas*, *Hunter* and *Falcon Crest*. He also shot pilots (for *Flag* and *Maximum Security*) and some television movies (including *The Johnnie Gibson Story*). As for many other directors, episodic television proved an excellent training: 'In terms of training for a director, I can't see how you can have a better training ground. First of all, you're under enormous amount of pressure all the

Photograph: Charles Burnett, by the camera, working on My Brother's Wedding.

time, because the budgets are relatively restricted, and so are the schedules. You have seven working days to shoot that film. No matter what happens, you have seven days – you do not go over. You have to shoot it within this budget – no more money. So if you're working consistently as a television director, you're coming in on time and you're coming in on budget. You're working with stars who may wake up one morning and say, "I don't like tall people, you're fired." I've seen television stars fire producers. So you're under that kind of pressure also. And you're working in an environment – particularly if you're a black director, so you're foreign to them and they're foreign to you – in which you have to learn the politics of surviving in a television atmosphere. I cannot tell you the value of those years working in television – it was like going to school.'

Duke believes that he was such a popular television director mainly because he was an actor himself. Episodic television directors usually work on the basis that the actors know their characters, so tell them to please move there, and get it over with quickly, 'but being an actor, I love actors. I always push for that ounce more. One of the reasons I was hired back on shows many times was that the actors appreciated that kind of attention, especially the major stars. Most directors were just intimidated by these stars, but I would relate to them as a fellow actor. And it's a sorry thing to say, but a lot of directors don't like actors. That gave me a leg up.' Sometimes, this did not help him so much and the severe constraints on directing episodic television came into play, 'I covered a scene in which a woman was sewing a button on her lover's coat. The scene was not about the button, but about their conversation and the conflict in their marriage. When the producer saw the scene, he loved the acting but he said I'd ruined it for him. Why? "You didn't get a close-up of the button. On our shows, we always do close-ups of everything we do, we always get inserts. You've ruined the whole scene for me." The fact of the matter is that shows like *Knots Landing* or *Falcon Crest* have certain formats and they expect you to get very close coverage of all the major principals. As a director, sometimes that was repugnant to me, because I felt I wanted to see the design of the whole frame. I'd say, the audience is intelligent enough, they know what's being said, why do we have to be here? "Well, because we want the camera there." "Well, that's what you get, because you're paying me, fine." You don't have very much say. And

Still: Alfre Woodard and Damien Leake in The Killing Floor.

your cut of the episode is only a formality: you turn your cut in, but the network and the studio determine what they want.'

Duke is certain that his being black had no effect whatsoever on the shows he was offered. As he says, there were no black characters on shows like *Dallas* or *Falcon Crest*. Duke was impressed that 'if you were a good director who gave shows an interesting look, they hired you. It was a much more democratic and liberal atmosphere to work in. Feature films are different.' This difference of attitude – it was not yet the period of the trend for black film-makers – plus the 'unwritten code' that made it hard for television directors to get features, posed a big problem for Duke: how to get out of television and make features? Trying to do so, he made two features for PBS, *The Killing Floor* (1985) and *A Raisin in the Sun* (1988). *The Killing Floor* is a powerful account, based on fact, of the conflicts between racial and union solidarity in the Chicago stockyards in the 1920s, centring on a black character who has migrated from the South during World War I and sacrifices himself for the struggle.

The producers were looking for someone who was good but inexpensive and looking for a break. Duke fitted this bill very well. Made on a very low budget, the film was financed by grants and, because it was a film about unions, the unions worked for half scale. Duke 'learned an incredible amount in a very short period of time,' during nine weeks or so of pre-production and nine weeks of shooting, but he also learned a lot of other things. First, the film was not much seen, being released in art houses in the United States and in Europe with little promotion. Second, it did not help Duke's career mainly because its pro-union stance and its raising of difficult questions about black allegiances made it too controversial. 'I learned very quickly that many people loved the film, but some people were offended by the content of the film. The politics of it just came crashing down, because it was not commercial.' Duke had expected that, because for him 'it was about something important,' it would achieve more. 'But it's one of the things I'm most proud of and I think in the near future I will be able to make films, God willing, of that nature. The irony is, I first have to prove myself as a

Still: Damien Leake, Clarence Felder (centre) and Moses Gunn (right) in The Killing Floor.

commercial film-maker. The films I make will have content commercially – not that kind of significant content, but I can't make a film I can't relate to.'

After *The Killing Floor,* Duke went back to directing television and to acting to survive – 'I do bad guys mostly,' – *Commando* (1985) and *Predator* (1987) are notable examples, and he has continued more recently with *Bird on a Wire* (1990), though he feels his talent as an actor far surpasses the kinds of role he is offered. Duke found himself making more money than he could spend from a very busy life directing television and became physically sick and disenchanted with the business: 'What am I doing? Did I get into this to make money, or did I get into this to say something?' 'Holding out for more significant material,' he refused all television offers for a while.

Making *A Raisin in the Sun* for PBS was a calculated move to make something as a bridge from television to features. As a classic of black theatre, Lorraine Hansberry's play posed none of the questions of controversiality which *The Killing Floor* had, 'I was able to say, this is difficult subject matter which I've made palatable, and it's not episodic television. It's significant writing, and I've shown I can handle a dramatic piece. Luckily, it paid off.' Duke had been, of course, 'on the look-out for features, but features weren't on the look-out for me. I was hungry to do something significant.' He had offers of projects that were wrong for him, but 'film-making for a director is such a gruelling experience. It's like a triathlon, it's an unforgiving process, and it's hard to do that on something you don't have faith in. The only thing that got me through *A Rage in Harlem,* which was a gruelling experience, was the fact that when I saw my dailies, I felt I was working on something I believed in. That got me through it. If I was going into the dailies and saying, "Oh, my God, what am I doing?". . .'

A Rage in Harlem (1991) was an $8 million production by the British production company Palace Pictures (in association with Miramax, its American distributors), which was in search of an American box-office hit. It took three years from work on the script and pre-production to being shot and finished. Based on a Chester Himes novel, *A Rage in Harlem* centres on crime and sexuality in Harlem in the 1950s. Duke had seen

Photograph: left to right, facing camera, Forest Whitaker, Gregory Hines and Bill Duke during the shooting of A Rage in Harlem.

other adaptations of Himes's work, like *Cotton Comes to Harlem,* in the 1970s but had not connected Himes's name to them; his attraction to the project now came to centre very much on the controversial figure of Himes: 'Was it possible to take this great writer and capture him on film, take the essence out of the novel and add to it those elements that would make it filmic without destroying his message? In addition, he dealt with fundamental universal issues, like good and evil, which I guess I'm old fashioned about but very much believe in.' While making the film, Duke described it as 'a combination of the Cain and Abel story and Porgy and Bess. The tolerance the brothers arrive at for each other is an important message for the black community. We are killing each other at a rate that's phenomenal . . . In his autobiography, *A Life of Absurdity,* [Himes] talked about rage. The rage in Harlem he was talking about is the kind of rage a black man feels who tries to bleach his skin, tries to straighten his kinky hair with lye, and allows him no iota of self-respect . . . The rage against being made to feel worthless. The rage that burns down its own neighbourhood in the riots. That's the kind of rage, and it's much more devastating than any physical bludgeoning because it tears the very soul of a man.'

A Rage in Harlem was another film which, many have argued, did not succeed as well as it might have because of inadequate promotion and marketing. Duke, having gone some way towards setting up a picture on the life of Otis Redding, *Try a Little Tenderness,* then went on to make another crime action movie, *Deep Cover* (1992, with Larry Fishburne and Jeff Goldblum). Can he work within commercial projects and still explore the racial and other human issues, which he is committed to? 'I think I can get some of those things explored, but I think the nature of the industry does not allow you to explore them fully, because to a certain extent it doesn't trust the intelligence of the audience. Whether or not that's right will have to be proven . . .' While this is a major concern of many in Hollywood, it is clearly most important to committed minority film-makers. All Spike Lee's work, for example, shows the tension between responsible subject matter and the demands of commercial film-making. As Lee said of *Malcolm X,* 'If I was solely in the business of entertainment, I would not be making the movies I make. There would have been *She's Gotta Have It 2, 3, 4* and *5.* I try to make entertainment that's also thought provoking and has some intelligence behind it.'

At present, the future of the whole new generation of black film-makers is uncertain. In some respects, there is a healthy distrust of Hollywood and its seductive ways.

Columbia's proud claim on billboards for *Boyz N The Hood* was that 'John Singleton wanted to tell the truth. Columbia Pictures gave him the chance to do it.' Singleton himself was reported as saying that 'the less I get mired in that Hollywood machine, the better my films will be. I think you write about what you know about. I'm black and I write about black folks.' Matty Rich was reported as resisting Hollywood's call to direct a big-budget picture: 'I don't want to make the leap from a $300,000 movie [*Straight Out Of Brooklyn*] to $20 million because you could be an overnight success who fails and they spit you out.' As several film-makers have noted, much may ultimately depend on access to power within the industry. As Melvin Van Peebles put it, 'We don't have any black heads of studios that can greenlight movies. Black agents, maybe five. Black managers, maybe six.' Spike Lee concurs: 'We've arrived? That's not the case at all. Not one person outside of Eddie Murphy, not one African-American in Hollywood who can greenlight a picture.'

Though it might give Reggie Hudlin satisfaction to prove movie executives wrong about the commercial prospects of a movie like *House Party*, 'it would give me greater satisfaction to see those experts replaced by black executives in the studios – that's the only way to overcome the institutional racism that still exists.' Bill Duke sums up and extends these perceptions: 'In the executive halls of Hollywood, there is not yet a black executive who has the power to greenlight a film, so that, without someone who has a sensibility to the needs of the black community, minorities hold a diminished position in the industry. There is not one minority represented by a major or minor distributor in the US, revealing another aspect of the business in which we are not participating. There are no black marketing executives of any significance who are in touch with the

Still: Forest Whitaker and Robin Givens in A Rage in Harlem.

black community, who would know how to save films like *To Sleep With Anger* or *The Five Heartbeats* by marketing them directly to the right audience; and, finally, on the exhibition side, there is only one movie house in America which is owned or operated by blacks. So when you put production within the context of the overall business, and then you put our participation in that production into the overall context, you can see how small our participation really is.'

A crucial question is what kinds and sizes of project will black film-makers be allowed to undertake. According to Warrington Hudlin, 'Overall, this industry sees us as cheap labour; we are a group of people they see as able to make films on very low budgets, that turn significant profits . . . Our experience is that there seems to be a $15 million budget ceiling on films by and about black people.' This ceiling may now be being breached, with Spike Lee's budgets moving up from $6.5 million for *Do The Right Thing* to $14 million for *Jungle Fever* and $35 million for *Malcolm X* (though the relative profitability of Lee's films has been steadily declining as their costs have risen, which must threaten his position); other big projects have included Reggie Hudlin's Eddie Murphy picture, *Boomerang* (1992). Warrington Hudlin argues that this change is essential, because 'Hollywood is geared towards the blockbuster; studios would rather spend $50 million on a film in the hopes of making $350 million. That's where blacks are at a disadvantage because again we have that ceiling where we can't get the money to have those production values.' The Hudlins have given a lot of thought to these issues: Warrington was one of the founders in 1978 of the Black Filmmaker Foundation which advises film-makers and acts as a pressure group. Among other things, it helped to find the financing for *She's Gotta Have It,* and its members include Spike Lee, Harry Belafonte, Michael Schultz, Bill Duke and Melvin and Mario Van Peebles. Others have argued strongly that the crucial thing is for black film-makers to remain as independent of the studios as possible, as Spike Lee has done and Ernest Dickerson has done with *Juice.* John Singleton has pressed home the point: 'Black film will always prosper – in an independent realm. We've been making films since the early part of this century, since the beginning of American cinema, and we'll continue to make films with or without studio help.' Spike Lee's situation on *Malcolm X* has become well known: Warner refused to put up an extra $5 million when the film went over budget, and Lee had to go to black stars like Bill Cosby and Oprah Winfrey for the funding: 'It shows that we don't always have to rely on funding from outside our communities.'

For the immediate future, the dependence of even independent films on studio finance and distribution raises questions about what kinds of film black film-makers will be able to make. For some, assimilation is the essential demand. Mario Van Peebles believes 'very strongly that if a white director can make *The Color Purple,* I can make *Home Alone.* We have to resist the temptation to make movies that are personal, and make movies that are entertaining stories and that will kick ass at the box-office. While we have the opportunity, I want to move away from the genres represented by *House Party* or *New Jack City* . . . we should be going further and asking, where is our *9¹/₂ Weeks,* where's our *Fatal Attraction,* where's our *Ordinary People.* If we don't stretch it now, we'll be shutting the door narrowly for the women and men that come behind us.' Charles Lane, who moved from the critically successful, silent independent feature *Sidewalk Stories* to the Disney comedy *True Identity* (1991), in which Lenny Henry has to disguise himself as white, also believes that black film-makers 'need to make more than one kind of film,' but, as Spike Lee put it, 'black artists aren't allowed the same diversity that white people have. It's just like one monolithic black group.' Lee argued long and hard that only a black film-maker could make *Malcolm X.* 'I have not said that only white people can interpret white subject matters and *vice versa* only black people, but there are specific cases where I feel that you should be of that background. A white person will never know what it means to be an African-American and you needed that for this film.'

Photograph: left to right, Annabella Sciorra, Spike Lee, Wesley Snipes and architectural consultant Jack Travis on the set of Jungle Fever.

Charles Burnett feels that even if the fad for black film-makers does not pass, the trend may be set for 'meaningless films'. Dickerson argues that 'at the moment, we have to think in terms of popular cinema, but later on we can turn to riskier ventures,' which is fundamentally the way Bill Duke has been thinking, but Duke has also expressed what is inevitably a strong commitment among most black film-makers and almost a *raison d'être* of their struggle to work in the industry: 'Every day in America, you are bombarded with a consciousness that the colour of someone's skin is important, so it's a constant struggle and evolution, and "black" is a significant factor in my cinematic equation. I'm not saying it's the only factor or even a major factor, but if we don't address it, we diminish its importance . . . we can't rely on white directors to create our aesthetics for us, we have to create them ourselves and proclaim their validity. What's wonderful about *Straight Out Of Brooklyn* are the images: those faces, the big lips, those brown wide noses, big beautiful eyes and kinky hair . . . My concern is the longevity of [Hollywood's] commitment . . . We're not asking to receive any special treatment; we want the same treatment given to other important directors in the community given to us – the opportunity to fail and experiment.' The way Duke was drawn to Chester Himes clearly had to do with the parallel he saw between Himes's situation as a writer in the 1950s with the current situation of black film-makers: 'Himes's brilliance was his blessing, his brilliance was his curse. The crime novels were written for money, and they're the least of his work, but as a black he wasn't taken seriously by the powers-that-be. He objected to being called the best of the black writers. He didn't want to be part of that microcosm when he knew that the macrocosm existed, and as a result he was a very tortured man and left this country.'

In terms of demographics, at least, the future for black subjects and black film-makers looks good. Statistically, it is reported that the black population, as well as going to the movies more often than whites, is younger and growing faster than other segments of the American population, except for Latinos. As Warrington Hudlin has put it, 'In twenty years, people of colour [are not going to be] minorities anymore, and if this industry is going to remain financially viable, they have to programme for the new majority.' That new majority will be, of course, not only black and not only male. As the 1990s begin, there are the first substantial signs of an American Hispanic cinema (though there had earlier been independent films like Robert M. Young's *The Ballad of Gregorio Cortez*, 1983), with Joseph B. Vasquez's *Hangin' With The Homeboys* and Edward James Olmos's *American Me* (1992), which is to be released by Universal. The representation of black women in the films of some of the new black male film-makers has often caused controversy, which implies the desirability of black women film-makers making their own breakthrough into feature films, rather than leaving it to something like John Singleton's second feature, *Poetic Justice,* to tell 'a story from a black woman's point of view'. So far, this does not seem to be happening, although, in television, Debbie Allen, having been a performer in *Roots* and *Fame,* has directed episodes of shows like *Fame, Quantum Leap, A Different World* and *The Fresh Prince of Bel Air* (for which she did the pilot), and Helaine Head, from a background in theatre, has directed since the mid 1980s, making episodes of *Cagney and Lacey* and *LA Law* and cable movies for Showtime. Allen, among others, has projects for theatrical features.

Black women have been much more active in the more experimental and political sector of independent film-making since the 1970s. A major figure here has been Julie Dash, who was assistant director on Burnett's *My Brother's Wedding,* and is best known for her 1983 short film *Illusions,* which directly confronted the 'invisibility of blacks' and women's roles in the movie industry. Dash is now coming to the end of a five-year struggle to fund and produce her 35mm feature debut, to be premiered on television, *Daughters of the Dust* (1991), the story of the women of a family descended from the freed slaves of the islands off the coast of South Carolina and Georgia at the turn of the century. The breakthrough of black women to feature film-making is a development to be awaited eagerly in the 1990s.

Still: Lawrence Gilliard Jr in Straight Out Of Brooklyn.

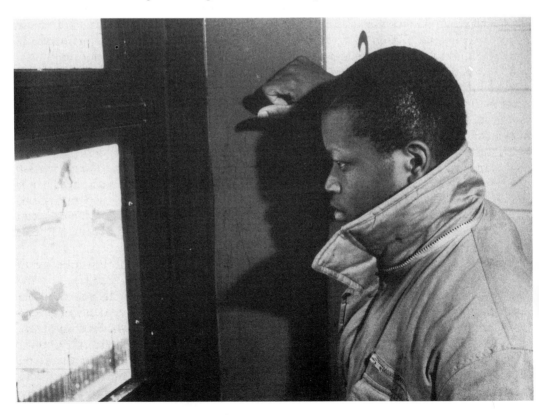

FOREIGNERS

Particularly since the advent of the studio system in the 1920s, Hollywood has actively attracted film-makers from other countries, but never more so than today. Ate de Jong, a young Dutch film-maker now working out of Los Angeles, calculates that some thirty-five per cent of the work in Hollywood today is being done by foreign film-makers, most notably directors, but also writers, directors of photography, art directors, and so on – those whose work can be categorised as creative and who have least problem, therefore, in being able to work legally in the United States. Predictably, foreign directors working in Hollywood are, with only a couple of exceptions, white and male. The German woman director Doris Dörrie followed her internationally successful 1985 German film, *Men*, with a project for Columbia, then under David Puttnam, *Me and Him* (1988), about male libido, 'him' being the male protagonist's talking penis; the completed film was buried by Puttnam's successor, Dawn Steel. The Martinique-born black woman director Euzhan Palcy, who had some art-circuit success with the French-made *Rue Cases Nègres (Black Shack Alley*, 1983) directed *A Dry White Season* (1989) in the United States after five years setting it up. Hollywood is mainly keen to attract film-makers who have established their credentials in their own countries, which, until recently, are likely to have been as slow as Hollywood in producing women and ethnic minority film-makers.

American revenues from the export of film and television to Europe run at around $700 million a year, compared with European revenues from the United States at under $50 million a year. Although a recent trend has seen Hollywood remaking successful European films such as *Three Men and a Baby,* the American film industry is not particularly attracted to films and television programmes made in Europe. But it is intensely interested in European film-makers, and it follows that what Hollywood wants from those film-makers cannot be exactly what they were making before. The foreigners – the vast majority of them European in origin – come from countries where attitudes to film and film-making are very different from those in the United States and from film and television industries (or film-making where 'industry' would be too presumptuous a term) that may be organised very differently. All in all, the likelihood of foreign film-makers experiencing difficulties of one kind or another in Hollywood is very great. What attracts them is not just being paid at levels they could not normally expect in their home countries, but also the technical expertise and funding for projects that Hollywood, almost alone, can provide, and access to the world-wide distribution system of the major studios that secures Hollywood's dominance of the world film marketplace.

Hollywood's interest in foreign film-makers has always reflected both a desire to attract the best possible talent in the world and thus make the 'best' movies, and the less laudable aim of depriving other national cinemas of their major talents and thus reducing competition for its own products. Both these factors were certainly operative in the 1920s in Hollywood's recruitment of the successful German director Ernst Lubitsch, who was in the United States from 1923, the Swedish directors Victor Sjöström (renamed Seastrom for his Hollywood pictures) and Mauritz Stiller, and the Dane Benjamin Christensen, who were in the United States from 1923, 1925 and 1925 respectively. More spectacularly, the Parufamet Agreement of 1926 allowed Paramount and MGM collaborative rights to the personnel of Germany's artistically vital but financially floundering UFA studios and led to the emigration in 1926-27 of many important directors, like F.W. Murnau, Paul Leni, Mihaly Kertész (a Hungarian working for UFA, who became Michael Curtiz in the US) and Ludwig Berger, as well as directors of photography like Karl Freund and Eugen Schüfftan (Eugene Shuftan in the United States) and art directors like Hans Dreier.

This flood of prime German talent to Hollywood became even greater during the 1930s when the growth of German fascism prompted the flight of many more German and Austrian film-makers to Hollywood, some directly like Fred Zinnemann, Otto Preminger, Edgar G. Ulmer, William Dieterle and Douglas Sirk (originally Detlef Sierck, a Dane who worked for UFA) – Ulmer had already worked in Hollywood with Murnau – and some, like Robert Siodmak, Fritz Lang, Billy Wilder and Max Ophüls after periods (prolonged for Siodmak and Ophüls) working in France or, in John Brahm's case, Britain. France, with a very different industrial and political climate in its cinema during the inter-war years, was much less likely to export talent, but important directors like Maurice Tourneur and Jacques Feyder worked in Hollywood in 1914-26 and 1928-31 respectively, and Jacques Tourneur, Maurice's son, went to Hollywood in 1939. Jean Renoir's 1940s work in the United States and René Clair's during the war years arose solely from the difficulties caused by war and occupation; neither really became genuinely American film-makers.

Inevitably, the experiences and achievements of the émigrés in Hollywood varied. Lubitsch stayed in Hollywood and became one of its most important directors of the 1930s. Sjöström did fine work such as *The Scarlet Letter* (1926) and *The Wind* (1928) but returned to Sweden. Stiller died only a few years after going to American having, despite *Hotel Imperial* (1927), managed to find little outlet for his talent. Murnau died early, at the peak of his career, having made only a handful of Hollywood films, including *Sunrise* (1927). Many of the earlier émigrés worked in the United States for some time and then returned home, but Curtiz, like Lubitsch, found success in the studio system. However, the circumstances in which the 1930s wave of German film-makers came to Hollywood (and the virtual absence until well after the war of a German film industry cinema to which they could return) meant that most of them stayed for the remainder of their careers, and they were responsible for some of the finest Hollywood films of the 1940s and 1950s.

Politics has continued to play some role in the passage of film-makers to Hollywood in more recent years. Milos Forman and Ivan Passer came from Czechoslovakia after the repression of the young film-makers there at the end of the 1960s. Political factors were also involved in the movements of Roman Polanski, from Poland after a spell in Britain, and Andrei Konchalovsky, from the Soviet Union, but the increasing flow of non-American film-makers to Hollywood has had its prime basis in the crises, generally economic, of other national cinemas and the ever-growing global dominance of the American entertainment industry.

The vast majority of the film-makers who have most recently come to Hollywood have English as their first language. Directors whose native language is not English still come, but generally when they have managed to make commercially successful – and preferably also Oscar-winning or nominated – films in their own countries or internationally: Wolfgang Petersen had made *Das Boot (The Boat*, 1981) and *The Never Ending Story* (1984) before moving to Hollywood and making *Enemy Mine* (1985) and *Shattered* (1991). Lasse Hallström went to Hollywood to make *Once Around* (1990), after making *ABBA, The Movie* (1977) and *My Life as a Dog* (1985). Costa Gavras, after a distinguished French and international career with political thrillers, has been able to make American films such as *Missing* (1981), *Betrayed* (1988) and *The Music Box* (1989). Barbet Schroeder, French *nouvelle vague* producer of Eric Rohmer's films and, among others, Jacques Rivette's *Céline et Julie vont en bateau* (1974) turned director in France with *More* (1969), *La Vallée* (1972) and *Maîtresse* (1984); he achieved surprise success in Hollywood with *Reversal of Fortune* (1990) and has subsequently released *Single White Female* (1992). Mira Nair had an international art house success with *Salaam Bombay* (1988); she went on to make *Mississippi Masala* (1991) in the United States.

But it is Britons and Australians who have made up most of the expatriate film-makers in Hollywood since the 1960s. The relative strength of the British film industry in the days of the Hollywood studio system meant that rather few British directors emigrated. Several important or prolific Hollywood directors during this period were British – including Charles Chaplin, James Whale, Edmund Goulding and Robert Stevenson – but they had not been movie directors before emigrating across the Atlantic. Alfred Hitchcock is, of course, Britain's most celebrated directorial export; Alexander Mackendrick made some sorties into Hollywood, directing *Sweet Smell of Success* (1957) and *Don't Make Waves* (1967); his British-made 1960s films, *Sammy Going South* (1963) and *A High Wind in Jamaica* (1965), like many others of the period, were British-American co-productions.

But it was only in the late 1960s, as the British film industry started falling into terminal decline, that many British directors started making films in Hollywood (though quite a few of them did not emigrate in the sense of settling permanently in Los Angeles and making only American films). American co-production in the 1960s eased the way for several frankly commercial directors, such as John Guillermin, J. Lee Thompson and Guy Hamilton to start working in Hollywood. A second group was made up of people from Free Cinema and British 'new wave' of the late 1950s and early 1960s: John Schlesinger (first Hollywood film, *Midnight Cowboy*, 1969), Tony Richardson *(A Delicate Balance*, 1973) and Karel Reisz *(The Gambler*, 1974); of those from Free Cinema, the only major figure who chose not to work in Hollywood at this time was Lindsay Anderson, though he has more recently done so with *The Whales of August* (1987) and the mini-series *Glory! Glory!* (1989) for cable producers Home Box Office. John Boorman and Peter Yates, initially from television rather than film backgrounds, were not part of this group but began to make American films around the same time, with Boorman's *Point Blank* (1967) and Yates's *Bullitt* (1968). All then continued to work intermittently on Hollywood movies, often prestige or high-profile projects, such as Schlesinger's *Day of the Locust* (1975), *Marathon Man* (1976) and *Pacific Heights* (1990), sometimes with very distinguished results, such as Reisz's *Who'll Stop the Rain* (a.k.a. *Dog Soldiers*, 1978), Boorman's *Deliverance* (1972) and Yates's *Breaking Away* (1979).

The dominant background of the next generation of British directors to be taken up by Hollywood (even if the films themselves were made in Britain) was advertising. Great prestige has become attached to British directors like Alan Parker (*Bugsy Malone*, British, 1976, then among others, *Midnight Express*, 1978, *Fame*, 1980, *Angel Heart*, 1987, *Mississippi Burning*, 1989, *Come See the Paradise*, 1990, and, on a much smaller scale, *The Commitments*, 1991), Ridley Scott (*The Duellists*, British, 1977, then *Alien*, 1979, *Blade Runner*, 1982, *Legend*, 1985, *Someone To Watch Over Me*, 1987, *Black Rain*, 1989, *Thelma and Louise*, 1991, *1492: The Conquest of Paradise*, 1992), his brother Tony Scott (*The Hunger*, 1983, *Top Gun*, 1986, *Beverly Hills Cop II*, 1987, *Revenge*, 1989, *Days of Thunder*, 1990, *The Last Boy Scout*, 1991), and Adrian Lyne (*Foxes*, 1979, *Flashdance*, 1983, *9½ Weeks*, 1985, *Fatal Attraction*, 1987, *Jacob's Ladder*, 1990).

Australian film-making, barely an industry before the 1970s, was encouraged by subsidies from the Australian Film Commission and by individual state bodies. It burst on to the international film scene in the 1970s with directors like Peter Weir (*Picnic at Hanging Rock*, 1975, *The Last Wave*, 1977), Phillip Noyce (*Backroads*, 1977, *Newsfront*, 1978, *Heatwave*, 1981), Fred Schepisi (*The Devil's Playground*, 1976, *The Chant of Jimmie Blacksmith*, 1978), George Miller (*Mad Max*, 1979) and Bruce Beresford (*The Getting of Wisdom*, 1977, *Breaker Morant*, 1980). Although many of these early films were identifiably Australian in character, and part of their generally art-house international success was undoubtedly due to this national quality, Australian productions began to be increasingly international in production and appeal, like Weir's *Gallipoli* (1981). The existence of English-language film-makers who had demonstrated that they could make pictures of international appeal inevitably attracted Hollywood, and several Australian directors have made critically and commercially successful Hollywood movies over the last decade, including Weir's *Witness* (1985), *The Mosquito Coast* (1986), *Dead Poets Society* (1989) and *Green Card* (1990), Beresford's *Tender Mercies* (1982), *Crimes of the Heart* (1986), *Driving Miss Daisy* (1989) and *Mister Johnson* (1990), Schepisi's *Roxanne* (1987) and *The Russia House* (1990) and Noyce's *Blind Fury* (1989) and *Patriot Games* (1992).

The fact that so many of the films by Parker, Lyne and the Scott brothers have been good commercial successes has helped to maintain the stock of British directors (or 'tea-bags', as they are sometimes called) in Hollywood, and keep a pretty constant flow of new names, fed by an exceptionally vital British commercials and music video industry and a television industry that can produce dramatic filmed material of a quality not possible in American network television, as well as by what is left of British commercial film production. Michael Apted is one of several directors from British television drama who has made Hollywood movies – *Coal Miner's Daughter* (1980), *Gorillas in the Mist* (1988) and *Class Action* (1990). He has been followed more recently by directors like Mick Jackson, who directed *A Very British Coup* for British television and made *LA Story* (1991) and *The Bodyguard* (1992) in Hollywood.

Television is the background of many of the newer British recruits to Hollywood, but often along with British features. John Mackenzie comes from television and a handful of British films including *The Long Good Friday* (1979); he has made *Blue Heat* (1990) and *Ruby* (1992) in Hollywood. Stephen Frears had a long association with television drama and independent British features like *Gumshoe* (1971), *The Hit* (1984), *My Beautiful Laundrette* (1985) and *Prick Up Your Ears* (1987) before working with or going to Hollywood for *Dangerous Liaisons* (1988), *The Grifters* (1990) and *Hero* (1992). Kenneth Branagh comes from the British theatre and directed and starred in the film of *Henry V* (1989); his first Hollywood feature was *Dead Again* (1991). James Dearden worked as a scriptwriter (for example on *Fatal Attraction*) and directed the British feature *Pascali's Island* (1988) and the Hollywood feature *A Kiss Before Dying* (1991).

Promising British features have led to Hollywood work for such directors as Malcolm Mowbray (from *A Private Function*, 1984, to *Out Cold*, 1989, and *Don't Tell Her It's Me*, 1990), Bernard Rose (from *Paperhouse*, 1988, and *Chicago Joe and the Showgirl*, 1989 to *Candyman*, 1992), Jonathan Lynn (from *Nuns on the Run*, 1990, to *My Cousin Vinny*, 1992), Bill Forsyth (from *Gregory's Girl*, 1980, *Local Hero*, 1982, and *Comfort and Joy*, 1984, to *Housekeeping*, 1987, and *Breaking In*, 1989), Neil Jordan (from *Angel*, Eire, 1982, *The Company of Wolves*, 1984, and *Mona Lisa*, 1986, to *High Spirits*, 1988, and *We're No Angels*, 1989), and Michael Caton-Jones (from *Scandal*, 1988, and *Memphis Belle*, 1990, to *Doc Hollywood*, 1991), and this by no means exhausts the list. An increasingly important source of new directors for Hollywood has been music video: Stephen Hopkins, for example, came to Hollywood features like *Nightmare on Elm Street: The Dream Child* (1989) and *Predator 2* (1990) from commercials and music videos via the Australian thriller, *The Dangerous Game* (1988), while the Australian Russell Mulcahy went from music videos to the Australian features *Razorback* (1984) and *Highlander* (1986) and then to Hollywood features *Highlander II: The Quickening* (1990) and *Ricochet* (1991).

Mike Figgis is one of the most recent and most distinguished of British directors to work in Hollywood, and his experience offers a British perspective on the way the American film industry works. He was born in Kenya and moved to Newcastle in the mid 1950s. His first interest was music, which he studied in the late 1960s, as well as playing in rock bands including Bryan Ferry's The Gas Board. In the 1970s, he was involved with the experimental theatre group The People Show, which toured widely. In the early 1980s, he wrote and directed theatre shows which often combined music and film with live action. One of these, *Slow Fade*, led to a commission from the then

Still: Tommy Lee Jones (left) and Sting in Stormy Monday.

new Channel 4 Television to write and direct his first film, *The House* (1984). With the encouragement of producers like David Puttnam, Figgis developed several film projects, the first of which to be realised was *Stormy Monday* (1987), a stylish British thriller, financed by the American company Atlantic Entertainment, set and filmed in Newcastle on a budget of about $2 million. Despite some difficulties, Figgis cast the rock singer Sting, who was also from Newcastle, as the owner of a jazz club and Americans Tommy Lee Jones as a ruthless American businessman and Melanie Griffith as an American who has an uneasy relationship with the businessman and becomes involved with a heroic drifter played by Sean Bean. The film has been criticised as too stylish and too American (though there is a very strong current running through it against the encroachment of American culture in Britain with its depiction of Newcastle celebrating 'America Week'). The criticism implied that the film felt as if it had been made as a 'calling card' for Hollywood. Certainly, the film's American backers liked the way the movie went, and it led immediately to offers from Hollywood: 'They really know how to court you, and it's very flattering.'

The project that Figgis liked and wanted to make was *The Hot Spot*, based on a Charles Williams thriller and, like *Stormy Monday* (and later *Internal Affairs*), centering on sexual obsession. It did not get made (at least not by Figgis – it was made by Dennis Hopper in 1990) but provided Figgis with vital experience of working in Hollywood. Figgis's interest in *The Hot Spot* was dependent on rewriting the script (as so often happens, Hopper went back to the original script) and the project went through four drafts and was then cast with financial backing from MGM/UA. The film was budgeted at about $7 million, mainly because the stars (Sam Shepard, Uma Thurman and Anne Archer) were not very expensive (under $1 million together) and it was to be a non-union picture shot in a small town in Texas. Figgis then 'lived through that process of a film collapsing.' Sam Shepard, cast in the male lead, dropped out because he felt insulted by one of the producers, and Figgis spent the next six months trying to resurrect the film. 'Having to deal with the studios as a project collapses, you learn more quickly than if a film goes well – I learned far more in many ways than I did with *Internal Affairs*' (which went well and was well supported). The first lesson for Figgis was to understand that far more films do not get made than do get made and not to be disheartened: 'Nobody blamed me for its collapse . . . Making a film that then fails puts you in a more debilitating position than to be on a film that did not get made but had a good script that people wanted to be made. Had it got made and been a stinker, the chances of going on to *Internal Affairs* would have been much slimmer.'

During the six or seven months Figgis was around and involved with *The Hot Spot* project, he was constantly having meetings to try to get it made, but he was also being offered other scripts, none very interesting to him, and meeting other people: 'I spent time here [Hollywood], and that, I realised, was the crucial thing, because people then knew who I was and it was vitally different from making phone calls from London.' Figgis realised that business could not be done by telephone and fax: 'They don't do business that way. It is very old-fashioned in a way. A lot of it's in a handshake and a lunch, and not in an ass-licking way. They say, let's do this. And they mean it. It might fall apart, but they mean it at the time.' He reckons that it takes about two years to get to know how the system works: 'It really is about a network of people who know each other here.'

Harry Hook, who on the basis of his British film *The Kitchen Toto* (1987) was hired to direct *Lord of the Flies* (1990) for Castle Rock and has since worked for Home Box Office on cable movies, believes that it is much harder to meet people in Britain: 'Here [in Los Angeles] people are set up to actively hunt out new talent and gobble it up.' Trying to set a film up in Britain is much more of a struggle: 'By the time you've knocked on three doors in Britain and they've turned you down for the project, you've got to come over here.' As Figgis has commented, there is a British film industry, but it happens to be in Hollywood: 'The reality is that thousands of British artistes connected with the film industry, be they cinematographers, writers, actors, designers, now work in the context of the American film industry. I feel that there is a very viable British film industry, it just doesn't have a cohesive national base . . . What we lack in Britain is any kind of commercial cinema which respects people's intelligence. You don't have to be stupid to be popular.'

In Figgis's experience, the system in Hollywood does allow directors to do what they want to. 'You have to be very careful what you choose, but the system here is very efficient, once you understand the subtleties about who the people are. Everybody might say the same thing but actually, you learn very quickly, when he says it, it probably will happen, when he says it, it might happen, and when he says it, it probably won't. The system will allow everybody to go quite a long way before something does not happen. There are so many meetings to make that the appearance of something being made is very deceptive, so you have to be very, very careful in your judgement, or you learn very quickly who's real and who isn't real. If you have the good fortune to get a decent script, things do get made – it's quite dependable. [As a British director,] you have to sort of "go to college" and be here. I think the mistake that a lot of European or British film-makers make is that they don't come here, they don't put in enough time actually studying the system. They go on faith and then they get terribly disillusioned rather quickly, and rather bitter, and say things like "the Americans don't want to make quality". That's a naive view. Quality doesn't come into it as a desire, but if you have a good script, it will get through, as long as you also supply them with A, B and C. For example, they're terrified about marquee casting – you have to go along with that, because of the problems with distribution. Those are the realities for these people, so you don't just say in a blanket way that these are bad people – there's a reality of work here which you have to go along with, that's all. You're naive if you don't acknowledge that. Of course, you can also make low-budget pictures here, but distribution is a nightmare.'

For Figgis, the scary moment of beginning to direct his first feature had come with *Stormy Monday:* 'There's this nightmare moment where you suddenly see this huge structure in front of you, with you as the focal point, and everybody's saying, "What do you want?" It's a bit like the nightmare of finding yourself in front of a large symphony orchestra and not knowing how to conduct. You feel like saying, "How the hell do I know? I was hoping you guys would know." ' Directing his first American studio picture, *Internal Affairs* (1990), for Paramount, did not hold this terror for him, and 'at the mundane but psychologically very important level of how they look after you' – bringing his family over, paying expenses, and so forth – he felt very secure, but there were some other unexpected problems. Although this was a Paramount picture, it was being made as a negative pick-up, that is to say, financed by the studio but through some 'independent' entity in order to avoid union regulations, a very common strategy – here done 'rather cheekily', as Figgis puts it, for a picture with a budget of over $11 million. Figgis had not been told about it, and rather unexpectedly found himself in the middle of a huge industrial dispute, with the production being picketed by IATSE and Teamster members. 'Also, coming from a British tradition of unions, one would not dream of crossing a picket line, but then you're dealing with the Teamsters and that's not like a British union – [they're] not very friendly people.'

Another area in which Figgis might have expected problems in making his first studio picture was dealing with a big star, in this case Richard Gere. In fact, however, when Gere expressed interest in the part of the main character, who is initially apparently generous and warm but is revealed as totally corrupt, Paramount were not keen and argued that no-one wanted to see Richard Gere any more. 'After the film came out – *Pretty Woman* had also come out by then – I read a big feature in *Vanity Fair* in which the studio was claiming credit for putting him in *Internal Affairs*. Complete gibberish. It was a huge fight to get them to use Gere. They thought he was a negative factor that would stop people coming to see the picture. So, psychologically, he was not difficult to deal with. In fact, he was great to deal with.' Gere subsequently starred in Figgis's next Hollywood picture, *Mr Jones* (1992).

Where *Stormy Monday* had had a shooting schedule of seven six-day weeks, *Internal Affairs* had a ten-week shoot of five-day weeks (since it was shot in Los Angeles, it was

Photograph: Mike Figgis (at camera) shooting Internal Affairs *with Richard Gere (right).*

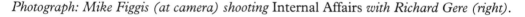

Stills. Above: Richard Gere in Internal Affairs. *Opposite: Kevin Anderson and Pamela Gidley in* Liebestraum.

a location picture only for Figgis – everyone else went home in the evenings and at weekends), but it also had nine weeks of pre-production and much more time in post-production. As a director for hire, Figgis was not passionately involved from the outset – he got into it through working on the script and casting – but he did not find the experience particularly different from his earlier films. Despite Figgis's conviction that the Hollywood system overall is efficient, he was surprised to find that the actual production was in some ways less efficient than for *Stormy Monday:* 'What was interesting was that you expect studios to be all-powerful and interfering but also well-oiled and efficient machines, and they're not. It's a shambles. It's like a big factory; nobody knows what's going on. People feel that once they have had the meeting and said something, it will happen, and then there's this appalling discovery that nobody has actually done it. For example, after they tested the film, everybody was clear they wanted to reshoot the ending, but no-one got around to commissioning or organising the rewrite. So the day before the reshoot, there was no script, no-one had done it. Richard Gere was panicking, saying he wouldn't come to the set because there wasn't a script. Eventually we did it on the set, which was by far the best way of doing it, as far as I'm concerned, but if you had suggested doing that, they would have fired you as being incompetent. So, they had spent another $¹⁄₂ million on rebuilding the set, and so on, and there was no script, and they were delighted I could just get on and do it, because everyone was panicking. It was most bizarre.'

Internal Affairs was a moderate commercial success; Figgis's own view of the success of his career so far is that it has depended partly on being prepared to 'go wider' on each project. However, his next work, *Liebestraum*, was 'a step down, if you like', a non-union picture based on a script he had written before *Stormy Monday* and shot entirely on location in a 'very strange upstate New York town'. It had no big stars – the leads were played by Kevin Anderson, Pamela Gidley and Kim Novak. Figgis mentions that Madonna was to have starred but there were things in the script she did not

understand and Warren Beatty persuaded her to not do something she did not understand. *Liebestraum,* then, was 'cheap', at $8 million, a scale of production that also allowed Figgis to do his own music to a much greater extent than on *Internal Affairs.* It is a very personal project, not at all a typical Hollywood picture, and not at all what MGM wanted or expected. The story mainly concerns an architect/writer who travels to a small town to meet his dying mother, from whom he was separated at birth, and becomes involved in a doomed love affair which in some strange and ambiguous way mirrors an earlier passionate liaison that ended tragically. 'What I want to get on the screen is some kind of nightmare of our own devising. *Liebestraum* is about sex and death, really, and I don't think Americans like the connection between the two.' By Figgis's account, the making of the film was both horrifically difficult and very strange, not helped by the fact that MGM/UA was beset with problems in trying to fend off the takeover by Giancarlo Parretti's Pathé. After a disastrous New York preview, a very forthright ten-minute scene in a brothel was cut out of the version released in the United States as too offensive. 'So it's going to go out as an "art film", with maybe two cinemas in Los Angeles and two in New York, then the art-house circuit, which I don't mind, because it is at least going out.'

As a personal project which did not fit easily with the kinds of product Hollywood wants to make, *Liebestraum* raises the question of how well Figgis feels he can adapt to the system. Hollywood products inevitably tend towards blandness, whereas one quality of *Stormy Monday* and *Liebestraum* is their quirkiness. Figgis argues that you don't need to avoid being quirky, but that it is easier to be so in Europe, where quirkiness is seen as a quality. In mainstream Hollywood films, quirkiness seems much more subversive, though Figgis feels, rightly, that even the more mainstream *Internal Affairs* is quirky by American standards. 'Strangely, though, they do want to allow you to do the sort of work you want, and they do try to help . . . I'm known as the guy who likes a dark script and is quite interested in sex. So they start pitching me all these dark and sexy stories, mostly very silly indeed . . . But if you work in a lunatic asylum, you can bend the rules quite a bit, and the last thing I'm ever going to do is your orthodox American commercial movie.' The possibility of being 'quirky' also depends to some extent on film-makers' familiarity with the culture in which they work. Here Figgis does not consider himself at a disadvantage, because he does not feel specially British ('a terrific advantage if you are a film-maker') and anyway does not like too much cultural 'texture', preferring his work to be rather stylised. He nevertheless feels that he is able to bring an 'outside eye' to American culture: his new picture, *Mr Jones,* about a manic depressive (Richard Gere) who has an affair with his therapist (Lena Olin), was originally scripted to be set in Boston or San Francisco, 'the two cliché American locations for people with brains, and in the Fall. So I'm going to shoot it in San Diego, in bright sunshine, because that's normally seen as "surf city".'

Figgis's feelings about working in Hollywood have been undergoing some change. He was setting up a feature for Universal with Al Pacino, a remake of Charles Vidor's *Love Me Or Leave Me* (1955), with a good, tough new script, but not set to go for some time, when Home Box Office sent him a Henry Miller short story which would be a segment of their cable movie, *Women and Men 2.* Although Figgis would consider working for British television, perhaps in documentary rather than fiction, he considers American television (apart from PBS) as 'dreadful . . . such a colossal lie . . . crippled by censorship.' But HBO's cable movies are different, and no danger to the status of theatrical movie directors – Figgis thinks they are much riskier for actors, who are more inclined to hesitate because it could be catastrophic for them to become labelled as television actors. HBO is widely regarded as almost the only place left in Hollywood where 'adult entertainment' can be made – Harry Hook considers that his HBO project, about death and bereavement, just would not be made for the big screen. Figgis read the Miller story in ten minutes, loved it and agreed to adapt and direct it. He was also able to decide on his own casting: Scott Glenn, who would normally not have worked in television, and Juliette Binoche, who was not much concerned with Hollywood's hierarchy of status. The project was also appealing in that it could be done quickly.

Miller's story was set in Paris, where Figgis's film was shot on location. 'The technique of making films was exactly as I had fantasised. I had a small crew, all of whom drank half a bottle of wine before we started work without it affecting their work. There was something immensely civilised about their way of making the film. All the crew members were film-literate and talked about Jean-Luc Godard as well as *Dances With Wolves*. There was a kind of intellectual awareness of film that was wonderful, and, at the same time, when you're dealing with a character like Juliette Binoche's in the film, there are nuances that you can call on that have to do with European culture which are more interesting than what's available here [in the United States].' Figgis's feelings about the experience were rather soured by what happened after shooting: 'Despite all their protestations to the contrary, HBO is an interfering television company that thinks it knows best.' Figgis remembers that with HBO having been involved in three different cuts and saying it was wonderful, he scored the film, finished dubbing it and sent it off, only to get a call ten days later to say that they had another editor and were already recutting it. Figgis wanted to take his name off the credits but to do so he would have had to sign a gag, so he left his name on it and did talk about it (he has not seen the new version, which lacks his score but seems otherwise only marginally different). 'To have this happen on something that you did for love, not for money, was a galling experience, so I wouldn't go near them again. Somebody said to HBO, why on earth would you want to alienate a director, who is obviously going to talk to other people, when you're desperately trying to attract directors – film directors, not television directors – to come and work for you?' Figgis's willingness to work for the BBC or Channel Four in Britain obviously has much to do with his feelings that such interference would be very unlikely from them.

'Having had this very charming experience of making a film in Paris, the love affair with the idea of being an American film-maker is coming to an end. If I were really honest, the most rewarding film-making experience that I can think of is the low-budget, European film, not using stars, using high energy, probably a short shooting period, etc. I'm trying to set up a film now to be shot on Super 16mm, for $2 million, in England, Italy and Northern Europe, twenty short stories, and that I have vowed will be the next film I'll make after this. I always set myself the task of doing one of my own films, and then a "commercial" film, then one of my own again, and I've done that so far. This next one [*Mr Jones*] is a commercial film. *Liebestraum* was my own script and a low budget by their standards. This one is by my standards huge – it's TriStar, Richard Gere again, and it'll be $25-30 million by the time they've finished. So I'd like to go down to $2 million and do another art film, or what they call an art film – I don't call it that.' If he does enough small deals for film, video and television rights, and produces as well as directs, the budget should not be too hard to raise or too great a risk for any individual investor.

'There is a very specific thing for sale here [in Hollywood], which is that fascination with American culture, the largeness of the culture and the country, the epic. The thing that's very hard to kick, because it is ingrained in us from birth, is American music and film, and wanting to be part of that. And having now been part of it for two or three years, you start to long for a European sensibility. Not in a bad way. I'd never put down anything here, because you can make interesting films, but you need to go away and change up, and come back.' With these recent thoughts, Figgis now feels very much based in Britain, where his family lives and where he has done post-production on *Women and Men 2* and *Liebestraum*. 'A year ago, I would have said I was "here" [in Los Angeles]. Nothing has changed' – except his way of seeing himself and his identity, since he still spends the time he needs to in Hollywood – 'except that I would now say I'm "there" [in London].'

The Dutch director Ate de Jong came to America as an established director, like his compatriot Paul Verhoeven, who despite an unimpressive first Hollywood feature *(Flesh and Blood,* 1985) has achieved big box-office successes with *RoboCop* (1987), *Total Recall* (1990) and *Basic Instinct* (1992). De Jong had already made six features, some critically and commercially very successful and of great variety, though all driven by character and story ('I don't think I knew what "high concept" meant at that point'). Given Holland's system of government subsidy for film-making, these films had to be in Dutch, which limited their distribution possibilities, and they tended to be more 'cultural' than most Hollywood films. Though more general European production was a possibility for him, this was not something that de Jong had much faith in. In 1986, at the age of 33, having achieved most of what he felt he could do in Holland, and with a relationship that had just broken up, he felt it was perhaps the last moment he might dare to change his life so radically. He left and came to Hollywood, feeling that 'it would be a big challenge on another level, it would be great to be a nobody again, and that definitely happens if you come here. Basically, I came here with a few of my films on video in my knapsack and a big bagful of dreams.'

At first, since everyone in Los Angeles is potentially a scriptwriter, he gave his cassettes to anyone who would listen, even the mailman: 'You have to be willing to sit here for a year and not do anything,' be a bum and be laughed at. In Holland, de Jong knew everyone in the film business. In Hollywood, the first thing for him, as with Mike Figgis to learn, was 'networking' – meeting as many people as he could and talking to everyone at parties, since that is what parties are for. 'You start to accept that people are your best friends after one meeting, and still your best friends even if you don't talk for three years.' When he first arrived, de Jong rented the house of a screen writer who was away for some months, and he was invited to a dinner party when the writer returned. The writers of what became de Jong's first released Hollywood feature, *Drop Dead Fred* (1991), were among ten guests at dinner, and four years later, they remembered him (though he did not remember them) – a good example of the way networking works. Though de Jong did not feel he had to prove he could direct, he recognised that there was a question of whether he could adapt to American film-making. Certainly, no-one was about to give him $5-10 million to prove himself with his own script, but he could not afford to sit and wait, and so he initiated meetings with his own material while being open to material that others might have. De Jong believes he was helped by a public radio comedy show he was doing about a young European film-maker trying to get rich in Hollywood, because executives often knew the show. He had given himself six months to get something, then extended the deadline, having it in the back of his head that he would wait two years. He now feels that 18 months to two years is the minimum to give yourself to wait: 'If I think about it, I don't know how I ever got the guts to do it.'

After waiting a year, he was offered one episode of *Miami Vice* to direct, because they had liked his work. He had never worked for television but, despite some doubts, he felt it could be a wise career move, and he was frankly flattered to be offered work on such a high-profile show. Since he was 'nowhere at all' in Hollywood career terms, he had no status to be harmed by working for television. He does not think his episode was very good, and 'the story was so bizarre I didn't even understand it.' In Hollywood, he had always initiated his own projects and had control over them: on *Miami Vice,* 'the first thing Don Johnson said was that he'd been doing this character for four years and I'd been doing it for four days, so don't tell him anything. If I did try, Johnson would run off the set if he didn't like it. That was an attitude I'd never seen before.' De Jong figured that they had hired him, as a European director, to bring something a little different, but 'they didn't need my talents.' What they did need, like most television shows, was 'a good traffic cop, someone who says go from left to right and do it as quickly as possible.' In what he thought were the best interests of the show, he tried to be more than a traffic cop, but just felt uncomfortable and restricted. He does not look down on such shows, recognising that there is much quality in their kind of craftsmanship, but he did not

Still: Phoebe Cates and Rik Mayall in Drop Dead Fred.

think he fitted and, unlike some directors learning the craft in television, he felt no need to prove himself. He was asked to do more episodes, but told them he was not masochistic enough.

Working on *Miami Vice* transformed his meetings: however impressed people might have been with the fact that he had made six features, when he said he had made six features plus an episode of *Miami Vice,* 'everything changed like that, because someone had invested $1·5 million [the cost of a *Miami Vice* episode] in me.' Although they never looked at his episode – they did look at the features – 'the fact that I had made *Miami Vice* made me a professional in this system,' and gave him legitimacy. This enabled de Jong to set up two script development deals at United Artists; one got nowhere, and the other was in pre-production when United Artists was sold. De Jong was also almost signed up by producer Joel Silver for *Road House* (subsequently directed by Rowdy Herrington, 1989, with Patrick Swayze), but was 'packaged out' – dropped as director when the nature of the overall package changed – which he thinks was probably a blessing in disguise. He was by now earning a living, though still experiencing some problems with Hollywood codes of etiquette, like not calling people at times when their blood sugars will be low. Now he just calls when he wants and needs to. He is still surprised by the level of formal dress code – in his first year, he had his Pierre Cardin suit, but he gave it up. He feels he's forgiven for some things because he is European.

One of the executives from United Artists went to Quantum Media and took a script that de Jong had liked and been involved with, and when Quantum fell apart, the project was taken to Hemdale, where it was set up as *Highway to Hell*. The film was a spoof on exploitation, a teenage comedy but with a lot of action, the story of a young Orpheus, in which a girl is kidnapped to hell. De Jong knew when he went in that Hemdale's record with directors was not always good, but he also felt they had a degree of taste in movies. It seemed to him a good film to do, as it was budgeted at a very respectable $8 million – he knew in any case that he would have to do a certain number of other people's projects before he could do his own. This then, was not a film he would have done if he had had a free hand, but it was something that he liked, at least somewhat. As he puts it, the opportunistic side of someone in his position leads him to think, ' "I'll do anything for the money," but then you get a script and you think, 'I'm not sure I can do that." ' So he is willing to compromise, though he felt that *Miami Vice* was going too far. The way Mike Figgis heard it, de Jong 'got really burned on *Highway to Hell* . . . gobbled up by Hemdale.' De Jong himself still supports the film, even though he fought its recutting, which in his view made it less funny and less commercial. Since Hemdale has a backlog of movies to release, *Highway to Hell*, completed in 1990, was not released until 1992.

The fact that *Highway to Hell* remained unreleased was problematic for de Jong's profile in the industry, but showing its first three reels helped him to get *Drop Dead Fred* (1991), which was made by Working Title for Polygram. 'Drop Dead Fred' (played by Rik Mayall) is an 'imaginary friend' from childhood who comes back into the adult life of the woman protagonist (Phoebe Cates). It has been aptly described by Kim Newman as mostly 'content to be *Harvey* re-imagined for the *Beetlejuice* generation,' but its broad comedy was appealing to de Jong. It cost about $7 million – pretty much the same scale of production as *Highway to Hell*, as there was less action, which is always expensive. *Drop Dead Fred* will probably gross about $15 million at the North American box office and will be quite successful on video (video money was invested in the film, and the video people had a say in the film's release), but it was not a big hit. If it had earned $50-60 million, de Jong guesses, this might have given him freedom to make a more personal project. Brilliant reviews would have helped, because people do take notice, but the reviews of *Drop Dead Fred* were mixed.

De Jong believes that he will need to do another $6 million film before he is allowed to do a small studio picture for maybe $10-12 million. He has turned down some $3-4 million pictures, not just because he did not like the scripts much, but also because inevitably the films would not get much distribution; they are therefore, in his mind, projects for people wanting to prove that they can make a film. His thinking is he should either go up in budget or do something because he really believes in it. Though he is busy with three or four projects, some of which look good, he has learned that 'until money is transferred into your bank account, a project isn't a go picture.'

De Jong does not see vast differences between making films in Hollywood and making films in Holland. Lead actors in Hollywood tend to be more prima donnas but they are also often better prepared than Dutch actors. However, since Dutch actors usually have theatre backgrounds, they are more willing to try different things than Americans, who are more reluctant to deviate from the script. A small point: de Jong has been most surprised by the luxurious production spending on catering, at a level that would be unheard of in Holland. The director is given much more overt authority and deference in Hollywood: Directors' Guild rules don't allow directors to drive their own cars, they have to be chauffeured; in Holland a director would just get on his bike. The life-style of a Hollywood director can be very seductive; De Jong guesses that a lot of people are directing for just that, and for the power, not because they want to make particular films.

Much like Mike Figgis, de Jong feels it is very important that Europeans do not look down on the industry in Hollywood but at least allow themselves to be intrigued by American society: 'It's good to confront this culture with your own attitudes and feelings, but that's not saying that everything is shit here,' a view he finds quite common in other foreign film-makers. 'To work here, you need to accept the society for what it is – even if you're still critical. You can't survive on just wanting to be rich and famous.' But when he talks to people about why he came, that's what he likes to say: 'I wanted to be rich and famous.'

Not all the traffic in directors is one way: American film-makers do on occasion make European films in Europe – recent examples include Robert Altman's *Vincent et*

Théo (1990), a French-British co-production, or Jerry Schatzberg's *L'Ami retrouvé* (or *Reunion*, 1989), a French-German-British co-production. It is conceivable that if Europe's economic power in general and media power in particular continue to grow, more movement of American directors to Europe may take place, though this is not to say that Hollywood's dominance of the world media entertainment market looks about to slip significantly. Some shifts in this direction may already be evident. Susan Seidelman's 1992 project, *Yesterday*, looked to Europe, and to territory-by-territory presales, for its financing: 'When Orion went under, this signified a major reshuffle in Hollywood, with European financing coming in. I had a choice of looking either East or West; I chose to look East because I like the way European sales agents put the deals together.' Jodie Foster has been developing a project with Studio Canal Plus about the life of Jean Seberg, commenting that 'Europe is becoming more important than the domestic market.'

Bobby Roth's *The Man Inside* (1990) was a long-cherished project. At the end of the 1970s, he read about the German journalist, Günther Walraff, who infiltrated organisations to expose them. He optioned the rights and wrote a script, naively thinking, as he sees it, that if something is interesting to you, it's a good idea for a movie, 'instead of realising that what's a good idea for a movie is something that Julia Roberts wants to do.' The studios were not interested, and even Goldcrest could offer only half the budget and could not raise the other half. Eventually, ten years later, the movie was made, with 75 per cent of the money from France, and a little from New Line in the United States; it was shot in France and Germany with a mostly French crew. The result, in Roth's words, was 'an interesting failure'. It suffers from being ten years in the making: too much was felt to be at stake, and ideas were being realised that had been imagined eight or ten years before (and Jürgen Prochnow, in the lead role, had been thinking about his performance over a period of some six years).

Some of the problems came out of his being an American making a film in Europe. Roth feels that some of his strength as a director is in nuance and detail, which are qualities harder to achieve in another culture and language. 'It's a big undertaking as an American, with all your ideas about how movies are made, to go to Europe and try to impose your style.' Although it was not very different, says Roth, only slightly tongue-in-cheek, it was different, 'just enough to make it intolerable. People's expectations of how hard and how long they are going to work are very different. The problem with the French is they have the nerve to have another life beyond the movie. So they don't want to work overtime, they don't want to work on the weekend, and they want to drink during the working day. All of those things are anathema to me, so I had trouble with that.' Though the crew was like crews anywhere, half really talented, half not so good, the hardest thing for Roth was getting used to the shorter working day and the slower pace, so that 'I was always on edge, pushing very hard.'

Compare Roth's experience with Mike Figgis's pleasure at working in France. Figgis's six nights of shooting in Paris were with 'the most efficient and hard-working crew I've ever had. Sure, we stopped and had a meal, but the minute I stood up, they all stood up and we went to work,' doing a phenomenal number of camera set-ups. While making *Liebestraum*, Figgis shot material for a 'making of' documentary and, looking at the footage, noticed how dynamic the crew looked, all in great shape, with shorts, hats, headphones 'and belts with things hanging from them, so many tools, it's like a fetish for leather belts and objects, whistles, torches.' But focusing on one crew member, Figgis realised that although he appeared to be talking on walkie-talkies and otherwise 'conquering the world,' in a sort of choreographed way, he wasn't doing anything. Figgis detects a sort of paranoia in American crews about being seen to be working, so everyone is always moving. With a French crew, people appear to be lying down or sleeping, but they're not – they only move when they need to. To him, it is simply a very different approach, which you need to relax and go with. Just as much work gets done. It just doesn't appear to be getting done.

Director Credits

Directorial credits are given below for the directors featured significantly in the book. All films are produced in the United States unless otherwise stated. Titles in bold capitals indicate features and short films; titles in upper and lower case bold are of series or mini-series. Episode titles are in quotes. The absence of episode titles after a series titles does not indicate that the director was responisble for all episodes, but merely that the episode titles are not known. 'n.d.' indicates an unknown date.

GEORGE ARMITAGE

Theatrical features

PRIVATE DUTY NURSES (1972) Crest/New World Pictures. With Kathy Cannon, Joyce Williams, Pegi Boucher. [Also producer, screenplay]

HIT MAN (1972) Penelope Productions, for MGM. With Bernie Casey, Pam Grier, Sam Laws.

VIGILANTE FORCE (1987) The Corman Company, for United Artists. With Kris Kristofferson, Jan-Michael Vincent, Victoria Principal. [Also screenplay]

MIAMI BLUES (1990) Tristes Tropiques, for Orion. With Fred Ward, Jennifer Jason Leigh, Alec Baldwin. [Also screenplay]

Television

Feature: **HOT ROD** (1979) ABC Circle Films, for ABC-TV. With Grant Goodeve, Gregg Henry, Robert Culp, Pernell Roberts.

KATHRYN BIGELOW

Theatrical features

THE LOVELESS (1981) Pioneer Films Corporation. With Willem Dafoe, Robert Gordon, Marin Kanter, Don Ferguson, Tina L'Hotsky. [Co-director and co-screenplay with Monty Montgomery]

NEAR DARK (1987) The Near Dark Joint Venture/An F/M Entertainment presentation. With Adrian Pasdar, Jenny Wright, Lance Henriksen, Bill Paxton. [Also co-screenplay]

BLUE STEEL (1990) Lightning Pictures, in association with Precision Films, Mack-Taylor Productions. With Jamie Lee Curtis, Ron Silver, Clancy Brown, Elizabeth Pena. [Also co-screenplay]

POINT BREAK (1991) Largo Entertainment, for Twentieth Century-Fox. With Patrick Swayze, Keanu Reeves, Gary Busey, Lori Petty.

CHARLES BURNETT

Theatrical features

KILLER OF SHEEP (1977) Charles Burnett Productions. With Henry Gayle Sanders, Kaycee Moore, Charles Bracy, Angela Burnett, Eugene Cherry. [Also producer, screenplay, photography, editor]

MY BROTHER'S WEDDING (1983) Charles Burnett Productions, in association with Zweites Deutsches Fernsehen. With Everette Silas, Jessie Holmes, Gaye Shannon-Burnett, Ronald E. Bell. [Also co-producer, screenplay, photography]

TO SLEEP WITH ANGER (1990) SVS Films, Inc. [subsidiary of Sony]. With Danny Glover, Paul Butler, Mary Alice, Carl Lumbly, Vonette McGee, Richard Brooks, Sheryl Lee Ralph. [Also screenplay]

Short films

SEVERAL FRIENDS (1969) **THE HORSE** (1977), **AMERICA BECOMING** (documentary, 1991)

ROB COHEN

Theatrical features

A SMALL CIRCLE OF FRIENDS (1980) United Artists. With Brad Davis, Karen Allen, Jameson Parker, John Friedrich, Shelley Long, Gary Springer.

SCANDALOUS (UK, 1983) Raleigh Film Productons, for Angeles Cinema Investors, Lantana. With Robert Hays, John Gielgud, Pamela Stephenson, M. Emmet Walsh, Nancy Wood. [Also co-story, co-screenplay]

DRAGON, A LIFE OF BRUCE LEE (1992) Old Code Productions, for Universal. Jason Scott Lee, Lauren Holly, R.J. Wagner. [Also co-screenplay]

Television

Episodic includes: **Miami Vice** episodes 'Evan', 'Made for Each Other' (both 1985), 'Definitely Miami' (1986), 'Sons and Lovers' (1987), Michael Mann Productions and Universal Television, for NBC-TV. **Thirtysomething** episode 'Competition' (1989), Bedford Falls Co. and MGM/UA Television, for ABC-TV. **Private Eye** Universal Television, for NBC-TC (n.d.). **A Year in the Life** Universal Television (1988?). **Almost Grown** Atlantis Films and Universal Television, for CBS-TV (1988?). **Hooperman** Adam Productions and Twentieth-Century Fox Television, for ABC-TV (n.d.). **Nasty Boys** Wolf Film Productions and Universal Pictures Television, for NBC-TV (1990). **Eddie Dodd** Lasker-Parkes Production with Columbia Pictures Television, for CBS-TV (1991). **The Antagonists** pilot, Universal Television, for CBS-TV (1990).

Other work as director includes commercials.

MARTHA COOLIDGE

Theatrical features

NOT A PRETTY PICTURE (1974) Films Inc. Semi-autobiographical documentary-drama. [Also producer, script, co-editor]

VALLEY GIRL (1982) Valley-9000 Productions, for Atlantic Releasing. With Nicolas Cage, Deborah Foreman, Elizabeth Daily, Michael Bowen, Cameron Dye, Michelle Meyrink.

THE CITY GIRL (1981) Moon Pictures. With Laura Harrington, Joe Mastroianni, Carole McGill, Peter Reigert. [Also producer, co-story]. Not released until 1983.

JOY OF SEX (1984) Paramount Pictures, in association with Cinema Group Venture. With Cameron Dye, Michelle Meyrink, Colleen Camp, Ernie Hudson, Lisa Langlois.

REAL GENIUS (1985) Tri-Star-Delphi III Productions. With Val Kilmer, Gabe Jarret, Michelle Meyrink, William Atherton, Patti D'Arbanville.

PLAIN CLOTHES (1988) Sierra Alta, for Paramount. With Arliss Howard, George Wendt, Suzy Amis, Diane Ladd.

RAMBLING ROSE (1991) Midnight Sun Productions/Rambling Rose Productions, for Carolco Pictures. With Laura Dern, Robert Duvall, Diane Ladd, Lukas Haas, John Heard.

LOST IN YONKERS (1992) Rastar Productions. With Richard Dreyfuss, Mercedes Ruehl, Irene Worth.

Short films

DAVID: OFF AND ON (1972) documentary, Films Inc. [Also producer, script, editor]. **MORE THAN A SCHOOL** (1973) documentary, Films Inc. [Also script, editor]. **AN OLD-FASHIONED WOMAN** (1974) documentary, Films Inc. [Also producer, script, editor]. **BIMBO** (1978) Films Inc. [Also co-producer]. **EMPLOYMENT DISCRIMINATIONS: THE TROUBLE SHOOTERS** (1979) documentary, Odyssey Communications Systems.

Television

Episodic: **Sledge Hammer!** pilot, Alan Spencer Productions/D'Angelo Productions & New World Television, for ABC-TV (1986). [Four shows, including Coolidge's, were combined as **HAMMERED: THE BEST OF SLEDGE** (1986) with David Raschel]. **The Winner** mini-series episode 'Strawberries and Gold', Canadian Broadcasting Corporation, Canada (1980). **Roughhouse** pilot, other credits not known. **Twilight Zone** episodes 'Night of the Meek' (1985), 'Quarantine' (1986), CBS Entertainment and Persistence of Vision, for CBS-TV.

Features: **TRENCHCOAT IN PARADISE** (1989) Ogiens/Kane Co., for CBS-TV, with Dirk Benedict, Bruce Dern, Catherine Oxenberg, Kim Zimmer, Sydney Walsh, Michelle Phillips. **BARE ESSENTIALS** (1990) Republic Pictures Corporation, for CBS-TV, with Mark Linn-Baker, Lisa Hartman, Gregory Harrison, Charlotte Lewis. **CRAZY IN LOVE** (1992) Ohlmeyer Communicatons Co./Karen Danaher-Dorr Productions, for Turner Network TV, with Holly Hunter, Gena Rowlands, Frances McDormand, Bill Pullman.

JOE DANTE
Theatrical features

HOLLYWOOD BOULEVARD (1976) New World Pictures. With Candice Rialson, Mary Woronov, Rita George, Dick Miller. [Co-director with Allan Arkush].

PIRANHA (1978) New World Pictures/Piranha Productions. With Bradford Dillman, Heather Menzies, Kevin McCarthy, Keenan Wynn, Dick Miller, Barbara Steele.

THE HOWLING (1980) Avco Embassy Pictures/International Film Investors/Wescom Productions. With Dee Wallace, Patrick Macnee, Dennis Dugan, Christopher Stone, Kevin McCarthy.

TWILIGHT ZONE - THE MOVIE Segment 3: 'It's a Good Life' (1983), Warner Bros. With Kathleen Quinlan, Jeremy Light, Kevin McCarthy, Patricia Barry.

GREMLINS (1984) Amblin Entertainment, for Warner Bros. With Zach Galligan, Phoebe Cates, Hoyt Axton, Polly Holliday, Dick Miller.

EXPLORERS (1985) Edward S. Feldman, for Paramount. With Ethan Hawke, River Phoenix, Jason Presson, Amanda Peterson, Dick Miller.

AMAZON WOMEN ON THE MOON (1987) Universal. With Rosanna Arquette, Ralph Bellamy, Carrie Fisher, Griffin Dunne, Steve Gutenberg, [Segments directed by Dante 'Reckless Youth' and 'Critics' Corner'; other segments directed by John Landis, Robert Weiss, Carl Gottlieb, Peter Horton]

INNERSPACE (1987) Amblin Entertainment, for Warner Bros. A Guber-Peters production. With Dennis Quaid, Martin Short, Meg Ryan, Kevin McCarthy.

THE 'BURBS (1988) A Rollins-Morra-Brezner production, for Imagine Entertainment. With Tom Hanks, Bruce Dern, Carrie Fisher, Rick Ducommun, Henry Gibson.

GREMLINS 2: THE NEW BATCH (1990) Amblin Entertainment, for Warner Bros. With Zach Galligan, Phoebe Cates, John Glover, Robert Prosky, Robert Picardo, Christopher Lee, Dick Miller.

Television

Episodic: **Police Squad!** episode 'Ring of Fear' (1982), Paramount Television, for ABC-TV. **Twilight Zone** episode 'Shadow Man' (1985), CBS Entertainment and Persistence of Vision, for CBS-TV. **Amazing Stories** episode 'Boo!' (1985), Amblin Entertainment and Universal Television, for NBC-TV. **Eerie, Indiana** episode 'Forever Ware' (1991), Unreality Inc., Cosgrove/Meurer Productions and Hearst Entertainment, for NBC-TV [also series creative consultant].

ATE DE JONG
Theatrical features

In Netherlands: **BLINDGANGERS** (BLIND SPOT, Horizon Films, 1977); **THE INHERITANCE; KNOWN FACES, MIXED FEELINGS; EEN VLUCHT REGENWULPEN** (A FLIGHT OF RAINBIRDS, Sigma Films, 1981); **BRANDENDE LIEFDE** (BURNING LOVE, Verenigde Nederlandsche Filmcompagnie, 1983); **IN DE SCHADUW VAN DE OVERWINNING** (SHADOW OF VICTORY, Sigma Films, 1986) [also screenplays].

HIGHWAY TO HELL (1990) Hemdale. With Patrick Bergin, Adam Storke, Chad Lowe, Pamela Gidley. [Not released until 1992].

DROP DEAD FRED (1991) Working Title Films (USA), for Polygram. With Phoebe Cates, Rik Mayall, Marsha Mason, Tim Matheson, Bridget Fonda, Carrie Fisher.

Television

Episodic: **Miami Vice** (Michael Mann Productions and Universal Pictures Television, for NBC-TV (1988?).

JONATHAN DEMME
Theatrical features

CAGED HEAT (1974) Renegade Women/Artists Entertainment Complex. With Juanita Brown, Roberta Collins, Erica Gavin, Ella Reid, Lynda Gold, Barbara Steele. [Also screenplay]

CRAZY MAMA (1975) New World Pictures. With Cloris Leachman, Stuart Whitman, Jim Backus, Ann Sothern.

FIGHTING MAD (1976) Santa Fe Productions, for Twentieth Century-Fox. With Peter Fonda, Lynn Lowry, John Doucette, Philip Carey, Scott Glen. [Also screenplay]

CITIZENS BAND a.k.a. **HANDLE WITH CARE** (1977) Fields Company, for Paramount. With Paul Le Mat, Candy Clark, Ann Wedgeworth, Marcia Rodd.

LAST EMBRACE (1979) Taylor-Wigutow Productions, for United Artists. With Roy Scheider, Janet Margolin, John Glover, Sam Levene.

MELVIN AND HOWARD (1980) Universal. With Paul Le Mat, Jason Robards, Mary Steenburgen.

SWING SHIFT (1984) Lantana, for Warner Bros, in association with The Hawn-Sylbert Movie Company, Jerry Bick Productions. With Goldie Hawn, Kurt Russell, Christine Lahti, Fred Ward, Ed Harris.

STOP MAKING SENSE (1984) Talking Heads Film/Arnold Stiefel Company. Featuring the band Talking Heads - David Byrne, Chris Frantz, Jerry Harrison, Tina Weymouth, Steve Scales, Alex Weir, Bernie Worrell.

SOMETHING WILD (1986) Religioso Primitiva, for Orion. With Jeff Daniels, Melanie Griffith, Ray Liotta. [Also co-producer]

SWIMMING TO CAMBODIA (1987) The Swimming Company. Featuring Spalding Gray.

MARRIED TO THE MOB (1988) Mysterious Arts/Demme Productions, for Orion. With Michelle Pfeiffer, Matthew Modine, Dean Stockwell, Mercedes Ruehl, Alex Baldwin.

THE SILENCE OF THE LAMBS (1990) Strong Heart/Demme Productions, for Orion. With Jodie Foster, Anthony Hopkins, Scot Glenn, Ted Levine.

COUSIN BOBBY (1992) Tesauro. Featuring Robert Castle.

Television

Episodic: **Columbo** episode 'Murder Under The Glass' (1978), Universal Television, for NBC-TV. **A Family Tree** a.k.a. **Survival Guides,** pilot episode, 'Trying Times', VisionArts Communications Inc., (1987).

Short films for television: **WHO AM I THIS TIME?** (1982) for American Playhouse. **ACCUMULATION WITH TALKING PLUS WATER MOTION** (1986) documentary. **HAITI - DREAMS OF DEMOCRACY** (1987).

Music videos include work for: Sandra Bernhard, New Order, UB40 and Chrissie Hynde, Fine Young Cannibals, The Feelies, Suzanne Vega.

BILL DUKE

Theatrical features

THE KILLING FLOOR (1984) Public Forum Productions, in association with KERA-TV Dallas, Fort Worth/American Playhouse; a presentation of the Made in USA series, with financial assistance from public television stations, the Corporation for Public Broadcasting, the National Endowment for the Arts, the National Endowment for the Humanities, Communications Workers of America, United Steelworkers of America, Ford Foundation, Rockefeller Foundation, Illinois Humanities Council, International Union of Operating Engineers, United Foot and Commercial Workers International Union, Xerox Corporation. With Damien Leake, Alfre Woodard, Clarence Felder, Moses Gunn, Jason Green. [Made for television, but also shown theatrically]

A RAGE IN HARLEM (1991) Palace Pictures, in association with Miramax Film Corporation. With Forest Whitaker, Gregory Hines, Robin Givens, Zakes Mokae, Danny Glover. [Made in the United States, but classified as a British production]

DEEP COVER (1992) Image Organisation Inc. With Larry Fishburne, Jeff Goldblum, Victoria Dillard.

Short film

THE HERO (1980) while at AFI.

Television

Episodic includes: **Miami Vice** episode 'The Baseballs of Death' (1988), Michael Mann Productions and Universal Pictures Television, for NBC-TV. **Cagney and Lacey** episode 'The Bounty Hunter' (1984), Mace-Neufeld Productions and Orion Television, for CBS-TV. **Hill Street Blues** episodes 'Death by Kiki', 'Blues for Mr Green' (both 1984), MTM Enterprises, for NBC-TV. **Crime Story** Michael Mann Co. and New World Television, for NBC-TV. **Twilight Zone** episode 'Junction' (1989), CBS Entertainment & Persistence of Vision, for CBS-TV. **Starman** Michael Douglas Productions/Henerson, Hersch Productions for Columbia Pictures Television, for CBS-TV. **Matlock** Fred Silverman Co., Dean Hargrove Productions in association with Viacom Productions, for NBC-TV. **Flag** pilot, Lorimar, (date not known). **Fame** Jozak Productions and MGM-Television, for CBS-TV. **Dallas** Lorimar Productions, for CBS-TV. **Knots Landing** episodes 'New Family', 'Celebration' (both 1987), 'Yesterday It Rained', 'Out of the Past', 'Deluge' (all 1989), Lorimar Television, for CBS-TV. **Maximum Security** pilot, Major H Productions and New World Television for Home Box Office (1984). **Call to Glory** Tisch/Avnet Productions and Paramount

Television, for ABC-TV. **Falcon Crest** episodes 'The Good, The Bad and The Profane' (1981), 'The Last Laugh' (1984), 'Forsaking All Others' (1985), Lorimar Productions, for CBS-TV. **Hunter** episode 'Hot Grounder' (1984), Stephen J. Cannell Productions, for NBC-TV. **Amen** Carson Productions, for NBC-TV. **Heartbeat** episode 'Paradise Lost' (1989), Aaron Spelling Productions, for ABC-TV.

Features: **THE KILLING FLOOR** (see above). **JOHNNIE MAE GIBSON** a.k.a. **THE JOHNNIE GIBSON STORY** (1986) Foolscap Productions for CBS Television, CBS Tuesday Movie, with Lynn Whitfield, Howard Rollins Jr, Richard Lawson, William Allen Young, John Lehne, Marta Dubois. **A RAISIN IN THE SUN** (1988) American Playhouse/PBS, with Danny Glover, Esther Rolle, Starletta Dupois. **THE MEETING** American Playhouse/PBS Television, with Dick Anthony Williams, Jason Bernard.

ABEL FERRARA

Theatrical features

THE DRILLER KILLER (1979) Navaron Films. With Jimmy Laine [Abel Ferrara], Carolyn Marz, Baybi Day, Harry Schultz. [Also, as Jimmy Laine, co-editor, co-songwriter]

Ms .45 a.k.a. **ANGEL OF VENGEANCE** (1980) Navaron Films. With Zoe Tamerlis, Bogey, Albert Sinkys, Darlene Stuto, Helen McGara. [Also, as Jimmy Laine, actor]

FEAR CITY (1984) Rebecca Productions, for Zupnick-Curtis Enterprises. With Tom Berenger, Billy Dee Williams, Jack Scalia, Melanie Griffith, Rossano Brazzi, Rae Dawn Chong.

CHINA GIRL (1987) Vestron Pictures, in association with Great American Films Limited Partnership/A Street Life production. With James Russo, Richard Panebianco, Sari Chang, David Caruso.

CAT CHASER (1988) Whiskers Production, for Vestron. With Peter Weller, Kelly McGillis, Charles Durning, Frederic Forrest, Tomas Milian.

KING OF NEW YORK (1989) King of New York Film Corporation, for Reteitalia/Scena Film, An Augusto Caminito Film. With Christopher Walken, David Caruso, Larry Fishburne, Victor Argo, Wesley Snipes.

BAD LIEUTENANT (1992) Pressman Films.. With Harvey Keitel, Frankie Thorne, Zoe Lund, Anthony Ruggiero. [Also co-screenplay]

Television

Episodic: **Miami Vice** episodes 'The Home Invaders' (1984), 'The Dutch Oven' (1985), Michael Mann Productions and Universal Pictures Television, for NBC-TV. **Crime Story** pilot (1986), Michael Mann Co. and New World Television, for NBC-TV [also released in cut version on video as **CRIME STORY**].

Feature: **THE GLADIATOR** (1986) New World Television, in association with Walker Brothers, for Warner Bros., ABC-TV Monday Night Movie, with Ken Wahl, Nancy Allen, Robert Culp, Rick Dees.

MIKE FIGGIS

Theatrical features

STORMY MONDAY (UK, 1987) The Moving Picture Company, for Film Four International, Atlantic Entertainment Group, in association with British Screen. With Melanie Griffith, Tommy Lee Jones, Sting, Sean Bean. [Also screenplay, music]

INTERNAL AFFAIRS (1990) Paramount. With Richard Gere, Andy Garcia, Nancy Travis, Laurie Metcalf, William Baldwin. [Also co-music]

LIEBESTRAUM (1991) Initial, for MGM. With Kevin Anderson, Pamela Gidley, Bill Pullman, Kim Novak. [Also screenplay, music]

MR JONES (1991) Rastar, for Columbia. With Richard Gere, Lena Olin, Anne Bancroft.

Television

Features: **THE HOUSE** (UK, 1982) for Channel Four, with Stephen Rea, Nigel Hawthorne, Dudley Sutton, Ingrid Pitt [also screenplay]. **WOMEN AND MEN 2: IN LOVE THERE ARE NO RULES** segment: 'Mara' (1991) cable movie, David Brown Production, for HBO Showcase, with Scott Glenn, Juliette Binoche [also screenplay].

MARK FROST
Theatrical Feature

STORYVILLE (1992) Edward R. Pressman Productions, for Davis Entertainment Company. With James Spader, Jason Robards, Joanne Whalley-Kilmer, Piper Laurie. [Also screenplay]

Television

Episodic: **Hill Street Blues** episode 'Washington Deceased' (1985) MTM Enterprises, for NBC-TV [also series writer]. **Twin Peaks** Lynch/Frost Productions, Propaganda Films and World Vision Enterprises, for ABC-TV (1990) [also series producer, writer]. **American Chronicles** stories 'Farewell to the Flesh' (1990), 'Champions' (1992), Lynch/Frost Productions/Propaganda Films, for Fox Broadcasting [also screenplays, executive producer].

MICK GARRIS
Theatrical features

CRITTERS 2: THE MAIN COURSE (UK title **CRITTERS 2**, 1988) New Line Cinema/Sho Films. With Terrence Mann, Don Opper, Cynthia Garris, Scott Grimes. [Also co-screenplay]

SLEEPWALKERS a.k.a. **STEPHEN KING'S SLEEPWALKERS** (1992) An ION Picture/Victor & Grais production, for Columbia. With Brian Krause, Mädchen Amick, Alice Krige, Cindy Pickett, Ron Perlman.

Television

Episodic: **Amazing Stories** episode 'Life on Death Row', Amblin Entertainment and Universal Television, for NBC-TV. **Freddy's Nightmares** Stone TV and New Line Cinema, for syndication.

Features: **FUZZBUCKET** (1985) Walt Disney Productions, for Disney Channel, Disney Sunday Night Movie, with Chris Herbert, Phil Fondacari [also producer, screenplay]. **PSYCHO IV: THE BEGINNING** (1990) Smart Money/MCA-Universal, cable movie for Showtime, with Anthony Perkins, Olivia Hussey, Henry Thomas, C.C.H. Pounder.

MARK GOLDBLATT
Theatrical features

DEAD HEAT (1988) New World Pictures. With Treat Williams, Joe Piscopo, Lindsay Frost, Darren McGavin, Vincent Price.

THE PUNISHER (Australia, 1989) New World Pictures (Australia), for Marvel Entertainment Group. With Dolph Lundgren, Louis Gossett Jr, Jeroen Krabbe, Kim Miyori.

RANDA HAINES
Theatrical features

CHILDREN OF A LESSER GOD (1986) Paramount. With William Hurt, Marlee Matlin, Piper Laurie, Philip Bosco.

THE DOCTOR (1991) Touchstone Pictures [Disney], in association with Silver Screen Partners IV. With William Hurt, Christine Lahti, Elizabeth Perkins, Mandy Patinkin.

Short film

AUGUST/SEPTEMBER (1975-76) at AFI's Directing Workshop for Women..

Television

Episodic includes: **Hill Street Blues** episodes 'Cranky Streets' (1982), 'Pestolozzi's Revenge' (1982), 'No Body's Perfect' (1983), 'The Russians Are Coming' (1984), MTM Enterprises, for NBC-TV. **The Family Tree** Saracen Productions and Comworld Productions, for NBC-TV (1983?), **Knot's Landing** episodes 'Willing Victims' (1982?), 'Best Intentions' (1986?), Lorimar Television, for CBS-TV.

Features: **UNDER THIS SKY: ELIZABETH CADY STANTON IN KANSAS** (1990) PBS, with Irene Worth. **JUST PALS** (1982) ABC-TV Afterschool Special. **SOMETHING ABOUT AMELIA** (1983) Leonard Goldberg Production of an ABC Theater Presentation, ABC-TV Movie-of-the-Week, with Ted Danson, Glenn Close. **ALFRED HITCHCOCK PRESENTS** (1985) four re-made teleplays from the original television series, including 'Bang! You're Dead' directed by Randa Haines [other stories directed by Steve DeJarnatt, Joel Oliansky and Fred Walton], Universal Television, for NBC-TV Sunday Night at the Movies, with Kim Novak, John Huston, Tippi Hedren, Steve Bauer, Melanie Griffith, Annette O'Toole.

Short film for television: **THE JILTING OF GRANNY WEATHERALL** (1980) for PBS American Short Stories, with Geraldine Fitzgerald, Lois Smith.

AMY HECKERLING
Theatrical features

FAST TIMES AT RIDGEMONT HIGH (UK title **FAST TIMES,** 1982) A Refugee Films production, for Universal. With Sean Penn, Jennifer Jason Leigh, Judge Reinhold, Phoebe Cates, Brian Backer, Ray Walston, Forest Whitaker.

JOHNNY DANGEROUSLY (1984) Twentieth Century-Fox. With Michael Keaton, Joe Piscopo, Marilu Henner, Maureen Stapleton, Peter Boyle, Griffin Dunne.

NATIONAL LAMPOON'S EUROPEAN VACATION (1985) Warner Bros. With Chevy Chase, Beverly D'Angelo, Jason Lively, Dana Hill, Eric Idle.

LOOK WHO'S TALKING (1989) Tri-Star Pictures. With John Travolta, Kirstie Alley, Olympia Dukakis, George Segal, Abe Vigoda, plus the voice of Bruce Willis. [Also screenplay]

LOOK WHO'S TALKING TOO (1990) Tri-Star Pictures. With John Travolta, Kirstie Alley, Olympia Dukakis, Elias Koteas, Twink Kaplan, plus the voices of Bruce Willis, Roseanne Barr, Damon Wayans. [Also co-screenplay]

Short films as student: **MODERN TIMES** (1973), **HIGH FINANCE** (date not known), **GETTING IT OVER WITH** (1977).

Television

Episodic: **Fast Times,** Universal Television, for CBS-TV (1986) [also series supervising producer, co-writer].

REGINALD HUDLIN
Theatrical features

HOUSE PARTY (1990) Hudlin Brothers, for New Line Cinema. With Christopher Reid, Robin Harris, Christopher Martin, Martin Lawrence, Tish Campbell. [Also screenplay; produced by Warrington Hudlin]

BOOMERANG (1992) Paramount. With Eddie Murphy, Robin Givens, Halle Berry, David Alan Grier. [Co-produced by Warrington Hudlin]

Short films (as student) include: Short version of **HOUSE PARTY**

TIM HUNTER

Theatrical features

TEX (1982) Walt Disney Productions. With Matt Dillon, Jim Metzler, Meg Tilley, Ben Johnson.

SYLVESTER (1985) Rastar, for Columbia. With Richard Farnsworth, Melissa Gilbert, Michael Schoeffling.

RIVER'S EDGE (1986) Hemdale. With Crispin Glover, Keanu Reeves, Ione Skye Leitch, Daniel Roebuck, Dennis Hopper, Joshua Miller.

PAINT IT BLACK (1990) Vestron. With Rich Rossovich, Doug Savant, Julie Carmen, Jason Bernard, Martin Landau.

Films as a student include: **THREE SISTERS** (1969) with Tommy Lee Jones and Stockard Channing, **THE DEVIL'S BARGAIN** (American Film Institute, 1970)

Television

Episodic includes: **Falcon Crest,** Lorimar Productions, for CBS-TV (1990-91). **Twin Peaks,** Lynch/Frost Productions, Propaganda Films and World Vision Enterprises, for ABC-TV. **Beverly Hills 90201** pilot (1990), Propaganda Films in association with Torand Productions, for Fox Network.

Feature: **LIES OF THE TWINS** (1991) Ricochet Productions, cable movie for USA Network, 1991, with Aidan Quinn, Isabella Rossellini [also screenplay].

AMY JONES

Theatrical features

THE SLUMBER PARTY MASSACRE (1982) Santa Fe Productions. With Michele Michaels, Robin Stille, Michael Villela, Debra DeLiso, Andrée Honoré. [Also producer]

LOVE LETTERS (1983) Millenium. With Jamie Lee Curtis, Bonnie Bartlett, Matt Clark, James Keach, Bud Cort. [Also screenplay]

MAID TO ORDER (1987) Vista Organisation. With Ally Sheedy, Beverly D'Angelo.

Short film as student: **A WEEKEND AT HOME** (1973?)

JONATHAN KAPLAN

Theatrical features

NIGHT CALL NURSES (1972) New World Pictures. With Patricia T. Byrne, Alana Collins, Mittie Lawrence.

STUDENT TEACHERS (1973) New World Pictures. With Susan Pamante, Brooke Mills.

THE SLAMS (1973) Penelope Productions, for MGM. With Jim Brown, Judy Pace, Roland 'Bob' Harris.

TRUCK TURNER (1974) Sequoia Pictures, for American-International. With Isaac Hayes, Yaphet Kotto, Alan Weeks, Nichelle Nichols.

WHITE LINE FEVER (1975) The White Line Fever Syndicate/International Cinemedia Center. With Jan-Michael Vincent, Kay Lenz, Slim Pickens, L.Q. Jones. [Also co-screenplay]

MR BILLION (1977) Pantheon/Kaplan-Friedman Production. With Terence Hill, Valerie Perrine, Jackie Gleason, Slim Pickens. [Also co-screenplay]

OVER THE EDGE (1979) Orion. With Harry Northrup, Andy Romano, Ellen Geer, Julia Pomeroy, Michael Kramer, Matt Dillon, Patricia Ludwig, Vincent Spano.

HEART LIKE A WHEEL (1983) Aurora Productions in association with Michael Nolin. With Bonnie Bedelia, Beau Bridges, Leo Rossi, Hoyt Axton.

PROJECT X (1987) Twentieth Century-Fox, in association with Amercent Films, American Entertainment Partners. With Matthew Broderick, Helen Hunt, Bill Sadler.

THE ACCUSED (1988) Paramount. With Kelly McGillis, Jodie Foster, Bernie Coulson, Leo Rossi.

IMMEDIATE FAMILY (1989) Columbia. With Glenn Close, James Woods, Mary Stuart Masterson, Kevin Dillon.

LOVE FIELD (1990) Jaqueline Productions, for Orion. With Michelle Pfeiffer, Denzel Washington, Dennis Haysbert, Louise Latham. Released 1992.

UNLAWFUL ENTRY (1992) Largo Entertainment in association with JVC Entertainment. With Kurt Russell, Ray Liotta, Madeleine Stowe.

Short film as student: **THE STATIONMASTER** (while at USC, date not known).

Television

Features: **11th VICTIM** (1979) Marty Katz Production, for Paramount, CBS-TV Movie-of-the-Week, with Bess Armstrong, Maxwell Gail, Harold Gould. **THE HUSTLER OF MUSCLE BEACH** (1990) Furia-Oringer Productions, ABC-TV Movie-of-the-Week, with Richard Hatch, Kay Lenz. **THE GENTLEMAN BANDIT** (1981) CBS-TV Movie-of-the-Week, with Ralph Waite, Julie Bovasso. **GIRLS OF THE WHITE ORCHID** a.k.a. **DEATH RIDE TO OSAKA** (1983) Hill-Mandelker Television Productions, NBC-TV Movie-of-the-Week, with Jennifer Jason Leigh, Ann Jillian, Thomas Byrd, Mako.

SPIKE LEE

Theatrical features

SHE'S GOTTA HAVE IT (1986) 40 Acres and a Mule Filmworks. With Tracy Camila Johns, Tommy Redmond Hicks, John Canada Terrell, Spike Lee. [Also screenplay, editor]

SCHOOL DAZE (1988) 40 Acres and a Mule Filmworks, for Columbia. With Larry Fishburne, Giancarlo Esposito, Tish Campbell, Kyme, Spike Lee. [Also producer, screenplay]

DO THE RIGHT THING (1989) 40 Acres and a Mule Filmworks, for Universal. With Danny Aiello, Ossie Davis, Ruby Dee, Richard Edson, Giancarlo Esposito, Spike Lee, John Turturro. [Also producer, screenplay]

MO' BETTER BLUES (1990) 40 Acres and a Mule Filmworks, for Universal. With Denzel Washington, Spike Lee, Wesley Snipes, Giancarlo Esposito, Joie Lee. [Also producer, screenplay]

JUNGLE FEVER (1991) 40 Acres and a Mule Filmworks, for Universal. With Wesley Snipes, Annabella Sciorra, Spike Lee, Ossie Davis, Ruby Dee. [Also producer, screenplay]

MALCOLM X (1992) 40 Acres and a Mule Filmworks/Marvin Worth Productions, for Warner Bros in association with Largo International. With Denzel Washington, Spike Lee, Angela Bassett, Kate Vernon. [Also co-producer, co-screenplay]

Short films as student: **THE ANSWER** (1980), **SARAH** (1981), **JOE'S BED-STUY BARBERSHOP: WE CUT HEADS** (1982)

Television

Short films for television include: one-minute spots for MTV (1986), **HORN OF PLENTY** (1986, for Saturday Night Live)

Music videos include work for: Miles Davis, Branford Marsalis, Anita Baker, Phyllis Hyman, Steel Pulse, Public Enemy, Perri, Tracy Chapman.

Commercials for: Air Jordan/Nike and Jesse Jackson's New York State 1990 Primary Campaign.

AARON LIPSTADT

Theatrical features

ANDROID (1982) New World Productions/Android Productions. With Klaus Kinski, Don Opper, Brie Howard, Norbert Weisser.

CITY LIMITS (1984) Sho Films/Videoform Pictures, in association with Island Alive. With Darrell Larson, John Stockwell, Kim Cattrall, Rae Dawn Chong.

Television

Episodic includes: **Miami Vice** episodes 'Payback', 'Yankee Dollar', 'El Viejo' (1986-87) Michael Mann Productions and Universal Television, for NBC-TV. **Crime Story** episodes 'Pursuit of a Wanted Felon', 'Abrams for the Defence', 'Battle of Las Vegas' (1986-87), Michael Mann Company and New World Television, for NBC-TV. **Private Eye** Universal Television, for NBC-TV. **The Equalizer** Universal Television, for CBS-TV (1986-88). **Tour of Duty** Zev Braun Pictures and New World Television, for CBS-TV (1987). **Wise Guy** Stephen J. Cannell Productions, for CBS-TV (1987). **Hard Copy** Universal Television, for CBS-TV (1987). **Houston Knights** Jay Bernstein Productions and Columbia Pictures Television, for CBS-TV (1988). **Quantum Leap** episodes 'Double Identity', 'Play It Again, Seymour', 'Honeymoon Express' (all 1989) Belisarius Productions and Universal Television, for NBC-TV. **Nasty Boys** Wolf Film Productions and Universal Television, for NBC-TV (1990). **Shannon's Deal** Stan Rogow Productions in association with NBC Productions, for NBC-TV (1990). **Law and Order** episode 'Life Choice' (1991), Wolf Films in association with Universal Television, for NBC-TV. **The Flash** Pet Fly Productions in association with Warner Bros. Television, for CBS-TV (1990). **Eddie Dodd** Lasker-Parkes Productions, for Columbia Pictures Television, for CBS-TV (1990). **Lifestories** story 'Steve Burdick' (1990) Ohlmeyer Communications Co. in association with Jeffrey Lewis Productions and Orion Television Entertainment, for NBC-TV. **The Antagonists** Universal Pictures Television, for CBS-TV (1990-91) [also series producer]. **The Young Riders** Ogiens/Kane Co. in association with MGM/UA Television, for ABC-TV (1991). **I'll Fly Away** Lorimar Productions, for CBS-TV (1991). **The Human Factor** Universal Television, for CBS-TV (1991). **The Untouchables** Paramount Television, for syndication (1992).

Features: **POLICE STORY: MONSTER MANOR** (1988) Columbia Pictures Television, for ABC-TV, with Brian McNamara, Clayton Rohner, Scott Burkholder, Claudia Christian. **A PAIR OF ACES** (1990) Once Upon a Time Films/Pedernales Films, CBS-TV Sunday Movie, with Willie Nelson, Kris Kristofferson, Helen Shaver, Rip Torn, [also producer].

SONDRA LOCKE

Theatrical features

RATBOY (1986) A Malpaso Production, for Warner Bros. With Sondra Locke, Robert Townsend, Christopher Hewett.

IMPULSE (1990) Ruddy Morgan, for Warner Bros. With Theresa Russell, Jeff Fahey, George Bzundza.

JIM McBRIDE

Theatrical features

DAVID HOLZMAN'S DIARY (1967) James McBride Production. With L.M. Kit Carson, Penny Wohl. [Also screenplay, editor]

MY GIRLFRIEND'S WEDDING (1969) Daradigm Films. With Clarissa Ainley, Dennis Dalrymple, Jim McBride. [Also screenplay]

GLEN AND RANDA (1971) Sidney Glazier Productions. With Steven Curry, Shelley Plimpton, Woodrow Chambliss. [Also co-screenplay]

PICTURES FOR LIFE'S OTHER SIDE (1971) American Film Institute. Other credits not known.

HOT TIMES (1974) Extraordinary Films. With Henry Cory, Gail Lorber, Amy Farber, Steve Curry. [Also screenplay]

BREATHLESS (1983) Breathless Associates (A Greenberg Brothers Partnership)/A Miko Productions production. With Richard Gere, Valerie Kaprisky, William Tepper, John P. Ryan. [Also co-screenplay]

THE BIG EASY (1986) Kings Road Entertainment. With Dennis Quaid, Ellen Barkin, Ned Beatty, Ebbe Roe Smith, John Goodman, Lisa Jane Persky.

GREAT BALLS OF FIRE! (1989) Orion. With Dennis Quaid, Winona Ryder, John Doe, Joe Bob Briggs, Stephen Tobolowsky, Alec Baldwin. [Also co-screenplay]

Short films

WE SHALL OVERCOME (1966), **THE FUTURE IS OURS** (1969).

Television

Episodic includes: **Twilight Zone** episode 'The Once and Future King' (1986), CBS Entertainment and Persistence of Vision, for CBS-TV. **The Wonder Years** episode 'Glee Club' (1990), Black/Marlems Co. in association with New World Television, for ABC-TV.

Feature: **BLOOD TIES** (1991) Shapiro Entertainment, for Fox Broadcasting, with Patrick Bauchau, Harley Venton, Michelle Johnson.

MICHAEL MANN

Theatrical features

THE JERICHO MILE (1979) ABC Pictures International. With Peter Strauss, Richard Lawson, Roger E. Mosley, Brian Dennehy. [Also co-screenplay] Originally an ABC-TV movie-of-the-week, but also released theatrically outside the United States.

THIEF (UK title **VIOLENT STREETS**, 1981) Michael Mann Company/Caan Productions. With James Caan, Tuesday Weld, Willie Nelson, James Belushi, Robert Prosky. [Also screenplay, executive producer]

THE KEEP (1983) CBS Theatrical Films/Paramount; with Scott Glenn, Alberta Watson, Jürgen Prochnow, Robert Prosky, Gabriel Byrne, Ian McKellen. [Also screenplay]

MANHUNTER (1986) Red Dragon Productions, for Dino De Laurentiis Entertainment Group. With William Peterson, Kim Greist, Joan Allen, Brian Cox, Dennis Farina. [Also screenplay]

THE LAST OF THE MOHICANS (1992) Morgan Creek, for Warner Bros. With Daniel Day-Lewis, Madeleine Stowe, Russell Means, Eric Schweig, Jodhi May. [Also co-producer, co-screenplay]

Short film

JUANPURI (UK, 1970).

Television

Episodic: **Police Woman** episode 'The Buttercup Killer' (1977), Columbia Pictures Television, for NBC-TV. **Crime Story** episode 'The King in a Cage' (1987), Michael Mann Company and New World Television, for NBC-TV.

Features: **THE JERICHO MILE** (see above). **L.A. TAKEDOWN** (1989) AJAR Inc., with Movies Film Productions B.V., Cia Ibero America de TV S.A. & World International Network, for NBC-TV, intended as pilot for series but unsold, shown as television feature, with Scott Plank, Michael Rooker, Ely Pouget, [also executive producer, script].

Short films for television: **INSURRECTION** (made in Britain, for NBC-TV, 1968), **SEVENTEEN DAYS DOWN THE LINE** (for ABC-TV, 1972).

Also several television commercials in UK.

ROCKNE S. O'BANNON

Theatrical feature

FEAR (1989) Richard Kobritz-Rockne S. O'Bannon, for Vestron. With Ally Sheedy, Pruitt Taylor Vince, Lauren Hutton, Michael O'Keefe, Dina Merrill. [Also screenplay]

BOBBY ROTH

Theatrical features

INDEPENDENCE DAY (1975?) University of Southern California graduation film, other credits not known. [Also producer, script]

THE BOSS'S SON (1977?) Production Co. not known. With Asher Brauner, Rita Moreno, Rudy Solari, Henry E. Sanders, James Darren, Piper Laurie. [Also script]

CIRCLE OF POWER a.k.a. **MYSTIQUE** (1981) Qui Productions, with Televicine International. With Yvette Mimieux, Christopher Allport, Cindy Pickett, John Considine.

HEARTBREAKERS (1984) Jethro Films/Bob Weis Production, for Orion. With Peter Coyote, Nick Mancuso, Carole Laure, Carol Wayne, Kathryn Harrold. [Also co-producer, screenplay]

BAJA OKLAHOMA (1988) Rastar Productions for Home Box Office. With Lesley Ann Warren, Peter Coyote, Swoozie Kurtz, William Forsythe. Made for cable, but also released theatrically.

THE MAN INSIDE (France/West Germany/US 1990) Philippe Diaz/Compagnie de Production International/Franco American Film Productions. With Jürgen Prochnow, Peter Coyote, Nathalie Baye.

Short films; **DOOMSDAY** (1972), **WORKSHOP** (1973?) both made while at USC and UCL. **THE AMERICAN ARMY** (collectively made, Group Production Workshop, 1973), **FIGHT BACK** (collectively made, Group Production Workshop, 1974).

Television

Episodic includes: **Miami Vice** episode 'Give a Little, Take a Little' (1984), Michael Mann Productions and Universal Television, for NBC-TV. **Crime Story** episodes 'Old Friends, Dead Ends', 'For Love Or Money' (1986-71), Michael Mann Productions and New World Television, for NBC-TV. **The Insiders** pilot, Leonard Hill Films and Universal Television, for USA Network (1986?) [also series executive producer].

Features: **THE MAN WHO FELL TO EARTH** (1987) MGM-UA Productions, for ABC-TV, intended as a pilot for television series based on Nicholas Roeg's film, but became television movie-of-the-week, with Lewis Smith, Beverly D'Angelo. **TONIGHT'S THE NIGHT** a.k.a. **THE GAME OF LOVE** (1987) Indieprod Production/Phoenix Entertainment, ABC-TV Monday Night Movie, with Ed Marinaro, Ken Olin, Max Gail, Belinda Bauer, Jack Blessing. **DEAD SOLID PERFECT** (1988) HBO Productions and David Merrick, cable movie for Home Box Office, with Randy Quaid, Kathryn Harrold, Jack Warden, Corrine Bohrer [also co-screenplay]. **BAJA OKLAHOMA** (see above). **RAINBOW DRIVE** (1990) cable movie, with Peter Weller, Sela Ward, David Caruso, Bruce Weitz, Kathryn Harrold. **KEEPER OF THE CITY** (1991) Huey Pictures, cable movie for Viacom, with Louis Gossett Jr, Peter Coyote, Anthony Lapaglia.

JOSEPH RUBEN

Theatrical features

THE SISTER-IN-LAW (1975) Crown International. With John Savage, W.G. McMillan, Anne Saxon. [Also co-producer, screenplay]

THE POM POM GIRLS (1976) Crown International. With Robert Carradine, Jennifer Ashley, Lisa Reeves, Michael

Mullins. [Also producer, screenplay, co-story]

JOYRIDE (1977) Hal Landers-Bobby Roberts, for American International. With Desi Arnaz Jr, Robert Carradine, Melanie Griffith, Anne Lockhart. [Also co-screenplay]

OUR WINNING SEASON (1978) Samuel Z. Arkoff/Cinema 77. With Scott Jacoby, Joe Penny, Jan Smithers, Randy Herman, Dennis Quaid. [Also screenplay]

GORP (1980) Jeffery Konvitz Production, for American-International Pictures/Filmways. With Michael Lembeck, Philip Casnoff, Dennis Quaid, David Huddleston, Rosanna Arquette.

DREAMSCAPE (1983) Bella Productions/A Zupnik-Curtis presentation. With Dennis Quaid, Max Von Sydow, Christopher Plummer, Eddie Albert, Kate Capshaw. [Also co-screenplay]

THE STEPFATHER (1986) ITC. With Terry O'Quinn, Jill Schoelen, Shelley Hack, Charles Lanyer, Stephen Shellen.

TRUE BELIEVER (1989) A Lasker-Parkes Production, for Columbia. With James Woods, Robert Downey Jr, Margaret Colin, Kurtwood Smith.

SLEEPING WITH THE ENEMY (1991) Twentieth Century-Fox. With Julia Roberts, Patrick Bergin, Kevin Anderson, Elizabeth Lawrence.

Television

Episodic: **Breaking Away** pilot, Twentieth Century-Fox Television, for ABC-TV (1980).

JOHN SAYLES

Theatrical features

RETURN OF THE SECAUCUS SEVEN (1979) Salsipuedes Productions. With Bruce MacDonald, Adam Lefevre, Gordon Clapp, Karen Trott, David Strathairn. [Also screenplay, editor]

LIANNA (1982) Winwood Company. With Linda Griffiths, Jane Hallaren, Jon DeVries, Jo Henderson, Jessica Wright MacDonald. [Also screenplay, editor, actor]

BABY, IT'S YOU (1982) A Double Play production, for Paramount. With Rosanna Arquette, Vincent Spano, Joanna Merlin, Jack Davidson, Nick Ferrari. [Also screenplay]

THE BROTHER FROM ANOTHER PLANET (1984) A-Train Films. With Joe Morton, Tom Wright, Caroline Aaron, Herbert Newsome. [Also screenplay, editor, actor]

MATEWAN (1987) Cinecom Entertainment Group/Film Gallery, a Red Dog production. With Chris Cooper, Mary McDonnell, Will Oldham, David Strathairn, Ken Jenkins. [Also screenplay, actor]

RIGHT MEN OUT (1988) Orion. With John Cusack, John Mahoney, Charlie Sheen, Jim Desmond, Studs Terkel, Michael Lerner, Richard Edson. [Also screenplay, actor]

CITY OF HOPE (1991) Esperanza Inc. With Vincent Spano, Joe Morton, Tony Lo Bianco, Barbara Williams, Stephen Mendillo. [Also screenplay, editor, actor]

PASSION FISH (1992) Atchafalaya Films. With Mary McDonnell, John Lithgow, Alfre Woodard, Nora Dunn. [Also screenplay, editor]

Television

Feature: **MOUNTAINVIEW** (1989) WGBH, Boston. With Jane Alexander, Mary Schulz, Fred Holland.

Music videos: for Bruce Springsteen/E Street Band, **Born in the USA, I'm On Fire, Glory Days.**

SUSAN SEIDELMAN

Theatrical features

SMITHEREENS (1982) Domestic Films. With Susan

Berman, Brad Rinn, Richard Hell, Nada Despovitch. [Also producer, co-story]

DESPERATELY SEEKING SUSAN (1985) Orion. With Rosanna Arquette, Madonna, Aidan Quinn, Mark Blum, Laurie Metcalf.

MAKING MR RIGHT (1987) Barry and Enright production, for Orion. With John Malkovich, Ann Magnuson, Glenne Headley, Ben Masters, Laurie Metcalf. [Also co-executive producer]

COOKIE (1989) Lorimar Film Entertainment Company. With Peter Falk, Dianne Wiest, Emily Lloyd, Michael V. Gazzo, Brenda Vaccaro. [Also co-executive producer]

SHE-DEVIL (1989) Orion. With Meryl Street, Roseanne Barr, Ed Begley Jr, Sylvia Miles, Linda Hunt. [Also co-producer]

Short films as a student: **AND YOU ACT LIKE ONE, TOO** (1976), **DEFICIT** (197?), **YOURS TRULY, ANDREA G. STERN** (197?)

Television

Short film: **CONFESSIONS OF A SURBURBAN GIRL** (UK 1992) documentary commissioned by BBC Scotland [also screenplay].

JOHN SINGLETON
Theatrical feature
BOYZ N THE HOOD (1991) Columbia. With Ice Cube, Cuba Gooding Jr, Morris Chestnut, Larry Fishburne, Nia Long, Tyra Ferrell. [Also screenplay]

PENELOPE SPHEERIS
Theatrical features
THE DECLINE OF WESTERN CIVILISATION (1980) Spheeris Films. Featuring live performances by Black Flag, Germs, Catholic Discipline, X, Circle Jerks, Alice Bag Band, Fear, and interviews with band members, fans, club owners, etc. [Also producer, script, additional photography]

SUBURBIA (original title in United States: **THE WILD SIDE,** 1983) Surburbia Productions, for New World Pictures. With Chris Pederson, Bill Coyne, Jennifer Clay, Andrew Pece, Wade Walston. [Also screenplay]

THE BOYS NEXT DOOR (1984) The Killing Venture, for New World Productions/Republic Entertainment. With Maxwell Caulfield, Charlie Sheen, Patti D'Arbanville, Christopher McDonald, Hank Garrett.

HOLLYWOOD VICE SQUAD (1986) A Cinema Group presentation of a Sandy Howard production. With Ronny Cox, Frank Gorshin, Leon Isaac Kennedy, Trish Van DeVere, Carrie Fisher.

DUDES (1987) Vista Organisation. With Jon Cryer, Catherine Mary Stewart, Daniel Roebuck, Lee Ving.

THE DECLINE OF WESTERN CIVILISATION PART II: THE METAL YEARS (1988) New Line Cinema/I.R.S. World Media. Featuring live performances by Lizzy Borden, Faster Pussycat, Seduce, Odin, London, Megadeth and interviews with members of Aerosmith, Alice Cooper, Kiss, Motorhead, etc.

WAYNE'S WORLD (1992) Paramount. With Mike Myers, Dana Carvey, Rob Lowe, Tia Carrere, Brian Doyle-Murray, Lara Flynn Boyle.

Television
Feature: **PRISON STORIES: WOMEN ON THE INSIDE** story 'New Chicks' (1991) cable movie, Home Box Office presentation, one of three short stories, others directed by Donna Deitch, Joan Micklin Silver, with Rae Dawn Chong, Annabella Sciorra, Grace Zabriskie, Leontine Guilliard, Desi Parker.

Rock promos include work for: Fleetwood Mac, The Doobie Brothers, 2 Live Crew (**Banned in the USA,** 1990), Lifers Group: World Tour (1992)

LEWIS TEAGUE
Theatrical features
DIRTY O'NEIL: THE LOVE LIFE OF A COP (1974) United Producers Production. With Morgan Paull, Art Metrano, Pat Anderson. [Co-director with Howard Freen]

THE LADY IN RED (1979) Lady in Red Productions, for New World Pictures. With Pamela Sue Martin, Robert Conrad, Louise Fletcher, Robert Hogan.

ALLIGATOR (1980) Alligator Associates, for Group 1. With Robert Forster, Robin Riker, Michael Gazzo, Dean Jagger, Henry Silva.

FIGHTING BACK (1982, UK title **DEATH VENGEANCE**) Dino De Laurentiis Corporation. With Tom Skerritt, Patti LuPone, Michael Sarrazin, Yaphet Kotto.

CUJO (1983) Taft Entertainment Company, for Sunn Classic Pictures. With Dee Wallace, Daniel Hugh-Kelly, Danny Pintauro, Christopher Stone.

CAT'S EYE (1984) Famous Films Productions/International Film Corporation, a Dino De Laurentiis presentation, for MGM/UA. With Drew Barrymore, James Woods, Alan King, Kenneth McMillan, Candy Clark.

THE JEWEL OF THE NILE (1985) The Stone Group, for Twentieth Century Fox. With Michael Douglas, Kathleen Turner, Danny DeVito, Spiros Focas.

COLLISION COURSE (1990) Interscope Communications, for De Laurentiis Entertainment Group. With Pat Morita, Jay Leno, Chris Sarandon, Ernie Hudson.

NAVY SEALS (1990) Orion. With Charlie Sheen, Michael Biehn, Joanne Whalley-Kilmer, Rick Rossovich.

Short film
IT'S ABOUT THIS CARPENTER (1963)

Television
Episodic includes: **Barnaby Jones** Quinn Martin Productions for CBS-TV. **Vegas** Aaron Spelling Productions, for ABC-TV. **A Man Called Sloane** Woodruff Productions and Quinn Martin Productions, for NBC-TV. **Shannon's Deal** pilot (1989), Stan Rogow Productions in association with NBC Productions, for NBC-TV.

Feature: **WEDLOCK** (1991) Spectacor Films, cable movie for USA Cable, with Rutger Hauer, Mimi Rogers, Joan Chen, James Remar.

MARIO VAN PEEBLES
Theatrical feature
NEW JACK CITY (1991) Warner Bros. With Wesley Snipes, Ice T, Allen Payne, Chris Rock, Mario Van Peebles.

Television
Episodic includes: **Wise Guy** Stephen J. Cannell Productions, for CBS-TV. **Jump Street** production details not known. **Top of the Hill** Stephen J. Cannell Productions, for CBS-TV.

Sources

Any work on the current state of the US film and television industry relies heavily on the trade paper *Variety*, a major source of information and opinion. References to *Variety* are too numerous to mention. *Variety* was subjected to particular scrutiny during the six or seven months from July 1991, on the basis that six months' concentrated study of its pages would provide a pretty accurate picture of US film industry trends and neuroses at a particular historical moment. Other useful sources of information and opinion, many of which (particularly the books) also provide material for further reading, are listed below.

Andrews, Nigel *Kaleidoscope* (Women Film-makers in Hollywood), BBC Radio 4, 5th January 1990.

Balio, Tino (editor) *The American Film Industry*, University of Wisconsin Press, Madison, Wisconsin, 1976.

Balio, Tino (editor) *Hollywood in the Age of Television*. Unwin Hyman, Boston & London, 1990.

Baron, Saskia, & Lipman, Amanda 'Consenting Adults in Public', *City Limits*, 15th-22nd May 1986.

Bates, Karen Grigsby 'Boyz with the Black Stuff', *The Guardian*, 27th July 1991.

Bergson, Phillip 'A Good Story Is a Good Story', *What's On in London*, 2nd May 1990.

Biskind, Peter 'Terminators', *Sight & Sound*, May 1991.

Biskind, Peter 'Synergetic', *Sight & Sound*, June 1991.

Biskind, Peter 'McMovies', *Sight & Sound*, July 1991.

Biskind, Peter 'The colour of money', *Sight & Sound*, August 1991.

Black, Larry 'The Visionary of Tinseltown', *The Independent on Sunday*, 17th November 1991.

Boorman, John & Donohue, Walter (editors) *Projections: A Forum for Film-makers*. Faber & Faber, London & Boston, 1992.

The Business of Film. Special issue on black film-making. June/July 1991.

Bygrave, Mike 'Killing Time', *The Guardian*, 3rd October 1987.

Case, Brian 'Harlem Hustle', *Time Out*, 27th June - 4th July 1990.

Chute, David 'Fear City', *Film Comment*, November-December, 1983.

Chute, David 'Dante's Inferno', *Film Comment*, May-June 1984.

Clarens, Carlos 'Demme Monde', *Film Comment*, September-October 1980.

Cook, Pam 'The Art of Exploitation, or How to Get into the Movies', *Monthly Film Bulletin*, December 1985.

Cook, Pam 'Looking for Rhett Butler, or the Art of Exploitation II', *Monthly Film Bulletin*, May 1986..

Cook, Pam 'Not a Political Picture - Martha Coolidge', *Monthly Film Bulletin*, December 1986.

Cook, Pam 'Good Girl/Bad Girl - Susan Seidelman', *Monthly Film Bulletin*, May 1990.

Corman, Roger, with Jerome, Jim *How I Made a Hundred Movies in Hollywood and Never Lost a Dime*, Random House, New York, 1990.

Cronenworth, Brian 'He Knew What He Wanted', *American Film*, January-February 1989.

DiMatteo, Robert 'Philadelphia Lawyer', *Film Comment*, July-August 1989.

Errigo, Angie 'Profile: John Sayles', *Empire*, December 1991.

Falk, Quentin 'Look Who's Directing - Amy Heckerling', *The Guardian*, 12th March 1991.

Floyd, Nigel *'Stormy Monday'*, *New Musical Express*, 21st January 1989.

Francke, Lizzie 'Her Excellent Career', *The Guardian*, 19th May 1992.

Gristwood, Sarah 'Past imperative', *The Guardian*, 4th May 1988.

Gristwood, Sarah 'Talk of the She-devil', *The Guardian*, 9th May 1990.

Gristwood, Sarah 'Look Who's Directing - Penny Marshall', *The Guardian*, 12th March 1991.

Hillier, Jim & Lipstadt, Aaron *Roger Corman's New World* (BFI Dossier no 7), British Film Institute, London 1981.

Hillier, Jim & Lipstadt, Aaron 'The Economics of Independence: Roger Corman and New World Pictures 1970-1980', *Movie* 31-32, Winter 1986.

The Hollywood Reporter, Independent Producers and Distributors Special Report, 7th August 1990.

Hugo, Chris 'American Cinema in the '70s: The Economic Background'. *Movie* 27-28, Winter 1980/Spring 1981.

Hugo, Chris 'US Film Industry: Economic Background Part 2', *Movie* 31-32, Winter 1986.

Izod, John *Hollywood and the Box Office, 1895-1986*, Macmillan, London, 1988.

Johnson, Angella 'Putting the X Factor on Celluloid', *The Guardian*, 16th January 1993.

Johnston, Sheila 'Harlem Nights', *The Independent*, 7th August 1992.

Kuhn, Annette, with Radstone, Susannah (editors) *The Women's Companion to International Film*, Virago, London, 1990.

Litwak, Mark *Reel Power*, William Morrow, New York, 1986.

McGregor, Alex 'Marshall Lore', Time Out, 13th-20th March 1991.

Malcolm, Derek 'Why the Picture's Black', *The Guardian*, 14th February 1991.

Malcolm, Derek 'Why Sayles Refuses to Sell Out', *The Guardian*, 12th November, 1991.

Malcolm, Derek ' When the Picture Goes Dark . . .', *The Guardian*, 9th January 1992.

Miller, Mark Crispin (editor) *Seeing Through Movies*, Pantheon, New York, 1990.

Newman, Kim 'Once and Future: Jim McBride', *Monthly Film Bulletin*, October 1987.

Newman, Kim 'The Street Where I Live - Abel Ferrara', *Monthly Film Bulletin*, January 1988.

Newman, Kim 'More Scenes from the Class Struggle in Beverly Hills', *Monthly Film Bulletin*, June 1989.

Pines, Jim *Blacks in Films*, Studio Vista, London, 1975.

Pye, Michael & Myles, Lynda *The Movie Brats*, Faber & Faber, London & Boston, 1979.

Reed, Christopher 'Revenge for Pearl Harbor - or How the Japanese Bombed in Hollywood', *The Guardian*, 13th November 1991.

Reeves, Phil 'Mighty Mouse of the Movies', *The Independent on Sunday*, 23rd February 1992.

Rochlin, Margy 'Vice is Nice . . .', *American Film*, September 1986.

Root, Jane 'Celine and Julie, Susan and Susan', *Monthly Film Bulletin*, October 1985.

Salisbury, Mark 'Hollywood's Macho Woman', *The Guardian*, 21st November 1991.

Sayles, John *Thinking in Pictures*, Houghton Mifflin, Boston, 1987.

Sherwood, Rick 'Anatomy of a Deal', *(Storyville)*. *Hollywood Reporter* (Independent Producers and Distributors Special Report), 7th August 1991.

Smith, Gavin 'Wall Street-Wise', *Film Comment*, January-February 1988.

Smith, Gavin 'Moon in the Gutter', *Film Comment*, July-August 1990.

Smith, Gavin 'Identity Check', *Film Comment*, January-February 1991.

Snow, Mat 'Profile: Lili Fini Zanuck & Richard Zanuck', *Empire*, April 1992.

Sragow, Michael 'Jonathan Demme on the Line', *American Film* vol.9, no.4 January-February 1984.

Stein, Eugene 'Interview with Jonathan Kaplan', *Films in Review*, March 1984.

Taylor, Paul 'Keep on Truckin' - Jonathan Kaplan', *Monthly Film Bulletin*, February 1989.

Thomas, Philip 'Don't Believe the Hype', *Empire*, September 1991.

Thomas, Philip 'Who the Hell Does John Singleton Think He Is?', *Empire*, November 1991.

Thompson, Anne 'Flatliners', *Film Comment*, March-April 1991.

Thompson, Anne 'Scenes from a Mall', *Film Comment*, March-April 1992.

Thompson, Ben 'Hudlin Together', *New Musical Express*, 1st September 1990.

Tran, Mark 'Nirvana for the Couch Potato', *The Guardian*, 28th March 1992.

Turner, Adrian 'One from the Heart', *The Guardian*, 18th November 1989.

Vaughn, Christopher 'Case Study: *To Sleep With Anger*', *Hollywood Reporter* (Independent Producers and Distributors Special Report), 7th August 1990.

Walter, Natasha 'A Rose among Hollywood's Thorns', *The Guardian*, 30th October 1991.

Walter, Natasha 'Fast Forward', *The Guardian*, 12th March 1992.

Weber, Jonathan 'Sony's Synergies', *Los Angeles Times*, 25th August 1991.

Wilson, David 'Of Anarchists and Alligators - John Sayles', *Monthly Film Bulletin*, June 1989.

Yakir, Dan 'Celine and Julie Golightly - The Mover: Susan Seidelman', *Film Comment*, May-June 1985.

Yakir, Dan 'Big League Teague', *Film Comment*, November-December 1985.

Index

189